Laruelle

CARY WOLFE, *Series Editor*

(continued on page 281)

Laruelle

Against the Digital

ALEXANDER R. GALLOWAY

posthumanities 31

UNIVERSITY OF MINNESOTA PRESS

MINNEAPOLIS • LONDON

Portions of the Introduction were published in *French Theory Today: An Introduction to Possible Futures* (Brooklyn: The Public School New York, 2011). A different version of chapter 5 was published as "Computers and the Superfold," *Deleuze Studies* 6, no. 4 (November 2012): 513–28. A different version of chapter 6 was published as "Laruelle, Anti-capitalist," in *Laruelle and Non-philosophy*, ed. John Mullarkey and Anthony Paul Smith, 191–208 (Edinburgh: Edinburgh University Press, 2012). Portions of chapter 7 were published as "What Is a Hermeneutic Light?" in *Leper Creativity: Cyclonopedia Symposium*, ed. Ed Keller, Nicola Masciandaro, and Eugene Thacker, 159–72 (Brooklyn, N.Y.: Punctum Books, 2012) and as "Rocket: Present at Every Point of the Remote," *Dark Nights of the Universe*, 89–100 (Miami: [NAME] Publications, 2013). Portions of chapter 8 were published as "Laruelle and Art," *continent.* 2, no. 4 (2013): 230–36. Portions of chapter 9 were published as "François Laruelle, *Théorie generale des victimes*. Mille et une nuits 2012," *Parrhesia* 16 (2013): 102–5.

Published by the University of Minnesota Press
111 Third Avenue South, Suite 290
Minneapolis, MN 55401–2520
http://www.upress.umn.edu

Library of Congress Cataloging-in-Publication Data
Galloway, Alexander R.
Laruelle : against the digital / Alexander R. Galloway. (Posthumanities ; 31)
Includes bibliographical references and index.
ISBN 978-0-8166-9213-2 (pb : alk. paper)—ISBN 978-0-8166-9212-5
  (hc : alk. paper)
1. Laruelle, François. 2. Philosophy, French—21st century. I. Title.
B2433.L374G36 2014
194—dc23

                                        2013051110

Printed in the United States of America on acid-free paper

The University of Minnesota is an equal-opportunity educator and employer.

20 19 18 17 16 15 14   10 9 8 7 6 5 4 3 2 1

for

EUGENE THACKER

Toute pensée est une capacité de saisir les divisions d'un tout . . . *les divisions d'un tout absolument quelconque.*

—RENÉ DAUMAL, *Le Mont Analogue*

Contents

Preface

Explanations, diversions, interpretations, polemics, songs, follies, and other unorganized bits fill these pages, at least mostly. I do not claim definitive knowledge of François Laruelle. I do not present this book as full and clear exposition of Laruelle's notoriously idiomatic endeavor. This is not an *Introduction to Laruelle*. I leave that task to others. Nor do these chapters try to enact the non-philosophical method. I leave that to Laruelle's army.

But there's love here, and more than a little fairy dust. Like many readers, I have tumbled deep down into the Laruellean abyss. It has taken a long time to reach the bottom, but every minute of it has been blissful, from the rigor and radicalism, to the profound ethical and monastic sensibility, to the unending commitment to immanence and materialism.

Some newcomers to Laruelle turn tail and leave after only a few pages. There is little in his work to serve as a familiar anchor, particularly for those of us reared on critical theory and cultural studies. Laruelle is no 1968 radical like Guy Debord or Michel Foucault. He is not a public intellectual cast from the Sartrean mold like Alain Badiou. He does not practice phenomenology or dialectics, and he has little sympathy for today's reigning Hegelianism championed by the likes of Slavoj Žižek. His is not a familiar way of thinking. It's a genuinely weird way of thinking, *a weirder thought*.

Recall Foucault's quip in *The Order of Things* concerning a certain mysterious Chinese encyclopedia: it's possible to think *like that*? With Laruelle the problem grows worse. *Why would you ever want to think that way?*

Still, there's a reason for all this weirdness. Laruelle has taken two of the most appealing traditions within Western thought, immanence and materialism—the former found in philosophers like Baruch Spinoza and the latter in thinkers like Karl Marx and his lineage—and has driven them all the way to the end of the night. Many have attempted such an experiment, only to flunk before finishing, as Laruelle is not shy about reminding his readers. Deleuze couldn't manage it; Michel Henry got very close but also came up short. No one in fact, provided we believe Laruelle, has yet had the nerve to pursue the full ramifications of immanence and materialism. If you follow that path, Laruelle warns, you'd better be ready to accept the consequences. The result is rather horrific, to be sure, as the individual is ripped from its humdrum routine and inserted directly into the one. A blissful horror though, a pleasure in pain, a terror of letting go, an abnegation of the self in allegiance to a dark, dark universe.

So there's love, but there's an argument here, too, divulged slowly if not always steadily throughout. Laruelle is an important thinker. Indeed, a Kant or a Heidegger or a Deleuze walks among us. My argument aims to highlight certain tendencies in Laruelle's overall project, tendencies labeled "univocal," "unidirectional," or "immanent"—or to use less subtle language, "oblivious," "autistic," or "prophylactic." In essence I suggest that we must be rather simple-minded about the one, taking it at face value and combining it again with its binary companion, the zero, in order to collide Laruelle with contemporary discourse on digitality. Laruelle almost never talks about the digital, it is true, yet I see evidence of the topic on almost every page. The goal is not to forge a new digital Laruelle, but on the contrary to show how, even in this day and age, Laruelle remains a profoundly nondigital thinker, perhaps the only nondigital thinker we have.

These last terms, though—oblivious, autistic, prophylactic—are controversial if not offensive to some, and are used here somewhat loosely. The one in Laruelle may appear neglectful, oblivious, even slightly sadistic. Yet this is no totalitarianism, no fascism, no Stalinism of the real. To be sure, Laruelle is docile as a lamb. Like Christ's kingdom (of the meek) or even Lenin's dictatorship (of the proletariat), the apparent oblivious totality of the one is only a quasi or false totality, precisely because it is a totality of insufficiency. The one is never the Whole or the All, but rather merely a finite and generic one: *this* one; this one *here;* this one here *in person.* A dictatorship of the meek, therefore, need not be feared, even if it demands complete fulfillment. For this is the only method adequate, truly and actually, to pursue a rigorous immanence.

All the Spinozian theorists of immanence are hawking a cake-and-eat-it-too duplicity, or so says Laruelle, because in flattening a formerly transcendental nature they merely proliferate difference. In righting one wrong they merely unloose a secondary corruption. Deleuzian mantras like "pure multiplicity across the plane of immanence" are simply nonsensical contradictions for Laruelle. Difference and immanence will never find common cause, because they are quite plainly opposites.

In fact, Laruelle will propose the inverse position, that immanence meshes best with *commonality,* not difference. Commonality and immanence mesh well because, according to Laruelle, the only kind of immanence worth talking about is one uncoupled from anything different from it, uncoupled even from itself (as a different self).

Or as Carla Lonzi put it in 1970, *Let's spit on Hegel.*[1] Here is where Deleuze and Laruelle agree: Hegel must be renounced; nothing good will ever come from something confronting its own alterity.[2] This is why the one plays such a large role in Laruelle—at times a maddeningly monotonous role—because, again, if immanence is driven all the way to the end of the night, if indeed nothing good comes from the staging of self and other, then the only thing left is the non-difference of the one. A most merciful obliviousness, then: the universe is everything and I am nothing, but the universe emanates a glorious peace.

Weird, yes, and more and more unfashionable today. How does Laruelle deviate from today's prevailing wisdom? Here are some characterizing viewpoints, in no particular order, that will be unpacked further in the pages to come: Laruelle endorses identity of the same, not heterogeneity or difference; his non-standard method requires ascetic withdrawal, not the kind of self-realization associated with the "me generation" of post-1968 philosophy; his ontology is rooted in a cryptography of being, not the more popular pornography of being (evident in the virtues of transparency, the strategies of capture, or the logics of *aletheia*); he requires a unilateral relation, not today's hegemony of multilateral ecologies of difference (assemblages, rhizomes, networks). No wonder that Laruelle has been overlooked for so many years.

The text is organized into ten chapters, bookended by an Introduction and short Conclusion. The discussion progresses by way of header sentences underscored for emphasis, among which include fourteen numbered theses. The header sentences and theses are meant to aid comprehension by outlining the arc of the book and highlighting its essential claims. Yet given the condensed nature of the headers and theses, it is necessary to elaborate on their meaning in normal prose, sometimes at great length. Such constitutes the continuous body of the work.

We begin in the crypt and end at the altar. The crypt (the Introduction and chapter 1) is the realm of the hidden, the secret, and the absolutely obscure. Although we will not borrow such hiddenness from our old friends Heidegger or Marx, that Heideggerian pathway toward a hidden truth that must be unconcealed, or those Marxian rational kernels that must be dragged out into the light of reason. Laruelle's crypt is a pure hiddenness, a secret that has never been divulged and never will.

Beyond the crypt lies the world, the *philosophical world,* replete with processes like reflection and differentiation. Chapters 2 and 3, perhaps the least Laruellean sections of the book, concern themselves chiefly with the philosophical world, exploring the various epithets of being in its rivenness and the larger forces of distinction and integration, dubbed here the "digital" and the "analog." Chapter 4 extends the discussion of the philosophical world by looking at the concept of the event. Typically understood as either relation or decision, the event in Laruelle takes on a very different meaning, and we conclude Part I of the book considering the static, final, and preemptive nature of non-standard action.

After dealing with the philosophical concept of digitality and its relation to Laruelle's non-philosophy, we continue in Part II by exploring two important aspects of actually existing digitality, computers and capitalism, with the goal of outlining some of the necessary conditions for withdrawing from the standard model of philosophy. Here the Laruelle–Deleuze relation will be tackled more directly by way of a specific subtheme existing in both authors, the politics and aesthetics of control society, including computers and cybernetics. As for capitalism, the surprise is that there is no surprise, because Laruelle is a Marxist, and in that sense quite on par with his intellectual compatriots and indeed with those who concern themselves with "theory" broadly conceived. But as might be predicted, Laruelle's Marx is subjected to the non-philosophical method, leading in chapter 6 to some rather interesting if not altogether unusual places, Louis Althusser for one.

Chapters 7 and 8 follow, both devoted to art and aesthetics. First, in chapter 7, we consider the question of blackness and light. Then, in the following chapter, we sift through some of Laruelle's writings on fine art with the hopes of defining a realist or non-standard aesthetics rooted in the concept of utopia.

Having crawled out of the crypt, we find ourselves at the altar. The book concludes with twin chapters on the ethical and the generic, including Laruelle's views on persons in their humanity. A black mass, though, not a holy union; Laruelle's altar is just as dark and gloomy as the lowest levels of the most colorless crypt. Laruelle's ethical universe is a universe of strangers and victims, a generic humanity if not exactly a "bare life." As with the previous chapters on computers, Marxism, and art, Laruelle's vertiginous twists and turns begin to pay off in the end, and the weird becomes wonderful.

What of non-philosophy as a whole? I am not pretending to be a Laruellean, nor do I necessarily aspire to promulgate the non-philosophical method and its attendant communities. The goal here is not to decamp to the shores of the a priori universe. But at the same time I have no intention of absconding with Laruelle and forcing him at gunpoint to sing the recessional as non-philosophy leaves the church. To kidnap Laruelle from non-philosophy is hardly feasible, much less desirable.

Yet to abscond with the one; to reinsert Laruelle into discussions of the immanence of the one begun in Lucretius, Spinoza, Deleuze, or Henry; not so much to sow Laruelle with a different seed, or to inseminate him with a mutant offspring, as others might want to do; but to think Laruelle himself in terms of the generic; to fortify and extend his project in new ways; to consider the commonality of the one in terms of the commonality of all being and thought; to withdraw from the long tradition of digital philosophy: these are activities worth pursuing.

introduction

The Oldest Prejudice

"Inebriated and bastardized by Plato, liquified and cogitated into concentrate by Descartes, moralized by Kant, whipped by Sade, devoured by Hegel, disgorged by Stirner, conscripted by Husserl, chewed out by Nietzsche, down the wrong pipe of Derrida, turned over by Heidegger, crapped out by Deleuze, thrown up by Laruelle. And it would ask for more if we let it!"[1]

With this litany, François Laruelle recounts the many crimes of the philosophers caught in the clutches of their depraved profession. Philosophy is "the oldest prejudice."[2] To do philosophy means to harbor a secret stance toward the world—pursuing it, eating and digesting it, beating it down, then building it back up again. And philosophy itself is forever a glutton for punishment, eager to be reenlisted for future abuses. It will always come back for more if we let it.

This insatiable beast, can it be avoided? Is it possible to leave philosophy behind, to abandon the prejudice? Or are we forever caught in a vicious circle, where any stance taken against philosophy becomes recast as merely a new instance of intellectual reflection, a different kind of philosophical intervention? What if philosophy is the problem, not the solution? What if the best response to philosophy *is to cease doing it*?

Laruelle is the most recent figure to take these questions seriously, but certainly not the first. The chief aim of his life's work is to consider philosophy without resorting to philosophy in order to do so. His chief aim is to think philosophy unphilosophically.

Why should such a pedantic exercise matter to anyone outside the micro niche of professional philosophers? Is Laruelle simply a virtuoso of the mind, performing intellectual backflips and other feats of reason? Laruelle had been writing and publishing regularly for around thirty years before his first book was translated into English. What would account for the sluggish pace of his reception both in France and abroad? Perhaps it is not clear to many readers what is at stake and why he should be viewed as anything other than a dazzling performer with equal parts acrobat and swashbuckler.

Yet there are a number of reasons to be attracted to Laruelle above and beyond the seductive beauty of his idiosyncratic way of thinking. One might seek a theory of immanence more rigorous than those offered by Michel Henry or Gilles Deleuze. One might be schooled in medieval mysticism and seek a new kind of heretical thought appropriate to the modern condition. One might seek a nonrepresentational politics. One might seek a realist aesthetics. These are some of the many things that may be found in Laruelle.

Although this book aims to address some of these topics, the ultimate focus here is slightly different. I hope not simply to interpret Laruelle's existing paper trail, but further to collide Laruelle with a theme and context largely missing in his writings, the theme of *digitality*. If this project is successful it will offer commentary and analysis relevant to a variety of issues cutting through a number of Laruelle texts, and at the same time provide a novel realization not explicitly evident in any of them.

Like philosophy, the digital is also an insatiable beast, and like philosophy, the digital is also inescapable today. Digital machines dominate the planet, in rich and poor regions alike, while so-called digital thinking—the binarisms of being and other or self and world—is often synonymous with what it means to think at all. By piggybacking on Laruelle's withdrawal from the philosophical decision, thereby discovering a non-standard real in parallel with philosophy, it also becomes possible to withdraw from the digital decision, likewise discovering a non-standard digitality in parallel with this one.

To that end, this book has essentially two goals. The first is to define digitality and demonstrate that philosophy and digitality share a special connection, no easy task to be sure. This will necessarily lure the discussion away from Laruelle proper, if only temporarily, as we investigate what digitality means and how it relates to philosophy as a whole. The second goal is to show that, given his withdrawal from philosophy, Laruelle too withdraws from the digital. In other words, if philosophy and the digital are structured in similar ways, then to decline to participate in philosophy means to decline to participate in digitality.

How could it be possible that philosophy and digitality are the same thing? The question will be engaged more fully in the first part of the book, but the crux of the matter is that philosophy is rooted in distinction. Whether the metaphysical distinction between essence and instance or the political distinction between friend and foe, philosophy relies on opposition, reflection, or relation between two or more elements. Likewise, digitality entails a basic distinction, whether zeros and ones or some other set of discrete units—the four nucleobases of the genetic code or the twenty-six letters of the alphabet are just as digital as the base-two numeric encoding used in binary computers. Any digital medium will have a bed of genetically distinct elements. These elements form a homogeneous substrate from which constructions are built.

But for Laruelle's non-standard method, distinction no longer holds sway, at least not in the way distinction has been classically defined. So just as he withdraws from the philosophical decision, Laruelle implicitly withdraws from the digital decision. Just as he bars distinction in favor of the single determining instance of "the One," Laruelle leaves any possibility of zeros and ones behind because he bars the essential condition of discriminating between the two elements in the first place. (Again, zeros and ones have a nice heuristic utility, and they will be deployed throughout the book, but any base mechanism for encoding value distinctions would serve equally well—the alphabet, the genetic code, and so on.)

Because of this, the present volume does not address digitality in terms of computers, software, the Web, or other kinds of existing digital technologies, as I have done in other writings. As counterintuitive as it may seem at first glance, this book examines digitality largely uncoupled from any sort of immediate technological referent. Instead we treat digitality as a strictly theoretical concept. It's not that computers have been mistakenly omitted from the argument. This apparent omission is the argument itself.

Thesis I. Definition of the media principle: the real is communicational, and the communicational is real. Before tackling philosophy and digitality directly, let us open the investigation into Laruelle by looking in some detail at a short essay titled "The Truth according to Hermes: Theorems on the Secret and Communication," first published in French in 1987.[3] I select this short essay not so much because it addresses non-philosophy as a whole but because it stands nicely on its own, is readily available online, and engages a kind of vocabulary—secrecy, communication, interpretation—that should be familiar to many even if they are unfamiliar with Laruelle.

What is Laruelle's general approach? To start, consider Laruelle's interest in radical immanence, illustrated in this text by a "pure" Hermes, that is, a Hermes unsullied by the sallies and wanderings of hermeneutics. Laruelle's Hermes is a non-Hermes, one who touches the truth as such, without any threat of deceit in exchange, without any metaphysical depth, and without the fog of semantic transfer. Laruelle's goal is to cut through the relational thinking associated with hermeneutics that forever breaks truth in half as truth and its communication or the secret and its manifestation. We must instead "let the philosophers in on the secret," so that they may pursue a rigorous science of truth.

"The unitary or dominant way of thinking is that of a *generalized hermeneutics*" (page 19, thesis 1), writes Laruelle at the opening of the essay. But what is a generalized hermeneutics? It is an "indissoluble correlation." It is "the undecidable coupling of truth and its communication" (page 19, thesis 1). In this way truth never simply stands on its own, because it always exists in a relationship of givenness vis-à-vis a human agent. The relationship of givenness is one in which truth is given over to humankind and made available for its consumption. It matters little whether truth is hidden or revealed. What matters is that truth is always already given over in advance to the possibility of being hidden or revealed. Similar to what Quentin Meillassoux has termed "correlationism," Laruelle describes a scenario in which truth as such is only ever given over to a receptive perceiver.[4]

If we were to extract a "media principle" from Laruelle it might be something like what he says in thesis 16 of the Hermes article: "The real is communicational, the communicational is real" (page 22, thesis 16). Such is the classical model of mediatic being handed down from antiquity and still prevalent today—handed down here as Hermes, the god of, among other things, transport into and out of foreign places.

Conceptions of mediatic being run deep in Western philosophy. They are evident in metaphysical models. They are evident in how we think about interpretation and communication. They structure the basic relationship between Being and *Dasein,* or "being-there," the uniquely human mode of being described in Heidegger. Hermes is the patron saint of mediatic being, a scenario in which something far away must be given over to something close at hand that becomes attentive to it. Hermes is the chaperone of travelers in foreign lands; the god of markets and merchants too, for they and their goods travel abroad just like the traveler. Hermes sits at the door hinge, for he is the god of thresholds. He gives his name to the art of literary interpretation, hermeneutics, for he is the god of translating what is obscure into what is known.

But to Laruelle this is all merely a picture of the "unitary and authoritarian" Hermes. Such a commonplace Hermes must be replaced by a non-philosophical one, a Hermes who does not take the correlationist bait. Thus Laruelle's Hermes

> defines the essence of truth as a secret, but as a secret that in order to exist and to be made known needs none of the light of *logos,* none of the tricks of meaning, the strategies of interpretation, the horizons of the World, or the transcendent forms of appearance. Truth as secret exists autonomously *prior to* the horizontality of appearance. The secret enjoys an absolute precedence over interpretation; it is itself the Uninterpretable. (page 20, thesis 4)

Alienation, translation, interpretation, reflection—these many vectors of the human mind are all steadfastly resisted by Laruelle. In our vanity we consider reason and logic to act in this way because we act in this way. But Laruelle is resolutely against such a narcissistic "we." His is a strong anti-phenomenology. That is to say, his is the rejection of any scenario in which a world or a thing is revealed to a solicitous subject. If Meillassoux opposes himself to correlationism in the hope of arriving at the absolute possibilities for thought and thus eventually for real matter, Laruelle opposes himself to correlationism in the hope of arriving at a finite and generic reason, itself existing in a superpositional matrix in the real. In any case, both thinkers wish to remove the normal human perceiver from the equation, because the human is considered to be a limiting factor vis-à-vis what may be known about the real.

What remains is pure essence, generic immanence. Laruelle's generic never enacts the media principle by propagating itself, and likewise his immanence is so entirely immanent to itself that it becomes generic or common (at best a quasi-propagation). "The secret is the strictly unreflected upon form of truth that, given to itself, gives nothing of itself and receives nothing of itself except the modality in which it is given" (page 20, thesis 5). Like data encryption, the secret admits nothing, except for the fact of it being communicated. Such a condition is named "the One" by Laruelle. Sometimes he offers alternative synonyms for the One: the "Indivision," the "Without-Division," or the "Non-interpretable."[5]

But this "One" is not infinite; it is not simply another name for God or the absolute. Entities in their generic immanence are still simply entities. Hence Laruelle labels these entities *finite* rather than infinite. "The secret is truth when it no longer needs to go out of itself and be for itself, when it is itself by staying in itself" (page 20, thesis 6). Such truth is finite in its immanent oneness.

Laruelle's is a Hermes as science, not a Hermes as art. The old "hermeneuts" of philosophy or literary interpretation are like astronauts or argonauts; these are people who travel, with Hermes at their elbow, to a foreign place. Laruelle dismissively calls philosophers the mere "mailmen of truth" (page 22, thesis 16). He subtracts the mailman from the equation, reaching directly through this mediating individual to touch Hermes himself. The secret "never reaches a consciousness, or vanishes when it does" (page 20, thesis 6). Removing the extra fluff of human mediation is necessary to break the philosophical circle, and ultimately to engage in the practice of non-standard philosophy.

The stakes are exceptionally high in such an endeavor, and we may now begin to catalogue the many enemies of Laruelle, the many traditions strewn by the wayside. Of course, hermeneutics is out, but so too are phenomenology and dialectics, because they also follow the media principle to the extent that they require mediative propagation via relation.

Listen to the direct assault on Heidegger and phenomenology in the following quotation: "To meditate on the essence of Being, on the forgetting of Being, is a task that has lost its sense of urgency" (page 21, thesis 10).[6] Or here, the assault on Barthes, Derrida, and the other post-structuralists: "The essence of the secret knows nothing of the play of veiling and unveiling, of the structure of difference in general" (page 21, thesis 9).

Shunning these philosophical traditions, Laruelle has essentially barred himself from entry into the intellectual currents of the twentieth century. What else was there among his potential confreres that was not dialectics, or phenomenology, or hermeneutics? All are taken off the table: Hegel, Marx, Nietzsche, Freud, Saussure, Husserl, Heidegger, Sartre, Cixous, Derrida, Kristeva, Barthes, Malabou. All that is left is a curious kind of immanence. It is natural, then, that Laruelle would have found a comrade, however remote, in Deleuze.

Yet Laruelle does not exactly reject these other figures. He recognizes and validates all hitherto existing philosophy. To be precise, Laruelle has no interest in overturning, rejecting, denying, or overcoming philosophy, and he never uses such language. (On this score, we should be clear that the *Against . . .* of my title is not entirely Laruellean.) Rather, in his parlance, such work becomes the "material" for non-philosophy. Laruelle's non-standard approach wishes merely to "clone" existing philosophy, and in so doing to discover the immanent identity of thought and reality residing within philosophy.

Laruelle illustrates what it means to do non-philosophy in theses 11 and 12 of the Hermes essay. Non-philosophy means, essentially, to select an existing philosophical system, hermeneutics say, and to analyze it exclusively for the generic logics that exist within it. These logics are what remain once the human, the person who decides to do philosophy, is removed. Thus even hermeneutics has a non-philosophical core, for it must propose something like an "absolute or finite experience of truth" (page 21, thesis 11) if it ever is able to meditate on the intractable difficulties of getting at such a truth (via interpretation or other methods). Even if it adamantly refuses that such a truth is graspable, *it has proposed it,* if only in silhouette.

The non-philosopher, then, enters the scene, removes the human decision to reflect, and rescues the logic of the situation that remains. If "truth" is the scene, and the communication of truth is removed, then what is rescued is the generic immanence of a secret truth that has been revealed to no living person.

Return to the age-old question, If a tree falls in the forest when no one is around, does it make a sound? For Laruelle, all trees only ever fall in forests where no one is around, and they always make a sound.

The philosophical decision and the principle of sufficient philosophy. We begin with Laruelle's short essay on Hermes because it presents in miniature all that is important in Laruelle. Let us continue now on to bigger things and explain how this small essay intersects with some of the larger concepts in his work.

First and foremost, non-philosophy hinges on a withdrawal of what Laruelle calls "the philosophical decision." To engage in the philosophical decision is to endorse the position that anything and everything is a candidate for philosophical reflection. Thus to do philosophy means to reflect on the world, and likewise, if one is being philosophical, one is necessarily also being reflective or metaphilosophical. (For Laruelle *philosophy* means primarily Western philosophy, and he tends to rely on examples from the continental tradition, such as Hegel, Nietzsche, and Derrida.)

Non-philosophy means simply *to decline to engage in such a decision.* In other words, non-philosophy declines to reflect on things. Non-philosophy withdraws from the decision (to reflect on things), and in doing so enters into a space of what Laruelle calls "theory" or "science." From this place "alongside" philosophy, non-philosophy is able to take philosophy as its raw material, extracting from it various kinds of pure, nonreflected, autonomous, and radically immanent logics.[7]

Although Laruelle's conception of the term science might be confusing—not to mention his late fascination with algebra, quantum mechanics, and imaginary numbers—it is perhaps best understood in terms of the distinction between immanence and transcendence. For Laruelle, philosophy means roughly "the thing that is transcendental vis-à-vis the real." Taken in this sense philosophy is always representational, reflective, or mediated. Philosophy reveals the conditions of possibility of things (but not those things themselves).

By contrast science means roughly "the thing that is immanent vis-à-vis the real." Science is always direct or radical, not reflective or mediated. Science reveals things immediately, unilaterally, and unconditionally. Thus when Laruelle refers to non-philosophy as a science of philosophy he means simply that it focuses on philosophy's radical or irreflective immanence, not its penchant for the transcendental.

(Such a distinction also helps categorize Laruelle's two most significant methodological volumes: the first, *Principles of Non-philosophy* [1996], is Laruelle's attempt to articulate a non-standard *philosophy,* while the second, *Non-standard Philosophy* [2010], is Laruelle's attempt to articulate a non-standard *science,* for which the chief representative is quantum mechanics.[8])

As John Mullarkey describes it, Laruelle is "abstaining from philosophy as such while simultaneously taking it as its own raw material."[9] The goal of non-philosophy is a rigorous theoretical knowledge *of* or *in* philosophy. Although even the word *of* becomes problematic for Laruelle, because through the structure of language it posits a relationship between two things—something is *of* something else. For this reason Laruelle will often quarantine the word by rendering it in parentheses, as with the term "force (of) thought."

In this sense, non-philosophy, being a science and not a philosophy, does not reflect back on itself. Laruelle is quite adamant on this point, repeating and clarifying it in almost everything he writes. Non-philosophy is not circular vis-à-vis philosophy, and thus there is nothing meta about it. Rather, according to Laruelle, non-philosophy is scientific and axiomatic.

The philosophical decision also goes by a second name in Laruelle, the *principle of sufficient philosophy.* Similar in form to Leibniz's principle of sufficient reason, which states that everything happening in the world happens for a specific reason—Whitehead's slight modification of the principle is elegant in its simplicity, "No actual entity, then no reason"—the principle of sufficient philosophy states that for everything in the world there must be a philosophy oriented toward it and bent on explaining and unpacking it. The principle of sufficient philosophy thus implicitly asserts that philosophy is an autonomous field, and that philosophy has the privilege and ability to tackle any subject whatsoever.

The subtext here is that Laruelle considers philosophy to be essentially a narcissistic enterprise, in that it turns the real world back on itself into the shape of something that can be looked at, reflected upon, absorbed in, and given over to mankind so it can be solicitous toward it.

Laruelle abstains from conventional discussions of dialectics, causality, and representation, but it is clearly the phenomenological scene that he avoids the most and that he most closely associates with the practice of doing philosophy. As the phenomenologists like to say, *The world is given to us so we can think about it.* But nearly everything in Laruelle is designed in order to avoid making such a claim.

Instead of a notion of ontology as the relationship between Being and existing, as the relationship between reality and its own communication, Laruelle speaks of the one as the real that is radically autonomous. Thus something like Catherine Malabou's basic plasticity of Being would be anathema to Laruelle, who would cast off Malabou as nothing more than the same philosophical tricks.[10] There is no low-level convertibility between the one and Being for Laruelle. The one is precisely the nonconvertible, the non-morphable. The one has no relationship to anything else. In general Laruelle abstains from any kind of logics that require reciprocity, reversibility, or exchange.

Traditional notions of causality must therefore be scrapped, because they typically imply a causality of two directions (as action/reaction, dialectical contradiction, and so on), even if we make allowances for the "frustrated" bidirectionalities of post-structuralism. Instead Laruelle's theory of causality is a strong *unidirectional* causality, for which he borrows the Marxian label determination-in-the-last-instance (DLI). Determination-in-the-last-instance is Laruelle's replacement for all the hitherto existing definitions of causality. The only causality proper to the one is a unidirectional and rigorously irreversible causality.

Causality is therefore given a new name in Laruelle. It is called "cloning," because cloning is a kind of logic that produces a dual entity through an identical copy. But the clone parent and the clone child never need establish a relationship with each other, and hence nothing is produced or synthesized during the act of cloning. The clone is thus a "duality which is an identity but an identity which is not a synthesis."[11] (Note that "dual" is acceptable to Laruelle, but he throws out concepts like pair or binarism. Dual is acceptable because it provides an avenue for thinking about two-ness without resorting to relationship.)

This also helps understand why Laruelle's "One" is not at all metaphysical in nature. The one is absolutely foreclosed to the clone, yet the clone as copy is entirely dependent on the one. Thus the one exerts total determination over the clone (determination-in-the-last-instance), yet is at the same time absolutely oblivious of the clone and therefore in a nonrelation with it.

Laruelle calls this a "unilateral duality." It is unilateral because the one, in its absolute totality, is never in a relationship with anything, and hence operates *unilaterally*. (If the one were merely one "side" pitted against another "side" we would be required to speak in terms of a bilateral relationship; but this is never the case in Laruelle. The one never takes a side.) Likewise it is also a duality, because the clone is a dual of the one, running "alongside" it or "according to" it. Laruelle's duality is thus never a two, or a pair, or a binarism, or an opposition. Binarisms exist only between *like* categories, between categorical equals; the one is not equal to anything, it *is* equality itself in the most radical sense. There can be no parity with the one, only the duality of a clone.

Materialism. Laruelle was labeled a materialist already in the preface to this book, but why exactly? Laruelle is indeed critical of the philosophical school known as materialism, just as he is critical of the contrary notion, idealism, along with realism and other philosophical positions. Of course, these terms are somewhat fungible and take on different meanings in different contexts. The term *materialism* is used here as a marker for a certain kind of thinking that refuses the primacy of idealist philosophy and transcendental metaphysics. Such a materialism refers to that special cocktail of empiricism, realism, and materialism in which may be found figures like Marx, Deleuze, Heraclitus, Lucretius, Spinoza, Hume, Bergson, or Whitehead.

To be clear, Laruelle's non-philosophy is neither a materialism nor a realism in the most narrow sense of the terms. He makes this evident on countless occasions, practically on every page. Although affiliated with materialist philosophy and particularly the historical materialism of Marx, Laruelle's conception of the real is not simply reducible to a kind of primary matter or empirical reality. He has no interest in debating whether or not the real world exists outside our ability to observe it, or whether or not the real world is constructed out of countless small material atoms. These are the squabbles of philosophy, after all. The real, as non-philosophical, is defined precisely and axiomatically by Laruelle. The real is the unilateral duality specific to an immanent one.

These caveats aside, and Laruelle's frequent use of the term *real* notwithstanding, I refer to Laruelle's project as a materialism throughout. This is not meant to mislabel Laruelle or sideline realism, but simply to indicate a larger set of concerns including immanence, anti-philosophy, historical materialism, determination-in-the-last-instance, generic humanity, critique of representation, critique of metaphysics, political militancy, ethical finitude, and so on. In my view the label *materialism* is ultimately the best way to describe the confluence of these various issues.

Indeed Laruelle is a materialist in a very basic sense, and he admits as much all throughout his work. First, despite a gargantuan and often onerous scaffolding of terms and concepts, Laruelle puts great stock in finite materiality, what the French call *vécu,* or lived experience. Just as Heidegger relies heavily on the concept of *Dasein,* the uniquely human experience of being in the world, Laruelle spends a great deal of time thinking about the real material experience of human life. Second, Laruelle is something of an unrepentant Marxist and adopts a number of theoretical principles from the tradition of historical materialism, including the concepts of the determination of the material base and the relation between forces of production and relations of production. Third, Laruelle builds the entire concept of matter and material into the non-philosophical method, such that the philosophical corpus serves as the raw material for non-philosophical investigation, a kind of empirical base, if you will, for theoretical inquiry. And finally, although there are many fine-grained distinctions that one might draw between realism and materialism, Laruelle's affection for the real, in particular his definition of the real in terms of generic insufficient finitude, could be read as an illustration of his materialist tendencies.

As for idealism, certainly there's no room in Laruelle for those stalwart idealist conceptions of infinity, abstraction, essence, or universal spirit. In fact Laruelle and his friend Michel Henry form a perfect mirror: both being theorists of radical immanence, Henry finds the ultimate condition of immanence in spirit, mind, and self, while Laruelle finds it in the real, the material, and the generic experience of human life.

The digital and the analog; analysis and synthesis. Since the remainder of this book freely employs the twin concepts of digital and analog, a word or two of introduction is required before getting underway. My view on these terms will be idiosyncratic to some, yet I believe my definitions are precise enough to generate a useful conversation. Indeed the conversation will begin only after the long arc of the book is complete.

There are many ways to define the digital and the analog. The digital is online, the analog is offline. The digital is new, the analog old. The digital means zeros and ones, the analog means continuous variation. The digital means discrete, the analog means integrated. The digital means the digits (the fingers and toes), the analog means proportion (ratios and correspondences).

Here the terms do not mean precisely these things. Here they delineate the broken and the smooth, the difference between discrete points and continuous curves. But even this forestalls the question: claiming "discrete points" explains little, because nothing has been said as to how such points became discrete in the first place. So the digital is something more fundamental. The digital is the basic distinction that makes it possible to make any distinction at all. The digital is the capacity to divide things and make distinctions between them. Thus not so much zero and one, but *one and two*.[12]

In chapter 3, the chapter in which the digital and analog are examined most closely, the digital is defined as "the one dividing in two," while the analog is defined as "the two coming together as one." As the one dividing in two, the digital describes processes of distinction or decision. Both distinction and decision involve the separation of a formerly indistinguishable mass into separate lumps. To decide means to choose, but it also means that the choice has been rendered into discrete paths that may be chosen. Likewise, distinction means to differentiate between formerly indistinguishable things, prompting variations and contrasts to become evident.

By contrast, the analog, as the two coming together as one, describes processes of integration or proportion. The analog brings together heterogenous elements into identity, producing a relation of nondistinction. Twoness is overcome by oneness; the transcendental is overcome by immanence.

These two expressions—"the one dividing in two" and "the two coming together as one"—have a storied past in postwar France, particularly in the wake of Louis Althusser. The expressions harken back to Mao, Lenin, Marx, and even Hegel, who used them to typify the two moments of the dialectic, the moment of *analysis,* where the one divides in two, and the moment of *synthesis,* where the two combines as one.

For his part, Hegel, while allowing for both distinction and integration, ultimately stresses the overcoming of alienation via synthesis ($2 \rightarrow 1$). History is an epic of synthesis in the work of Hegel. Contradictions can and will appear, but only so they may be reintegrated into the whole. But if Hegel viewed history as an epic synthesis, Lenin, following Marx, viewed history as an epic struggle. Analysis, not synthesis, takes center stage in Marxism and Leninism, as commodities are demystified into shells and kernels, society is disintegrated into factional classes, and the union of the common, while perhaps achieved in certain ways, remains ever elusive. As Lenin famously wrote, the essence of dialectics lies in analysis (1 → 2), that is, the division of the whole into its parts, which in fairness he attributed to Hegel as much as to Marx.[13]

What is the essence of the dialectic? Is it analysis, synthesis, or both together? In his book about the art and politics of the twentieth century, Alain Badiou recalls one of the classic mid-century debates concerning the digital distinction between one and two:

> Around 1965 there begins in China what the local press—ever inventive when it came to the designation of conflicts—calls "a great class struggle in the field of philosophy." On one side stand those who think that the essence of dialectics is the genesis of antagonism, and that it is given in the formula "one divides into two"; on the other, those who argue that the essence of dialectics is the synthesis of contradictory terms, and that consequently the right formula is "two fuse into one." The apparent scholasticism harbours an essential truth. For what is really at stake is the identification of revolutionary subjectivity, of its constituent desire. Is it a desire for division, for war, or is it instead a desire for fusion, for unity, for peace? In any case, in China at that time those who espouse the maxim "one divides into two" are declared "leftists," while those who advocate "two fuse into one" are called "rightists."[14]

Affirming Lenin's interest in contradiction and struggle, Mao expressed his preference for the analytic motion of the dialectic, the motion of the one-to-two, in various statements. The world teems with contradiction and it calls out for analysis, he said in a 1957 speech:

> There is no place where contradictions do not exist, nor is there any person who cannot be analysed. To think that he cannot is being metaphysical. . . . As a matter of fact, the secretaries of our Party branches understand dialectics, for when they prepare reports to branch meetings, they usually write

down two items in their notebooks, first, the achievements and, second, the shortcomings. *One divides into two*—this is a universal phenomenon, and this is dialectics.[15]

In 1963 the international communist movement split longitudinally into two basic wings, the Soviet and the Chinese, and under Mao the analysis–synthesis debate was recontextualized along the China–Soviet axis. Those who endorsed coexistence with the Soviets endorsed the "analog" moment of synthesis (2 → 1), while those who endorsed distinction from the Soviets and a continued revolution within China, the Cultural Revolution that would arrive only a few years later, endorsed the "digital" moment of analysis (1 → 2).

Already heated, the debate grew more furious after a lecture given in November 1963 by Yang Xianzhen, a Chinese philosopher and member of the Central Committee, ideas from which were reproduced by two of his students, Ai Hengwu and Lin Qingshan, and published in the Beijing newspaper *Guangming Daily* on May 29, 1964, under the title "'Dividing One into Two' and 'Combining Two into One': Some Realization Gained in the Study of Chairman Mao's Thought in Materialistic Dialectics." In the article Ai and Lin found value in the two movements of the dialectic, in both division and combination. Yet they committed a mistake in the eyes of certain of their comrades by placing such an emphasis on the second moment, the combining of two into one:

The action and reaction between bodies are "combined from two into one" to become the mechanical motion of bodies. The attraction and repulsion between molecules inside bodies are "combined from two into one" to constitute physical motion. The combination and dissociation of atoms are "combined from two into one" to constitute chemical motion. The assimilation and dissimilation of protein organic bodies which are formed with carbon, hydrogen, oxygen and nitrogen among the chemical elements are "combined from two into one" to constitute the vital motion of metabolism. The productive forces and the relations of production, the economic foundation and the superstructure are "combined from two into one" to constitute the cognitional motion of mankind. . . . From all kinds of natural phenomena to human society, thinking, etc., there is nothing which is not a case of "combining two into one."[16]

A week later Hsiang Ch'ing published a rebuttal bearing the unambiguous title "'Combining Two into One' Is Not Dialectics," and the debate was on. One camp used two-to-one (analog) as a way to push for peaceful coexistence, while the other camp used one-to-two (digital) as a way to push for a more permanent class struggle.

By the next year Yang's synthesis of two-to-one had been thoroughly renounced by Mao and his adherents in the analysis camp; by 1966 Yang was in jail. The results were clear: division would be favored over combination, analysis over synthesis, digital over analog.

The identification of such a great class struggle in the field of philosophy has been an inspiration to many in recent decades, particularly in the context of postwar French thought; not only Badiou, but also Guy Debord, Pierre Macherey, and others including Bruno Bosteels, Alenka Zupančič, and most recently Michael Hardt and Antonio Negri, who during the conclusion of their *Empire* trilogy find cause to discuss how and why "the one divides into two."[17]

These thinkers do not all agree by any means, yet contra Hegel and subsequent to Marx, Lenin, and Mao, a new normal had more or less been established in the late twentieth century: to be political means to favor distinction over integration, struggle over coexistence. Those advocating the integrity of the whole are labeled bourgeois and reactionary, while those advocating the disintegration of existing relations are labeled revolutionary and progressive.

"Truth is what has *no identity other than from a difference*," wrote Badiou, "hence the being of all things is the process of its division into two."[18] Or as Hardt and Negri unambiguously put it, "The old three-part dialectic, which would make a unity of the two conflicting subjectivities, will no longer work. Its claims of unity and integration at this point are just false promises."[19]

Yet while a consensus had emerged around division, opinion was certainly not universal on this point. Mao's "One becomes two," wrote Deleuze and Guattari near the start of *A Thousand Plateaus*, describes the sad efforts of "the most classical and well reflected, oldest, and weariest kind of thought."[20] Indeed for Deleuze and Guattari, contra the Maoist and Leninist tradition, digitality is the oldest kind of thought, the oldest prejudice, because it requires a decision made between two elements forever held apart in distinction. These elements may be zeros and ones, as with the binary mathematics driving modern computers. But they may also be any number of other things, such as the binary pairs of man and woman, self and other, industrialist and proletariat, or essence and instance.

For Deleuze and Guattari both versions of the mechanism of distinction are equally unappealing, whether the one dividing in two or the two fusing into one. (Hence their nomination of the rhizome as an alternative to all trees, roots, and radicals, the rhizome as a form of propagation irreducible to both division and fusion.) Yet although they have little use for the dialectic, Deleuze and Guattari were fully committed to multiplicity, not so much Mao's teeming contradictions but something closer to the proliferation of difference. Spinoza's immanence of nature provided the necessary path to retain both the unity of things and their endless differentiation. And thus with the Spinozists comes the grand compromise of immanence: pure multiplicity within the univocity of being. In other words, what *exists* is digital, but *what* exists is analog.

Yet today there exists an alternative option, irreducible to the syntheses of Hegel, the struggles of Mao, or Deleuze's grand compromise of immanence. Enter Laruelle and the grand non-compromise of immanence, defined by him in terms of the generic finitude of the one. Instead of arguing analysis or synthesis, one-in-two or two-in-one, digitality or analogicity, pro or con, Laruelle pleads indecision and exits the vicious circle entirely.

And so, given Laruelle's abstention from the decision of philosophy, any examination of his work will necessarily involve an examination of analysis, division, distinction, and indeed digitality. Although computers and the online world are not central in his work, the digital itself is indeed central, particularly if the digital is defined in a more capacious sense than merely the electronic machines and networks of millennial life.[21]

The digital is, in crass terms, Laruelle's chief enemy. His nonparticipation in the analysis–synthesis debate is a nonparticipation in the digital. His abstaining from binary relation is an abstention from the digital. His withdrawal from decision is a withdrawal from the digital. The many technical terms that he invents, as onerous as they sometimes are—unilateral duality, One-in-One, vision-in-One, cloning, and so on—are all attempts to suppress and supersede a fundamentally digital world.

Of course, the digital does not ultimately mean computers. It is imperative to consider the digital above and beyond the micro niche of twentieth- and twenty-first-century technology. Digitality is much more capacious than the computer, both historically, because there simply is no history without digitality, but also conceptually, because the digital is a basic ingredient within ontology, politics, and most everything in between.

From all of this may be distilled a principle of sufficient digitality motivated by the digital decision. The principle of sufficient digitality is defined similarly to its philosophical counterpart. To arrive at the principle, one need only conjure the spirit of Alan Turing: the computer is a machine that can reproduce the functionality of any other machine, provided its functionality can be broken down into logical processes. Likewise the principle of sufficient digitality states that *for everything in the world there is a process of distinction appropriate to it.* The principle asserts, in essence, that digitality is an autonomous field able to encode and simulate anything whatsoever within the universe. Adjacent to the principle of sufficiency and working in concert with it, the digital decision is simply the decision to start down such a path, the decision to decide at all, the decision of distinction.

The digital computer "is endowed with the capacity for synthesis, connection and communication, interfacing and exchange, all of which are inherently philosophical or world-bound," writes Laruelle, explicitly linking computers and philosophy. "Hegel is dead, but he lives on inside the electric calculator."[22]

The digital logic is deeply rooted within the core of philosophy, Laruelle claims, and it is the goal of non-philosophy to unilateralize the digital decision and withdraw from it:

> The duality of the discrete *[numérique]* and the continuous, of the mathematical and the philosophical . . . is a constant throughout history and permeates all of Western thought. The discrete regularly claims victory, even as the continuous continues to survive. . . . Non-philosophy is, among other things, a way to register this survival without pretending that one side will crush the other. Rather, non-philosophy connects each to an instance that is neither the continuous (dominant in philosophy) nor the discontinuous (dominant in science).[23]

In sum, although we explore Laruelle's body of work from a number of different angles, including the political, ontological, and aesthetic, the goal of this book is to superimpose Laruelle onto digitality, resulting in a new unilateral posture vis-à-vis both digitality and philosophy. The outcome is potentially quite interesting, because it means that Laruelle's non-standard theorization and axiomatization of the philosophical infrastructure may also be applied to the digital infrastructure. The same kinds of things that Laruelle says about philosophy and non-philosophy can also be said about digitality and non-digitality. The same kind of withdrawal, the same generic, the same immanence, the same materiality—all of these things offer a real, tangible parallel to the computerized world, not to resist or reflect on it so much as to demonstrate that it never was determining in the first place.

Part I

Laruelle and the Digital

William Edouard Daege, *The Invention of Painting*, 1832. Oil on canvas, 176.5 × 135.5 cm. Photograph by Jürgen Liepe. Nationalgalerie, Staatliche Museen, Berlin. bpk, Berlin / Nationalgalerie, Staatliche Museen / Jürgen Liepe / Art Resource, NY.

one

The One Divides in Two

"It should be taken quite seriously that the 'one' is a number," wrote Badiou in *Being and Event,* only partially in jest.[1] Indeed, the one is a number, and as a number it has something to say about how things are. Things are one, or things are not one. And if things are more than one they are a multiplicity. To say something *is* is to say it is *as one*. To utter *exists,* as Parmenides does in his poem, means implicitly to cry *exists as one!*

Indeed, Badiou begins his treatise on the one and the multiple by returning to Parmenides, who was himself the first to consider the question philosophically:

> Since its Parmenidean organization, ontology has built the portico of its ruined temple out of the following experience: what *presents* itself is essentially multiple; *what* presents itself is essentially one. The reciprocity of the one and being is certainly the inaugural axiom of philosophy . . . yet it is also its impasse. . . . For if being is one, then one must posit that what is not one, the multiple, *is not.*[2]

Having wedged himself into this undesirable corner, that the multiples of the world *are not,* Badiou is forced to do great violence to Parmenides—albeit a dramatically creative philosophical violence—by taking the ultimate step. For it is not the case that the one is and the multiple is not, but rather the reverse: "The one *is not.*"[3]

Badiou's leap is one of the most virtuosic moments in recent philosophy. In taking this step Badiou proposes that we retain the one but in the form of a deflated one. Not the God-like one of neoplatonism, Badiou's one is merely the "oneness" or "one-effect" of being.[4] So what began as a riff on the Parmenidean word play—The one is? The one is not?—ends up in Badiou as a new ontological foundation in which "the One is not, there are only actual multiplicities, and the ground is void."[5]

Masquerading as a friend, Badiou also does great violence to Deleuze in his book *Deleuze: The Clamor of Being* by trying to demonstrate that Deleuze is secretly a Platonist (like Badiou himself).[6] But Badiou borrowed much more from Deleuze than is commonly acknowledged, and in the course of his commentary he rearticulates clearly perhaps for the first time Deleuze's basic ontological contribution, his defense of *the univocity of being*.

What follows are some of Deleuze's claims, filtered through Badiou's prism: "Being is formulated univocally as: One, virtual, inorganic life, immanence, the nonsensical donation of sense, pure duration, relation, eternal return, and the affirmation of chance."[7] Being is "univocal" for Deleuze, and likewise the one refers to the "univocity" or "oneness" of Being.

Univocal means that there is a sameness between being and its expression. Deleuze explained this condition most eloquently in his *Difference and Repetition,* first at an early point in the text:

> There has only ever been one ontological proposition: Being is univocal. . . . From Parmenides to Heidegger it is the same voice which is taken up, in an echo which itself forms the whole deployment of the univocal. A single voice raises the clamour of being. . . . In effect, the essential in univocity is not that Being is said in a single and same sense, but that it is said, in a single and same sense, *of* all its individuating differences or intrinsic modalities. Being is the same for all these modalities, but these modalities are not the same. It is "equal" for all, but they themselves are not equal. It is said of all in a single sense, but they themselves do not have the same sense.[8]

Then again in the climactic final sentences:

> A single and same voice for the whole thousand-voiced multiple, a single and same Ocean for all the drops, a single clamour of Being for all beings.[9]

These same sentiments reappear in similar phrasing at the midpoint of Deleuze's *Logic of Sense,* in the powerful 25th Series devoted to univocity.[10] Interestingly, here Deleuze is forced to push beyond philosophy's typical binarism between Being and beings, making an additional distinction between Being and what he enigmatically calls "extra-Being."

Depending on how neoplatonic one wishes to be, "extra-Being" can be interpreted as synonymous with a "One" that is structurally outside of and prior to Being, in essence a kind of a priori core of Being, or Being understood purely from the perspective of its univocity. Thus the normal metaphysical model, consisting of two terms, Being and beings, could be supplemented with a third, "prior" term, the one:

Extra-Being (the one) / Being / beings

This risks taking things too far, however, because Deleuze's one should be understood neither as some sort of transcendental category, nor as a codeword for God, nor anything else of the sort. In Deleuze the one is simply the oneness of being, being as considered in it most minimal or neutral condition of univocity, being understood as a generic *aliquid.*[11]

But why not take things too far? A more radical discourse on the one, inaugurated by Parmenides, reappears in the neoplatonists, particularly Plotinus and Proclus, and today is most evident in the work of Laruelle, albeit in altered form. Although Deleuze and Badiou speak often of the one, it does not ultimately take center stage in their work, eclipsing all else. In neoplatonism, however, and, differently, in Laruelle, the one is absolutely central, so much so that it ceases to act as a synonym for Being.[12]

In Laruelle the one is the real. Yet even in being real the one remains firmly autonomous both from philosophy and from Being. The one is *radically immanent,* meaning that it is absolutely nonconvertible with anything whatsoever. It never goes outside of itself to form a relation with anything. The one has nothing to do with existence, understood in its strict etymological sense of "being out of," because the one is not "being" and nor is it "out of" anything. "The One is immanence," Laruelle says, "and is not thinkable on the terrain of transcendence (ekstasis, scission, nothingness, objectivation, alterity, alienation, *meta* or *epekeina*)."[13]

In its immanence, Laruelle's one is understood as identity. That is, the one is an identity or commonality with itself without ever being construed as a transcendental. In fact, in a reversal of the classical metaphysics evident in everyone from Plato and Kant to Hegel and beyond, in which the transcendental is considered to be the primary precondition or grounding for reality, Laruelle asserts the one *as the immanent real* from which transcendental instances are, in his terminology, "cloned."[14] In this way, Laruelle can not be called a metaphysician, at least not any type of metaphysician currently known, because he denies the basic mechanics of metaphysics such as manifestation, representation, or existence.

So although Laruelle and Deleuze both reference the one, they have almost nothing similar to say about it. The main difference is that Deleuze's one is ultimately not differentiated from Being. Rather for Deleuze, a good materialist, the oneness of the one is expressed in all the multiple permutations of Being. Whereas for Laruelle it is impossible for the one to "appear" or even be "voiced" across all the multiplicities of being because the one would then have to be "in" Being, and thus would cease being in itself. In other words, the one is not the one by virtue of having been *realized in Being*.[15] So although they share an equal interest in immanence, Laruelle considers Deleuze too timid, accusing him of not being immanent *enough*.[16]

One of Badiou's masters, Lacan, will help expand this brief synopsis of the one. In Lacan the one is understood as an assemblage of the self. While speaking about love and sexuality, Lacan evokes the image of the "intuitive, fusional, amorous" self as one: "'We are but one,'" say the lovers, who, as it goes, are as one flesh. "Everyone knows, of course, that two have never become but one, but nevertheless, 'we are but one.' The idea of love begins with that."[17]

Then the playfulness subsides slightly and Lacan adds, "The One everyone talks about all the time is, first of all, a kind of mirage of the One you believe yourself to be. Not to say that that is the whole horizon. There are as many Ones as you like—they are characterized by the fact that none of them resemble any of the others in any way—see the first hypothesis in the *Parmenides*."[18]

Lacan clearly lacks a reverence for this particular one, which is but a "mirage" constitutive of the subject. The one is something to be picked up and modified as new symbolic economies impinge upon the constitution of the self. Although this is no ontology, Lacan has not deviated very widely at all from the tradition of "monist" or univocal being set out in Parmenides, Deleuze, and the others. These ones—"as many Ones as you like"—are but the multiplicities of the instances of being, concordant with how Deleuze defined univocity.

But the next paragraph begins to complicate the matter and reveals the real source of Badiou's affection for this particular passage in Lacan's seminars, as Lacan makes reference to set theory:

> Set theory bursts onto the scene by positing the following: let us speak of things as One that are strictly unrelated to each other. Let us put together objects of thought, as they are called, objects of the world, each of which counts as one. Let us assemble these absolutely heterogeneous things, and let us grant ourselves the right to designate the resulting assemblage by a letter. This is how set theory expresses itself at the outset.[19]

The two lovers, the two relatively heterogeneous things, join together as one. But they do so only under the aegis of a letter, which Lacan reveals to be his famous *a*, the supplementary other that always accompanies the one.

> In other words, there are three of them, but in reality, there are two plus *a*. This two plus *a*, from the standpoint of *a*, can be reduced, not to the two others, but to a One plus *a*. . . . This identification, which is produced in a ternary articulation, is grounded in the fact that *in no case can two as such serve as a basis*. Between two, whatever they may be, there is always the One and the Other, the One and the *a*, and the Other cannot in any way be taken as a One.[20]

Although Lacan shares little with the previous philosophers of the one, they all pursue a similar goal, to avoid the classical binarism of metaphysics. Lacan again: *In no case can two serve as a basis.* Philosophers of immanence wish to collapse the binarism back to the singularity of the one, while here Lacan, in a move that can be properly labeled poststructuralist, wishes to exceed the binarism by always already supplementing it with a tertiary level. In Lacanian algebra this is expressed in the delightful formula, $1 + 1 = 3$. (Whereas our previous chaperones of the one would likely have expressed it in the purely affirmative sense of $1 + 1 + 1 \ldots$ etc. [Deleuze], or even more simply in the identity equation $1 = 1$ [Laruelle].)

Now a crossroads, for we arrive at a decision point that remains unresolved. The one can be understood in quite different terms. The one can simply be *another name* for Being, putting the stress on the continuous, full, indivisible nature of Being. Or the one can refer to the *univocal way* of Being, allowing a proliferation of real multiplicities that despite their real differences are nevertheless all vocalized in terms of their oneness. Or in a more extreme sense, the one can *cease to be a synonym* for Being and assume its own space apart from it, either as an a priori precondition, or as a radically immanent real, unmanifested and irreflected. Or other options still: the neoplatonic transcendental One, the Lacanian post-structuralist one, and still others not yet itemized.

The question is *Which one?* Is it best to side with Deleuze, who maintains his univocity of Being precisely to avoid having to speak about a real metaphysical split between the one and its instances? Is it best to accept the upside-down Platonism of Badiou in which the one is not, multiplicities are, and events again are not? Or is it best to adopt the weird materialism of Laruelle, who admits that the one is real and immanent to itself, while we, the science-bound "clones" of the one can only run alongside the real and think "according to it" but never "of" it or "about" it?

In order to answer these questions we need to address a number of things more closely. We start with three questions: What is philosophy? Where did philosophy come from? And what is it like without philosophy? Following Laruelle's own tendencies, we limit ourselves to Western philosophy and focus on the continental tradition. Yet the claims made about philosophy may be easily extended into adjacent literatures and discourses.

What is philosophy? (the standard model). Philosophy is rooted in a grand illusion. The illusion is vividly evident in philosophy's most archetypal mode, metaphysics, which suggests that the ultimate task of philosophy is to watch over a grand division. What division, if not the division between appearance and presence, essence and instance, and Being and beings (see William Edouard Daege, *The Invention of Painting,* the frontispiece of this chapter)? To do philosophy means to assent to the fact that the universe is structured in this way. It means to assent to these particular conditions of possibility. To live means to mediate life by way of the grand illusion. And to live means to assume that the illusion was made to be grasped by us, that it is the special mode of being that is *ours* or *mine,* as Heidegger says. To live philosophically means to live in a world "by and for" us.[21]

Why call it the grand illusion? Is this to hint of a grand delusion, and thus to excoriate the metaphysical gambit as something less than serious? Not exactly, for the grand illusion is indeed impressive, an epic construction of colossal proportion. By *illusion* is meant a construction, and thus something like an ideological construction, just as consciousness itself requires a certain kind of construction (a scaffolding of intention and absorption between self and world).

But *illusion* also contains the root meaning "play"; it means to put into play against something else, from the Latin meaning "to play with or mock." Hence, withholding any derisive presuppositions about the term, "illusion" is quite appropriate for the metaphysical condition because it gives a basic architecture of relations in play. The beings of Being are "in play." Thus to call the basic practice of philosophy a grand illusion is nothing like a normative judgment—indeed normative judgments themselves are only possible within the regime of philosophy—it is simply a theoretical observation: in uncoupling from the Godhead, what simply *is* transforms into something that *is being,* and the core modes and categories of being are inaugurated as such. The inauguration is a "putting into play" of the mechanics of our world, and hence like an oversize ontological cinema, or the simultaneous firing of every synapse in the human brain, or the masses storming the Winter Palace, or the annual migration of the monarch butterfly—like all these, a grand illusion.

What is philosophy? Thankfully Laruelle has made this question relatively easy to answer, despite how daunting it might seem. To address the question we may simply itemize the various root-level conditions of philosophy, because they all tend to coalesce around something like a philosophical principle or a philosophical decision. In the same way that physicists agree, more or less, on a standard model that describes the elementary forces of the universe, philosophers agree, more or less, on their own standard model for what it means to do philosophy. Thus the following paragraphs all describe a similar mode. They all describe a similar model for philosophy.

¶ *The media principle.* Recall the opening sections of the book, for the media principle already illustrates the basic architecture of philosophy. As discussed in the introduction, Laruelle states the media principle elegantly as "the real is communicational, the communicational is real."[22] What this means is that philosophy assumes the real to be something that can be grasped and communicated beyond itself into a receiving mind, the mind of the investigating philosopher. Even a skeptic, while doubting the availability of such knowledge, implicitly assents to the basic parameters of the discussion (the real, communicability, interpretation, philosophy). Laruelle uses the technical term *amphibology* to describe this condition. By amphibology he means anything in which there is an ontological ambiguity established between the real and the represented, or between Being and beings. He means anything that is "amphibious" across two zones, just as frogs and newts are amphibious across land and water. This is why we began the book with Hermes, for he is the most amphibious of all the gods. Anything that follows the media principle can be labeled an amphibology. Hence metaphysics is an amphibology, and so is phenomenology and many other—Laruelle would say all—philosophical pursuits.

¶ *The architecture of distinction.* As Badiou puts it, philosophy means three things: "What is to be understood by Being? What is thinking? How does the essential identity of thinking and Being realize itself?"[23] Parmenides put philosophy on this course, and it has scarcely diverted in the many years since. In her fantastic book on Heidegger, Luce Irigaray phrases it like this: "The proposition at the origin of metaphysics: *to be— to think—the same*"; or in less asyndetic language: "Metaphysics always supposes, in some manner, a solid crust from which to raise a construction."[24] The architecture of metaphysics therefore requires a fundamental distinction between ground and construction, or between materiality and the relations formed "above" or "on top of" it. The many synonyms for such a ground include *object, body, entity, a being, extension, thing, matter,* and *substance.* Likewise the many synonyms for the forming of relation include *information, thought, reason, middle,* and *language.* The notion that these two lists of terms have anything to do with one another, indeed as Heidegger argues that they naturally *belong* to one another as a structure of "appropriation," is the philosophical gesture par excellence.

❡ *The ontological principle and the principle of sufficient reason.* These two principles, which are similar, appear in the work of a number of philosophers. My preferred version is the one already stated, the version that appears in Whitehead: "No actual entity, then no reason."[25] It is similar to the previously described architecture of distinction, in that it requires something like an object–relation dualism. The "actual entity" plays the role of the object, while the "reason" plays the role of relation. In coupling them, Whitehead asserts that one cannot exist without the other, and indeed that the condition of the world is one in which these two things are teammates. Whitehead's phrasing is a mirror image of how the principle appears in Leibniz—"Anything that happens does so for a definite reason"—but in the end they both achieve the same result. Heidegger concurs as well: during a discussion of Parmenides and identity, he translates Parmenides's important third fragment as "For the same perceiving (thinking) as well as being" *(το γαρ αυτό νοείν εστίν τε και είναι),* and uses the fragment as a launch pad to explore the primordial relation of identity at the heart of being.

❡ Yet the topic of mediation and distinction is but a minor note to a much larger discourse in Laruelle concerning the question of what philosophy is. Recall the two main concepts defined in the introduction: the *philosophical decision* and *principle of sufficient philosophy.* The philosophical decision refers to the decision, made willingly or unwillingly, Laruelle argues, by all philosophy and all philosophers, to reflect on anything whatsoever. Likewise the principle of sufficient philosophy refers to the privilege of doing such a thing, the privilege to relate to anything whatsoever. With the swagger of its privilege, philosophy brazenly assumes that there can be a philosophy of being, a philosophy of art, a philosophy of sport, a philosophy of anything and everything under the sun. Philosophy is thus exceedingly immodest; it is up to any task, and thus is "sufficient" for any and all practices of philosophizing.

In fact Laruelle takes pleasure in pointing out that the question "What is philosophy?" is something only a philosopher would pose. It fits the philosopher's personality perfectly. Philosophy is an endeavor that endlessly seeks to establish rational relations spanning the two categories of mind and matter, and hence endlessly poses the question "What is *x*?" In this sense, any and all philosophical pursuits are merely secret allegories for the question "What is philosophy?"[26]

***Thesis II. This reveals the basic law of the standard model,* whatever given is riven.** Having briefly described the root-level conditions of philosophy—the media principle, the architecture of distinction, the ontological principle, and the philosophical decision—we now summarize a few key points having to do with the rivenness of being.

First and foremost, philosophy is a *digitization of the real* because it is predicated on the one dividing in two. Laruelle describes it well in a late work devoted to the topic of generic science:

> The most general structure of philosophy—and I mean the structure of all philosophical and in particular epistemological systems—is built from the varying combinations of unity and duality, of One and Two. We call this a becoming-world whenever a pair of these heterogenous terms, in fusing immanently together, nevertheless allows one of the pair to obtain primacy over the whole and assume responsibility for the immanent relation, thereby uncoupling and asserting itself anew as a third transcendental term.[27]

The splitting of the real and the digitization of the real are synonymous. The term *being* is simply a contracted way of stating "being riven," and the standard model is the state in which there exists a riven being placed in conjugation with itself as being-riven.[28]

In other words Plato cheated. He *forced* the one, forcing the one to birth philosophy: "Seeing it as the transcendental rival to Being, Plato 'forced' the One—but forcing only in a negative sense—separating the One from Being, before cleaving them together again and forcing them to orbit each other. Philosophical forcing means to undo contraries that have been sutured together, to separate the contraries."[29] Such cheating (dubbed here "negative" forcing), to which we return in the final chapter, entails the inauguration of a structure of distinction or auto-alienation. And this is nothing other than philosophy itself.

So it is easy to agree with Michel Henry when he observes that "for Hegel the Concept is nothing other than *the very fact of alienating oneself*, the process of alienation as such."[30] If the concept is the process of alienation as such, then the same is true about relation, information, language, or thought: they are all the process of alienation as such, for they all depend upon a fundamental digitization between things. In the case of relation, it is a digitization between whatever two terms are brought into relation; for information, the digitization between two discernible forms; for language, the digitization between represented and representation; for thought, the digitization between thinker and whatever is being reflected upon.

Likewise it is easy to agree with Kant on his basic description of philosophy: "There can be nothing more desirable to a philosopher, than to be able to derive the scattered multiplicity of the concepts or the principles, which had occurred to him in concrete use, from a principle *a priori,* and to unite everything in this way in one cognition. . . . He has attained a *System.*"[31]

Kant's "system" is a newfound conjugation of the pure and the concrete, the universal and the scattered multiplicity. The point is not to quibble over details. It does not particularly matter whether one can or cannot defend the a priori, or whether "concrete use" consists of scattered multiplicities. The point is the architecture itself: a system, internally variegated according to the law of two.

Why stop there? For the concept or the system are not the only illustrations of the process of internal alienation via variegation. Within the condition of being-given, *all categories are equally riven.* This includes the concept (relation, preposition, link, sense), but also bodies (beings, entities, objects, nodes) as well as events (force, fiat, cause, will, process). Hence bodies must also be considered in terms of alienation: in their extension and transcendental persistence bodies are alienated from themselves through space and through time. Likewise events must be understood in terms of alienation: an event inaugurates a differential of evental states as a "before" alienated from an "after." In short, under the standard model, bodies, languages, and events are all equally riven.

In specifying that all *categories* are equally riven, it will not hurt to specify an additional corollary that follows directly from the ontological principle: all *modes* of being-given are equally riven. I have yet to itemize these modes, that being the task of the next chapter, so I speak now only in very general terms. But the notion is already contained within the grand illusion: being in the world means being in a condition of division and relation. And hence being requires the recognition of a fundamental alienation.

Being is on the side of the world, which means it is part of a universe in which things relate to or uncouple from other things. In the world, entities may virtualize or dissolve into other entities just as they may be "solved" or actualized. This, then, is the basic architecture of the standard model of philosophy . . . the primordial distinction *that there must be a distinction.*

The Standard Model,
or the essential digitization
of philosophy as being-riven:

God—humanity
essence—instance
relation—object
mind—body
affect—comportment
information—data
Being—being
ontology—ontics
life—the living
spirit—matter
ideal—actual
subject—object
orientation—world
form—content
representation—presentation

Where did philosophy come from? (the advent). One of Heidegger's most powerful concepts concerning ontology is *Ereignis,* which has an almost absurd translation history into English. *Ereignis* has been rendered awkwardly but technically as both "enowning" and "the event of Appropriation"; the term refers to a sense of belonging, a sense of being owned within something and thus becoming assimilated as proper or "appropriate" to it. Heidegger uses the term when he speaks about the special relationship of belonging forged between humanity and being. Man and being belong together, he writes in the essay "The Principle of Identity," "A belonging to Being prevails within man, a belonging which listens to Being because it is appropriated to Being."[32]

Heidegger also speaks of *Ereignis* in terms of the enigmatic expression "It gives" *(es gibt)*. The "It gives" is the closest Heidegger ever gets to Laruelle, the closest he gets to the one. For in partially suspending the subject of the verb—but he is too timid, leaving in place that pathetic little pronoun "it"—Heidegger begins to speculate about the advent of Being. It is crucial for Heidegger that the phrase have an impersonal subject, as in "It gives being" or "It gives time," not "Being gives . . . ," for there must be some sort of generic condition of possibility for being, some sort of advental precondition. This advent is simply the belonging-togetherness of the ontological categories. "What determines both, time and Being, in their own, that is, in their belonging together, we shall call: *Ereignis,* the event of Appropriation. *Ereignis* will be translated as Appropriation or event of Appropriation. One should bear in mind, however, that 'event' is not simply an occurrence, but that which makes any occurrence possible."[33]

Ereignis thus describes the event that establishes belonging—the notion that certain aspects of being belong together—and hence the event that establishes relation. *Ereignis* is therefore a digitization and is compatible with the standard model. Heidegger's being is *distinctive;* in stating "It gives" he is simultaneously stating the advent of digital being. For Heidegger there is a distinction to be made between man and Being, or between Being and time.

Yet what is ultimately most important about *Ereignis* is not so much the question of belonging, but rather the question of the event. So although the presence of Being constitutes a relation, the advent of Being is an *event* for Heidegger, not a relation or an object or some other ontological category. (This is part of the genius of Heidegger; it allows him to make his argument about the historicity of Being, namely that Being might have begun and that it might end.)

By putting the stress on Being as advent or event it is possible to strike an unholy alliance between Heidegger and Laruelle. The world is not the result of a thing (another world to spawn this one; the acorn and the oak), nor is it the result of a relation (metaphysics; God the Father and God the Son). Being carries the condition of relationality as such within itself as one of its attributes, yes, but this does not mean that Being is the result of a relation. In fact Being is the result of an event.

In other words, the standard model *is the result of an event not a relation.* There is no relation between the one and Being. It is not possible to convert one into the other through the alchemy of metaphysics. Because it is an event, the advent of the world is an unexplained arrival. One can quite technically label it, without irony or pomposity, a miracle.

Was the world created, yes or no? Of course the answer is yes. But there is no glory in referring to something called "creation" or "the advent," because the event of being is continually being renewed and reactuated. Just as Peter Hallward describes Deleuze's work as a "philosophy of creation," the structure of advent-event is a constant push and pull into and out of the real.

What is it like without philosophy? (the prevent). If the advent is a digitization, then the practice of philosophy, particularly in its most archetypal mode as metaphysics, is also a form of digitization, in that it requires the division into two of Being and beings, essence and instance, Life and the living, the pure and the practical, a priori and a posteriori, foundation and logic, genesis and structure, metaphysics and physics, and so on. The suggestion is not that these pairs are mere iterations of one another, or that they refer to the same thing, simply that they *are pairs,* that something has been rent apart and cleaved back together again. Such is the essence of the standard model.

What would happen if the advent were reversed? What would happen if, instead of being created, the standard model was uncreated? What would happen if we decline to make the decision? It will require a new term, the *prevent,* which means two things at once: the prevent is both what comes before the event (pre-event) and what hinders the event (prevention). To think the prevent is to think a universe without the standard model, and thus without both philosophy and digitality.

Admittedly it is difficult to speak about the prevent because the normal way of speaking about the world assumes a non-real world, which is to say a world of division, alienation, manifestation, and representation. However this should not discourage us, because such difficulties are a comment not on the speculative or impoverished nature of the real, but on the impoverished nature of our alienated languages.

So let us begin with language itself, as a soft segue into what follows. The easiest way to approach the prevent is to convert "being" from gerund back to infinitive. So from "being" to "be." Alternately one might strip the third person singular by removing its implied subject. So from "it is" to simply "is." The challenge is to deprive language of its transcendental aspects, leaving an immanent core, which itself will gradually fade away once the transcendental policeman has been silenced. So the continuous nature of "being" as a presence that persists through time and space—in other words as the sufficient transcendental—shifts to the much more generic "be." And the coupling of pronoun and verb in "it is," which cannot help but presuppose a transcendental relation between actor and action, if not a transcendental "it" itself, shifts to the unqualified "is." These are some of the primary names of the one revealed by the prevent: *be, is, real*. But never: *being, it is, reality*.

Why put the stress on uncoupling words from their transcendental forms? The one requires an uncoupling of the transcendental pairings, arriving not so much at a "divorced" language but an unconjugated or preconjugated language. A similar argument could be made about the way in which nouns are declined, the aim of which is to account for all the distinct cases of the word. But what if there are no cases of the word? Such is the condition of the one. It requires indistinguishing between cases, an indistinction of the declination.

But there is a danger, for in these kinds of discussions there is the ever-present danger of narrating the story of the one as a story of the fall, as a story of the before and the after. To be sure, the one is neither a place beyond, nor even a place right here, hiding in plain sight. The one is not from a special time, a time forgotten or a time to come. The story of the one is not the story of the Garden of Eden. The one is not transcendental, nor is it mythological. On the contrary, it is real, which means it is the closest to us, quite literally the least theological, the least speculative.

Laruelle "apriorizes" the world. Under classical Kantian metaphysics the a priori is the realm of the transcendentals (space, time, identity, scientific truths, and so on) and the a posteriori is the realm of the actuals, the real, the empirical (you, me, my thoughts, my body, this place, this world). Kant's approach is to maintain a distinction between these two realms. He privileges the transcendental, of course, but he also demonstrates that the transcendental is just one component of experience even if it perpetually infuses and subtends it.

Of course, many thinkers working in the wake of Kant have reconfigured these terms—for Deleuze, the point is to flatten the division entirely, such that the virtual is real, and any transcendental categories are defined and experienced purely and immanently in the self-expression of matter. And for Hegel, via Fichte and Schelling, the point is to embolden the realm of idea into a pure logical science of self-expression.

It has been said that Kant is to Laruelle as Hegel is to Marx, the elder figures producing a bourgeois idealism that must be inverted into a new science, be it the science of political economy for Marx or the science of non-philosophy for Laruelle. Hegel was standing on his head, after all, so why not Kant too? Although partially helpful, this formulation does not entirely capture Laruelle's precise intervention into philosophy, Kantian or otherwise. Under Laruelle the realm of the analytic a priori is no longer the minority realm, but the majority realm. The a priori is no longer simply the transcendental but the real as well. Likewise the things formerly considered real (you, me, my body, this place) are now transcendental, for they are the transcendental clones of the one.

To borrow a term of his own creation, Laruelle "apriorizes" the world. He reverses the real and the transcendental (from their Kantian positions) and recasts both real and transcendental as a priori. Hence the real, which Laruelle calls the one, is a priori by virtue of being an immanent identity: true immanence can only be obtained if the real is a priori. Likewise the transcendentals are also a priori, including the subject, axiomatic and theorematic claims, and even non-philosophy itself.

(The only domain that remains steadfastly a posteriori is philosophy itself, and the regional knowledges and sciences that ape the basic philosophical conceit. They are the new "data," the new empirical knowledge offered up for non-philosophical axiomatization and dissection.)

But although Laruelle seems to collapse the a priori/a posteriori distinction, in essence *apriorizing* it, this does not necessarily mean that non-philosophy is the domain of the prior, the pure, or the original. On the contrary, non-philosophy is the domain of the *last,* not the first, as evidenced by it being causally determined in the last instance. Laruelle never summons us to *go back to first principles* or *determine the universal possibility of cognition,* as philosophers like Kant or Heidegger do. Rather he entreats the non-philosophical subject to *withdraw from the decision, and dwell along side the last, the least, the finite.*

Thesis III. The one is a prevent, is part of the prevental mode, and hence has no concourse with the standard model. A synonym for this is virtualization. The event of Being is what establishes a world of transcendental presence as the "present continuous," a world of figure and ground, a world of objects and relations.

By contrast the prevent is a radically passive abstention from the event. The prevent means *withdrawal of decision*—"decision" meaning literally to "cleave" or "differentiate"—and thus a withdrawal of the event. To speak of Being means implicitly to speak of "trenchant" or "riven" Being. But the prevent or the virtual indicates a metastasis of Being within the totality of insufficient and undifferentiated alternative states. As prevent, the real pertains to no decision, to no event, to no presence.

The real indicates a withdrawal of the event of being, and in so doing shifts over to the purely a priori realm of the all. And here even formerly stalwart terms like *be* and *is* begin to dissolve. For in the strictest sense, the one forms no mixture at all with the existence or inexistence of things.

Here Laruelle exceeds even Parmenides: be, is, not be, not is—who cares? The one is oblivious to such worldly concerns. The real one is a condition of pure virtuality, and thus requires that standard notions of the event and the transcendental be suspended in favor of the prevent and immanence. Be, is, virtual, real, a priori—these are some of the primary names of the one.

No actual object, no actual relation, no actual event. Next let us interrogate the one from the reverse perspective, from the three co-original attributes of the standard model: *object, relation,* and *event.* From the perspective of object, the one is not a thing; it has no physical or corporeal continuity with being. From the perspective of relation, the one does not relate; it has no formal relation with being. Likewise from the perspective of event, the one does not happen; it does not occasion itself or actualize itself as an event.

To reiterate, the real is the condition of the prevent. Although it is true that thought does not hold sway within the real as real (because relation does not hold sway), it is still possible to think the real directly. If White-head's ontological principle states "No actual entity, then no reason," through which he describes the state of being-given into a world of orga-nized or rational entities (entities with rationales; rationales as entities), then to understand the prevent one must simply undo the ontological principle. It requires only the subtlest redaction: *no actual entity and no reason.* Simply underscore the force of the no. The prevent is a condition in which there are *no* actual entities (no bodies, no objects, no matter, no extension, and so on) and in which there is *no* reason (no language, no relation, no information, no media, and so on).

Still this only addresses two of the three co-original attributes of the actual. The reversal of Whitehead's ontological principle offers a rudi-mentary description of the condition of bodies and languages in the pre-vent of the real, yet what of the event?

As we already learned from Heidegger, *Being is the result of an event.* This point is absolutely crucial; it is another way of understanding the previous claims about the advent and the creation of the standard model. Being, as Being-given, is itself the homeland of relation, but it is not the *result* of a relation. Being-given unto the terrain of the three co-original attributes necessarily means that relationality exists, as bodies relate through relations and likewise bodies and relations are modi-fied via events. Yet the act of being-given is precisely that, an act, never a relation.

To put it in Laruellean language, one cannot bring together "One" and "Being" under the banner of a relation, stating something along the lines of "The One has a relation to Being" or even "Being has a relation to the One." This is impossible within the non-standard model. Instead it is necessary to bring together "One" and "Being" under the banner of the event, stating that "the One is cloned as Being," or, as Deleuze might put it, that "the actualization of the virtual is an event." This is why the philo-sophical decision is a *decision,* because a decision is an event.

Laruellean events are thus a kind of *static preemption.* They are static because the agency of the event is not predicated on the execution of the event; static realities are "known in advance" of any actualization. Like-wise, Laruellean events are a preemption because of the attractive gravity of the prevent, which acts in advance of the event and prevents it. In this sense, static preemption is simply a synonym for destiny.

Iterate the Laruellean logic across the other attributes to reveal their appropriate non-standard cousins. For the prevent reveals that Laruellean objects are in fact *black monads,* smooth globes of an almost infinite flimsiness, irresistibly dense and stubbornly opaque. Laruellean objects might best be understood as "actual inexistents" for as they span the advent they move into the realm of the actual, but in so much as they are immanently real they cannot "exist" (in the sense of *ekstasis*). Laruellean objects are labeled black because they "have no windows" and are thus absolutely opaque. And because they have no relation they may be said to "withdraw completely." They are labeled monads because they represent the entire universe of the one within them, and hence are structurally metastable or incontinent.

Likewise Laruellean relation is defined as *unilateral determination.* Such relation is not combinatory and synthetic, like the dialectic. It is not differential and classificatory, like empiricism. Neither is it efficient or occasioning, like metaphysics. Rather, unilateral relations are rigorously irreversible and nonreflective. Unilateral relations are oblivious and prophylactic because they impede the legibility of the agents involved and prohibit subsequent circuits of call-response or action-reaction.

These three aspects—black objects, unilateral determination, and static preemption—only briefly defined here, are taken up in greater detail throughout the book.

The horror of philosophy. Because philosophy requires sufficiency, the *insufficiency* of objects, relations, and events poses something of a threat. It catalyzes a great violence against philosophy.

As Eugene Thacker writes, the equiprimorder is supernatural horror, the horror of the supernature of the one. Claims made about the supernature are thus claims made directly about the real. And, as Laruelle would say, the supernature is just another word for the a priori.

Never the world-for-us, nor even the world-in-itself, the equiprimorder of the one is the world-without-us. "The world-without-us is the subtraction of the human from the world," Thacker writes. "The world-without-us lies . . . in a nebulous zone that is at once impersonal and horrific."[34] This is why the real seems so terrifying from the perspective of the world. But it is the philosopher who is horrified, not us, for only philosophy is threatened by the one.

In other words, what is "prior" as a priori is also at the same time a profoundly horrific priority. The a priori is thus properly labeled "ancient" or "primeval"—not so much in terms of a historical ancestrality but rather in terms of a structural priority or preemption.[35] What is last is also prior or preemptive.

Deleuze was on to something when he remarked that "thought 'makes' difference, but difference is monstrous."[36] Still, he didn't go quite far enough. Digitization is monstrous, but it does not hold a candle to the glorious, monstrous cataclysm of the one.

Artist unknown, *[Student in Bicycle-Bird Costume]*, 1924–1925. Gelatin silver print, 12.5 × 8.9 cm. The J. Paul Getty Museum, Los Angeles.

two

The Standard Model

Hang gliding, bungie jumping, ice climbing. Hulk Hogan, Tony Hawk, John Rambo. In a world of extreme sports and extreme weather, of super-sized portions and long tails, is anyone really surprised by the advent of "extreme philosophy"? Laruelle has arrived in America, but couldn't we see this coming? Like when the CIA funded the Afghani mujahideen during the Cold War only to have it come back to haunt them, we funded post-structuralism in the 1970s and '80s and are today engulfed in the ultimate blowback.[1] You planted the seeds of destruction, and Western metaphysics was shaken to its core. But nothing could have prepared you for what would come next. You thought Derrida was extreme, *but you ain't seen nothing yet. . . .*

Indeed Laruelle risks being co-opted as just another extreme continental philosopher. Kant systematized the conditions of possibility for knowledge; Heidegger chronicled the end of metaphysics; Derrida upended the foundations of Western thought; and Deleuze signaled the end of the dialectic. Laruelle could be described as simply the latest continental thinker to up the ante on philosophy, to be more meta than those who came before, to trump philosophy in the ultimate act of one-upmanship.

Yet this is not an accurate portrayal of the non-standard method, as I hope to show over the course of this volume. Laruelle has no intention of extending philosophy, supplementing it, strengthening it, or even competing with it. There is nothing meta about Laruelle, and there is nothing particularly extreme about his position. Indeed, Laruelle never uses such terms, but instead describes his own endeavors as axiomatic and generic.

Rather than pushing philosophy further, Laruelle simply abstains from participation. He *declines to make the decision*. Like Bartleby's "I would prefer not to" or the Occupy movement's "We have no demands," Laruelle declines to participate in philosophy, and likewise declines all structures or relations that mimic the basic philosophical stance. But an abstention is not a transcendental withdrawal, that much is clear, for in his abstention Laruelle does not "go meta" by stepping backward in order to gain better perspective on that raving beast called philosophy. He does not wish to reflect on philosophy, nor represent it, nor deconstruct it, nor recast it in another mold, for these are all simply the tricks and conceits of philosophical technology crafted and perfected over the course of the past few millennia. "Philosophical technology has been withdrawn mimetically from the World, in order to reflect and reproduce it," he remarked in one of his short experimental texts. But "such technology is inadequate for thinking the Universe."[2]

To be sure, Laruelle acknowledges the existence of the world, escaping that special gnostic trap in which the world is cast as a mere fallen illusion obscuring a heaven yet to come. Indeed, the world exists. But the world *is philosophical*.

Thesis IV on the epithets: (A) the one has no epithets. Prefixes and prepositions reek of metaphysics. Only a metaphysical universe would allow some things to be *for* other things or *of* or *from* them. The true one would do away with such connectors and qualifiers, for the one has no epithets.

"Where are they, the instruments of this thinking *in*, *by* but not *of* or *within* the One?"[3] What a grand lament, so generative, so instructive. Through his lament Laruelle indicates the crucial importance of the preposition, how the preposition acts philosophically by determining structures of belonging between one thing and another thing. Prepositions are one of the important ways in which language demonstrates relation, and thus any critique of relation would need to devote some time to the preposition. In fact, as a critique of relation, Laruelle's entire project might be usefully described as little more than an extended treatise on the preposition.

It would be hasty to conclude that Laruelle is against the preposition, even as he tends to suppress certain ones and suspend other ones in parentheses, in an incongruous nod to the syntactical mannerisms of post-structuralist writing. Laruelle generally avoids any linkages that indicate belonging, which is to say a relation that determines the object. So he steers clear of prepositions like *of, within, from, against, for,* and *with.*

Nevertheless some prepositions, contrary to their grammatical role, tend to obscure the object's determination in favor of a linkage of nonrelation. Such nonrelational linkages are often structures of parallelism in which two entities remain separate and nonequal even as they are brought together. Two entities might persist in parallel without ever exchanging anything, or their parallelism might be so radically and rigorously superimposed that, counterintuitively, they achieve mutual immanence. Prepositions useful to embody such structures include *in, as, by, according to, alongside,* and *without.*

So with little anxiety Laruelle will speak of things like given-without-givenness, vision-in-One, or thinking according to the real even as he hedges with parenthetical expressions like force (of) vision. Similar to Hermes, the chaperone god who runs alongside travelers as they venture into foreign lands, Laruelle seeks a parallelism or accompaniment. But such parallelism is a nonrelation in which no mutual exchange or correspondence transpires between the parties in question. In this sense Laruelle seeks *relation without exchange.*

This is why we might describe the one as *autistic.* Of course, this is not to pathologize autism, much less to pathologize the one. This is not to insinuate some new kind of neuro-normativity into the conversation. On the contrary, if anything Laruelle's autism should convince us that cognitive norms are something of a fraud, just as Deleuze and Guattari's use of the term *schizophrenia* was meant to overturn the apple cart of what healthy subjects were thought to be. To label Laruelle's theory of relation as autistic is simply to point out that the one is, as it were, non-normative in its relationships. Like the autist who does not form relationships using the typical linking techniques of language, object orientation, or eye contact, the one does not establish a relation with the clone, and in fact is not even party to the act of cloning because nothing of the one is advanced or synthesized during cloning. This is why the one requires such a radical rethinking of the preposition, and why the one has very little use for relation, at least in the way relation is commonly construed.[4]

Without relation, without exchange, without many prepositional arrangements, a basic thesis emerges: *the one has no epithets.* The one lacks
qualification conferred through aspects, adjectives, monikers, or titles.[5]

"The One is like a substance-without-attributes," writes Laruelle,
momentarily adopting the Spinozist vocabulary of substance and attribute.[6] The one is indecisive vis-à-vis the epithets of being. It quite simply
has no opinion about them. The one is not a "suspension" of epithetal
attribution, because there is nothing to suspend. Rather, the one occu-
pies the a priori position vis-à-vis both the epithets and the conditions of
possibility for any epithet whatsoever.

But *what is an epithet?* An epithet is an aspect of appearing. Given
the nature of being, multiple epithets will surround the same appearing
being. An epithet is a way of speaking, and therefore an epithet is a way
of speaking Being according to the one (univocity).

This speaking is not grounded on a principle of pure difference or
assemblage, such that each epithet is an isolated singularity, equally removed from each and every other aspect. In fact, an epithet demonstrates
that the attributes of an entity can be rooted in a principle of aspective
difference even while the elemental appearance of the entity (a being) is
rooted in a principle of identity (a being the Same). Each epithet speaks
difference through the singularity of the same Being. In this way epithets
present multiple aspects of an entity while remaining univocal vis-à-vis
the appearing of the being.

The epithet follows none of the logic of the normal connective gram-
mars like dative, genitive, or accusative. The epithet is never a question
of being *to* or being *for*. The epithet is, but only because it is *as*. In other
words, an epithet speaks the aspects of a being by saying "It is *as*."
Hermes only appears *as* Hermes Diaktoros or *as* Hermes Dolios, just
as water only appears *as* ice or *as* liquid. Philosophers call this the
as-structure: something appears as something else.

An epithet is an aspect of appearing, which means it pertains to the
phenomena and thus to phenomenology. Yet it is not a predicate, and
thus does not participate in the system of predication. This means that, in
withdrawing from the system of additive predication, an epithet is neither "analytic" nor "synthetic," to use the Kantian vocabulary. Following
Spinoza instead, one might call it "attributive." In the language of Marx,
an epithet is called a "form of appearance." Appearing as one epithet

rather than another represents attributes of the same body, not additive descriptions attached to a body.

To repeat, the one has no epithets, for it is insufficient to itself. But worldly being is always given in specific modes that are sufficient unto themselves. Hence being is always attributed, which is to say it is always given as and with an epithet. Being given means "being as." Being is an epithetal mode (an attributed sufficiency), while the one is a non-epithetal mode (a non-attributed insufficiency). Being is *appropriate,* as Heidegger says; and hence by contrast, as Henry says, the one is, merely and modestly, *proper.* To live within presence means to appropriate in an appropriate way, but to withdraw from presence means an inappropriateness of the merely proper.

Thesis V on the epithets: (B) the epithets of being are fourfold. As stated in Thesis II, the modes of being are equally riven. Now it is possible to consider these modes more explicitly. As any student of philosophy can attest, it is bewildering to read the great thinkers, particularly when they appear to disagree on so many issues, not least of which being the fundamental nature of things. Is the world metaphysically riven, following Plato? Or immanent, following Spinoza? Do contradiction and alienation drive history, following Hegel and Marx? Or is the world the result of an affirmative creativity, following Deleuze?

But must we choose? Why not simply shoot the moon and assent to a whole series of these claims simultaneously? Following the example of Heidegger, who described a "historicity of being" in which ostensibly different philosophers ultimately ventriloquize the same truth of being modified accordingly through history, can we not also propose a co-present, multimodal being that accommodates most if not all the possible scenarios of being-given?[7]

Many have described the different materializations of the as-structure: an essence appears *as* a particular thing (Plato), concrete human labor appears *as* exchange-value (Marx), and so on. Many have counted and classified the various aspects of being. We do not risk cosmological speculation and claim that the as-structure is infinite, as Spinoza said of the attributes of substance. Nor is there any reason to limit ourselves to two or one, or any other magical number. Here we explore four modes of Being, through four epithets.

Are these the special four? Do they claim exclusive rights? Perhaps not. Being is by definition the condition of historical being and hence has a historicity. It would be a mistake to anoint these four as the four absolute modes of being. These are simply the four modes of being that hold sway most powerfully now and within the context of the present conversation. If they are special, they are special simply because they appear. The following four modes are offered not as the last word on attributed being, or even the first, simply the most appropriate for today.

Each mode displays a different interpretation of the standard model. Each resolves, or fails to resolve, the standard model in its own particular way. Each bears an epithet. Each conditions the world through specific regimes of sense. Each has its own special physics, its own special theory of the event, and its own special matheme.

As a first step, it is possible heuristically to present the fourfold as four quadrants arrayed around two perpendicular axes. The first axis is the axis of affirmation and negation. The second is the axis of immanence and transcendence.

Transcendental as affirmation	Transcendental as negation
Immanence as affirmation	Immanence as negation

Affirmation here means the realm of positivity. It is a sacred realm, a realm devoted to the enchantment of things. Raw affirmation is visible in Foucault's discussions of power as *puissance,* or Deleuze's descriptions of creative becoming as a purely additive process. Likewise the poetic mysticism of being, evident in Heidegger, is evidence of a rudimentary affirmation. And Marx's description of the inexhaustibly generative nature of labor is also a question of ontological affirmation.

Affirmation leverages the affirmative operator, written either in terms of incrementation as $x++$ or $x + 1$, or as the absolute value operator $|x|$, the operator that removes the sign of negation. Through such operations, affirmation reinforces the positive, productive presence of entities.

Negation has its own genealogy. Marx too trades in negation, borrowing his contradiction engine from Hegel, with a renewed devotion to the darkly generative powers of the negation of the negation. Negation is not positive, but critical. It is not sacred, but profane. It seeks not to re-enchant the world, but to disenchant it, to shatter illusions, to denaturalize mystifications.

For negation consider Bataille's concept of unemployed negativity. Consider the movement of subtraction in the work of Badiou. Or consider Tiqqun's concept of civil war, a condition of pure agitation in which processes of social transformation arise strictly from the relentless friction between various warring factions.

Negation leverages the negative operator, written either in terms of decrementation as $x--$ or $x - 1$, or via a multiplicative inversion of valence ($x \times -1$).

Laruelle offers the following useful definition of immanence and transcendence: "We call radical immanence . . . the element to which anything whatsoever may be added or taken away without changing the fact of its immanence. And transcendence . . . the element for which adding or taking away compels a complete reworking of what is divided and undivided from it, a complete shift in its truth."[8] Note, however, the slight irony in Laruelle's definition. He modifies the typical way in which philosophers define the transcendental, as "the thing that doesn't change while weathering all change." In Laruelle we must understand the transcendental as essential or sufficient, and immanence (or the generic) as *inessential* or insufficient. In other words, essence is the thing that cannot be meddled with without altering it; yet the generic may be plied and revamped endlessly without a single change. The reason is that the generic is, essentially, *nothing,* or as close to nothing as it is possible to be while still remaining "something." Here Badiou helps shed light on Laruelle: the generic is an "essence" *but of the void only;* generic immanence is an "essence of the void," the thing that is "at the edge of the void."[9]

In this way, the *transcendental* refers to an entity's essential relationship with itself as it persists. Moreover the transcendental provides the conditions of possibility for persistence as such and, by extension, relation as such. In other words, what allows an entity to persist as it is, without vanishing or losing its own identity as itself, is the transcendental quality of the entity. Likewise what allows an entity to enter into relationships, either with itself or with other entities, is its transcendental quality. This is not to say that all entities must have a soul or an essence, simply that if an entity relates or persists it may be labeled transcendental. In this way the transcendental is a question not of immanence ("remaining within," from *manere*) but of emanation ("flowing out," from *manare*): an entity flows out of itself when it enters into relation, and likewise it flows out of itself only to meet and replenish itself again when it persists. The transcendental thus in no way prohibits change; persistence and relation have nothing to do with stasis. Quite the opposite, change is possible *only* via the (intransigent) transcendental.

Immanence too has its own genealogy, which can be framed in contradistinction to that of the transcendental. The three most developed theories of immanence in contemporary times come from Deleuze, Henry, and Laruelle, but the tradition of immanence goes back much further to Spinoza and beyond.

In rejecting both metaphysics and the dialectic, Deleuze describes a plane of immanence in which matter has no need to go outside of itself in order to actualize itself. (Whereas in metaphysics matter is actualized only through the outtering of essence into instance, and in dialectics matter is actualized only through a process of negation, and therefore externalization, along the lines of self/other.)

Henry goes in a slightly different direction, avoiding Deleuze's "democracy of immanence" that grants immanence to an aggregate of pure multiplicities. Instead Henry proposes that immanence, if it is understood correctly, must lead to an examination not of an aggregated plane but of a singleton. Because of this Henry focuses on the immanence of one thing, the only thing knowable, the Ego, and as a result he produces a pure immanence of the self. Instead of examining the exterior manifestation of things, as other phenomenologists do, Henry turns inward to an internal manifestation of the interior life of the self. "More original than the truth of Being," he writes, "is the truth of man."[10] Thus Henry arrives at the concept of immanent revelation, which he considers to be more fundamental than Hegel's concept of manifestation.

Such a solution is not rigorous enough to satisfy Laruelle, who does not simply submit a single philosophical practice, that of phenomenology, to the rule of immanence, as Henry does. Rather, Laruelle subjects the entire practice of philosophy to the axiom of immanence. If Henry's is an immanence that evacuates the outside, and hence must always be understood against a phenomenological stance rooted in space and time, Laruelle's is an immanence that evacuates the sufficiency of ontology, itself understood against a philosophical stance rooted in the various logics of being (appearance, manifestation, and so on).

By this token Laruelle's immanence is an immanence *within methodology*—a rather startling and unprecedented undertaking to be sure—not simply an immanence of nature (Spinoza, Deleuze) or an immanence of the self (Fichte, Henry). So, when certain critics claim that Laruelle is a Kantian, what they really mean is that, in the fashion of Kant but without parroting him, Laruelle is performing heavy surgery on philosophical method as such, not simply making this or that claim about nature or humanity.

The two perpendicular axes given earlier, transcendental–immanent and affirmation–negation, contain their own set of force fields and vector transformations. The forces along the vertical axis are the forces of distinction and integration. To follow a vector from immanence into transcendence is to follow the vector of *distinction* or *digitization,* to divide from one into two. But moving in the opposite direction, to follow a vector from transcendence into immanence is to follow the vector of *integration* or *analogicity,* to superimpose as one.

The forces along the horizontal axis, by contrast, are the forces of consecration and profanation. The force field that moves from affirmation into negation is a force of *profanation* in which hitherto associated entities are uncoupled and dissociated. Captured well by the double meaning of words like *splicing* or *cleaving,* this vector involves the simultaneous actions of both cutting and rejoining. Hence it is a vector of divorcement or rivenning. Profanation uncouples two entities only to bind them together again in an unbreakable uncoupling.

In counter transit to profanation is the vector of *consecration* moving from negation to affirmation. Along this path are the acts of association and connection. Belonging and appropriation are also acts of consecration, as are the acts of mixing (as opposed to separating) and interfacing (as opposed to defacing). Being still remains inescapably riven of course. Yet along the vector of consecration lies an irresistible impetus driving things away from their rivenness toward communion.

These two basic axes produce a fourfold space for the epithets of being. It is possible to assign proper names to the four quadrants: (1) transcendental affirmation refers to the One Two of differential being, (2) transcendental negation refers to the Not-One of dialectical being,

(3) immanent affirmation refers to the One-as-Multiple of continuous being, and (4) immanent negation refers to the One-and-the-Same of generic being.

After amending the previous table the four quadrants now appear as follows:

Differential being or "One Two" (transcendental as affirmation)	Dialectical being or "Not-One" (transcendental as negation)
Continuous being or "One-as-Multiple" (immanence as affirmation)	Generic being or "One-and-the-Same" (immanence as negation)

Not all four modes of being are equal in stature vis-à-vis the real base of the supernature. There are modes that are nearer to the base, and modes that are further from it. There are modes that cling to the supernature. There are other modes that flee the real base, only to consummate a new kind of supernatural intimacy, even at a distance. There are still other modes that revel in the rivenness of their own being-given, unapologetic that nature acts in the way it does.

For this reason the One Two of differential being is defined first, because it lies at a slight remove from the real, although it is not the most remote. The One-and-the-Same of generic being is defined last because it is the closest to the real, as close as is possible to get while remaining riven.[11]

(1) The One Two of differential being. In the opening pages of *Principles of Non-philosophy,* Laruelle defines the philosophical decision in terms of what he calls a "2/3 matrix." In such a matrix two terms come together to form a third synthetic term. For this reason philosophy is fundamentally "in a state of lack with itself," because it must come face to face with something else that exists in opposition or counterdistinction to it. Self and world make 2, establishing a relation of solicitude or orientation, which in turn is synonymous with the philosophical decision as 3. Or in an equivalent but inverted sense, philosophy will also tend to adopt a 3/2 matrix, because of its own irrepressible vanity, wherein philosophy begins "in excess of itself" as 3, and thus insinuates relationships of representation (the 2) into every nook and cranny.[12]

Such is the classic definition of metaphysics, not simply any old investigation into first principles, but a very specific stance on the construction of the universe in which the cleaving of the one is reorganized around an essential twoness rooted in difference. This is true just as much for Plato as it is for Heidegger, Derrida, or Badiou. The twoness of difference might be as simple as adjudicating the authentic and the inauthentic life. It might refer to the difference between self and world, or self and other.

In this way, metaphysics leads to a kind of *staccato* being in that it differentiates and detaches God from humanity, creation from the created, life from the living, and the sacred from the profane. The specific form of staccato being is the binarism; the generic form of staccato being is digitality (shared too by dialectical being, as we shall see in a moment). The specific form differentiates and detaches all from nothing, one from zero, man from woman. The generic form describes the basic conditions of possibility for making distinctions as such, and therefore the possibility of difference and differentiation.

Important passwords for differential being are *particle, sphere, binarism, detachment, digitality,* and *difference.* Under the modal condition of the One Two, being goes outside of itself into difference. The state of rivenness is not elided or ignored. Neither is it fueled and accelerated. It is ossified as it is. Rivenness is not given over as a force vector or "line of flight," nor is it resolved through synthesis. One could think of this as a fetishization of digitization, in the Marxian sense, to the extent that it seizes upon the relationality of digitization and injects a type of illusory value into the basic fact of distinction.

Rooted in difference and representation, the One Two of differential being is at home in the company of the transcendental. It is quite comfortable with the metaphysical relation. It is, in fact, the philosophical stage par excellence. Aesthetics is also typically found here—although not exclusively, as we will see in chapters 7 and 8. Likewise the One Two of differential being is the domain in which morality best flourishes, for having been endowed with the possibility of discrimination, the One Two considers all events in terms of the morality of the law. This is why metaphysicians can speak of the difference between essence and instance in terms of morality. Under this framework, the moral entity is defined as the entity that conforms most closely with its essence.

(2) The Not-One of dialectical being. If the One Two is a kind of *positive* dialectics or a dialectics of positivity, the Not-One of dialectical being is best understood as *negative* difference and hence truly a dialectics of negation.

"In the Dialectical stage," Hegel writes in the lesser *Logic*, "finite characterizations or formulae supersede themselves, and pass into their opposites."[13] In similar fashion Marx describes a number of different dialectical relationships, including the union of use-value and exchange-value within the commodity and the relationship between concrete and abstract labor. Dialectical being functions through direct and continual negation in the form of opposition or critique. If in the previous mode twoness was fetishized for its own sake, here twoness is understood not as a positivity of two but as a negativity of not one. The one and the not one form a new twin. So while previously the binarism held sway (man/woman, self/other), now the binarism has been profaned. It still exists as two, only it has lost its effervescence as an abstract, incorruptible binary. The dialectic pays homage to no one. There are no permanent categories, no grand narratives to sculpt the formation of the two.

The Not-One is thus a form of disenchanted being in which entities emerge and disappear through structures of contingency and metamorphosis. Malabou's plasticity is, in this sense, following Hegel, the consummate organon of dialectical being. The same is true for *stasis* in the work of Tiqqun. Dialectical being forever establishes relationships of antagonism, be they logical or political, in which entities or groups are formed and pitted against other entities or groups. And although such antagonisms can and will be resolved locally and historically, the essential architecture of antagonism itself persists eternally within dialectical being.

The passwords of dialectical being are *point* and *position, thesis, argument, resistance, critique, faction* and *factionalization, struggle, counterpoint,* and *opposition.* Dialectical being requires an intransigent immiscibility, but also mutual corruption and synthesis.

At root, dialectical entities are not particles but *points.* Unlike differential being they do not establish a local field bound by terminal transitions into and out of other states. Rather they occupy a point within space, defined exclusively by coordinates without extension or volume. They are a point within a field, measured against another location in the field. In this way, the rivenness of the dialectic leads to a *harmonic* being, a tone entity that resonates only in counterpoint to another tone. Under the modal condition of the Not-One, being is a semi-entity within a procession of translation and reconfiguration across an expanding field of time and space.

As a transcendental mode of the law, dialectical being is the realm of the workaday event. It is the normal way in which things happen, subsequent to the changes precipitated by action, reaction, stress, and force. The Not-One is not the only way to be political, but certainly it's one of the most common and prevalent political mechanics. Through position and negation, dialectical being mobilizes the law as political. Thus, just as the law provides a legal infrastructure for the management of bodies and behaviors, dialectical being manages the appearance, disappearance, and transmutation of entities.

(3) The One-as-Multiple of continuous being. Differential and dialectical being are both rooted in the transcendental. As such they appeal to the law, either in the form of a moral imperative or a political dynamic. Across these realms is found the Father and the Prince, the law and the commandment. These realms have been incredibly powerful historically, yet have changed in recent years because of sustained critiques of the transcendental. Such critiques have come from both the left and the right; they target things like hierarchy, repression, and social exclusion, as well as more exotic maladies such as logocentrism and ontotheology.

So now leave the realm of the transcendental and enter the realm of immanence. The One-as-Multiple achieves immanence by way of multiplicity and continuity. It is best understood as a "natural" immanence, or an "immanence of everything." Shunning the repressive laws of difference, continuous being affirms any and all entities as participants and grants them an open invitation to the multiplicity of the world.

Hence nature, for thinkers like Deleuze, is at root a smooth aggregation of heterogenous entities, all on equal footing within a material substratum. Crystals grow, and animals procreate. Elements catalyze chemical reactions just as nations surge together in battle. Each entity is a heterogenous singularity. But taken as a whole, they constitute a single plane of being, the plane of immanence, broad, flat, and continuous. There is no vacuum in a Deleuzian universe, no absence or lack, no unconscious, no repression, no binarisms like self/other or man/woman, only variations in intensity, fields of attraction and repulsion, local crystallizations of material habit and corruptions of structure leading to dissolution and subsequent recombination. Deleuzian immanence is an immanence at the level of ontology. Nature is immanent to itself; it does not need to go outside itself in order to realize itself.

The generic is therefore not unknown to Deleuze. But he locates the generic at the level of the totality. This is why continuous being is an "immanence of everything." Its totality is a "whatever totality"; any and all or whatever.

Here the one reappears not as the singleton but as the universe, not an entity in its finitude but the infinite undulations of the Earth. Deleuze's One is always a One All. Collectivity, for Deleuze, is a question of the totality of matter and the totality of physical processes. Deleuze is thus properly labeled a *physicist*, not a metaphysicist. His philosophy is that of physics and sensation, empiricism and aestheticism, not things like essence or teleology or truth. But while dialectical being achieves totality via negation, continuous being achieves totality via affirmation.

The passwords of continuous being are terms like *integration, multiplicity, wave, attractor, continuum, univocity, analogy, indifference, promiscuity, miscegenation, hybridity, mixing, process, emergence, autopoiesis, contagion, intensification,* and *modulation.*

And as Deleuze and Guattari so rightly pointed out, because of the propensity for multiplication and parallelization, the chief malady for continuous being is the "split mind" of *schizophrenia* (not fetishization, as was evident previously for differential metaphysics), as the traditional linkages among thought, emotion, and behavior break down and are replaced with various kinds of mental fragmentation. In the face of such developments Deleuze and Guattari made a virtue of necessity by advocating a new kind of schizophrenic subject—not uncontroversial in some circles—based in metastatic existence, the multiplication of affects, and the proliferation of desires.

"To reverse Platonism," Deleuze remarked, "is first and foremost to remove essences and to substitute events in their place, as jets of singularities."[14] Admittedly it is incorrect on the face of things to call Deleuze a theologian. But the vitality of pure matter that he describes; his obvious love for Spinoza's God-Nature; the One All that he credits also to Duns

Scotus and Nietzsche: these things point to an underlying mystico-theological core within Deleuze's world. Is it new age mysticism, a weird twist on neoplatonism, or simply garden variety vitalism? Regardless of the answer, continuous being will tend toward a sacred, enchanted, if not entirely theological explanation for things.

These "jets of singularities" that surge and shoot, these counter-Platonic non-essences, are pure events. Continuous being is, in this sense, the converse of dialectical being. They both locate the event at the core of things, making events the very building blocks of all existence. Yet although the dialectic proceeds through a chain of negation, formulating dynamic oppositions in series, continuous being proceeds immanently via inductive, emergent affirmation. So Badiou is ultimately correct to pounce on the "clamor" in Deleuze's being. Deleuze's events are these never-ending clamorous occasions. They happen all the time, and everywhere. In fact, for continuous being, the world is *nothing but* such clamorous occasions.

Entities become less important, while processes more important. For the One-as-Multiple of continuous being, the universe is no longer divided up into objects so much as nexuses of relation, forever ebbing and flowing in and out of equilibrium. The law, the commandment, and other grand structures start to fade from view, to be replaced by common convention. Indeed both continuous and generic being shun the law in favor of the immanent mode of practice. Yet although practice may pertain to both things and nature, continuous being (for which Deleuze is the exemplar) places practice ultimately in the lap of nature. So while Deleuze and Guattari sing beautifully of the nomad with its war machine, or the child who hums a tune to fend off the dark, their most reverent words are saved for the strata of the Earth, which Deleuze describes so mystically as "the primary order which grumbles beneath."[15]

In this way, continuous being renounces metaphysics in favor of *legato* being, in which an undivided continuum of smooth, flowing aggregates attach fluidly to themselves across space, bounding into the unbroken continuum of time.

(4) The One-and-the-Same of generic being. For Badiou, philosophy consists in thinking the generic as such. Philosophy consists in thinking the elemental condition of subtractive being, in which the specifities of

discrete entities, including the apparatuses required to mold and main-tain them *as* discrete entities, are dissolved in favor of a newfound agnos-tic totality of the particular entity.

If continuous being approaches immanence at the scale of nature, generic being approaches immanence at the scale of the person. If con-tinuous being is thus ultimately a question of the affirmative infinity of nature, generic being is ultimately a meditation on the finitude of com-mon existence and experience.

This is why Laruelle can speak of an immanence that is finite (as opposed to an immanent infinitude, which can only ever resemble God or some God proxy such as nature or the absolute). Likewise it is why Badiou can speak of truth, not in terms of grand overarching absolutes, but in terms of the generic fidelity to truth furnished to all persons. Hence the label One-and-the-Same: it affirms the generic sameness of unadorned personhood; it affirms the oneness evident in raw common-ality. Here is Badiou:

> What we know about inventive politics at least since 1793, when it exists, is that it can only be egalitarian and non-Statist, tracing, in the historic and social thick, humanity's genericity, the deconstruction of strata, the ruin of differential or hierarchical representations and the assumption of a com-munism of singularities. What we know about poetry is that it explores an unseparated, non-instrumental language, offered to everyone, a voice founding the genericity of speech itself. What we know about the math-eme is that it seizes the multiple stripped of every presentative distinction, the genericity of multiple-being. What we know about love, at last, is that beyond the encounter, it declared its fidelity to the pure Two it founds and makes generic truth of the fact that there are men and women. Philosophy today is the thinking of the generic as such.[16]

In Badiou the generic revolves around these four truth procedures: poli-tics, art, science, and love. Politics illuminates a generic humanity; poetry, a generic language; mathematical science, a generic multiple; love, a generic miracle of an intimacy that is "ours."

But Badiou does not exhaust the sources of the generic, and we are not obligated to think about generic being strictly in these terms. Laruelle men-tions in particular Feuerbach's rupture with Hegel and his endorsement of "generic man," as part of a longer tradition of "minor or minoritarian thinkers":

> Hamann (against Kant), Jacobi (against Fichte), Eschenmayer (against Schelling), the Young Hegelians up to Stirner, and fully realized with Kierkegaard (against Hegel). A single key feature unites all these figures: *how to break with philosophy, with its systematic nature*, in the name of passion, faith, feeling? in the name of actually existing religious individuals? in the name of non-philosophy?[17]

At the intersection of both immanence and negativity, generic being operates through a subtractive logic. If dialectical being deploys the negative in the service of transcendental transformation (the persistence of the party through struggle, the persistence of spirit through actualization, and so on), generic being deploys the negative as a kind of pure bunker for thought. The One-and-the-Same hunkers down within immanence; its negativity is not that of negation, resistance, or opposition, but of solitude, absence, peace, and love. If the dialectic is an instance of provisional negation, the generic is an instance of pure negation. Its passwords are *oblivion, withdrawal, subtraction, nothingness, commonality, something, whatever, equality, disappearance, exodus,* and *the impersonal.*

Both Badiou and Deleuze have written on the generic. But perhaps the most well-developed theories of generic being come from Henry and Laruelle. If Deleuze and Guattari wrote about the dangers and affordances of a schizophrenic immanence, Henry and Laruelle gravitate instead to what I've been calling an autistic immanence. Their concern is not so much the fragmentation or multiplicity of the subject but a purely autonomous entity that need not go outside itself in order to realize itself, not so much an unbridled proliferation of relation running to and fro within the subject but a static parallelism consisting of the one and the person in superposition. "We must radicalize the Two (after first radicalizing the One)," writes Laruelle. "The generic shall be the Two fleeced of its totality or system."[18]

Indeed, generic being summons not so much an "immanence of everything," as with continuous being, but an "immanence of something." Deleuze's immanence of everything views the plane of being as a space of endless multiplicity. But an immanence of something redirects focus from the plane to the entity, be it a person or the one itself. These something-entities are no longer elongated horizontally, like the subterranean offshoots of the rhizome, but instead persist modestly and finitely without differential multiplicity. Generic being is generic in its immanence. Not so much a generic totality, but a generic particularity. Not a generic infinity, but a generic finitude.

So while formerly the rivenness of being was resolved by proliferating such rivenness into endless repetitions of difference, here the rivenness of being is resolved *by pretending it never happened*: the fundamental cleavage is not repeated or rehearsed, it is not fetishized or ossified, and it is not reduplicated or multiplied; rather, the fundamental cleavage is deprived of itself and dissolved into a new state of impoverishment.

Like the three previous modes of the standard model, generic being has its own theory of the event. Instead of politics, morality, or theology, the generic event is understood as *ethical practice*. The generic is a lived relation, and therefore defined as an ethos. It follows no explicit goal and is subservient to no state of affairs, and is thus rooted strictly in practice. Practice may be the practice of nature, but it can also be, as it is here, the practice of entities themselves.

But this is an ethos of negation, not affirmation. The slogan now is not "Liberate your desires," as it was with continuous being. The new slogan for generic being is "We have no demands" or "Withdraw, and leave being behind." The mission is no longer to identify and legitimate new subject positions, as in the socially visible monikers of *woman, proletarian, queer,* and so on, but to slough off the very apparatus of subject formation that obliges a person to assume such a position. Yet even then, through the very rejection of subject formation, the generic being achieves a generalized woman, a generalized proletarian, or a generalized queer.

In this way, we should speak not of a staccato being, nor a harmonic, or legato being, but a *quiescent* being, a mode of living that grows quieter and quieter with each passing day, even as it passes more fully into whatever it is. Its virtues are rarely those of liberation—more like withdrawal, abstinence, or discipline, that same discipline that has today been so thoroughly discounted and demoralized by the forces of liberation, in everything from May 1968 to capitalism itself.

Instead of the queer consumer, generic being produces something like a queer communism, in which the absence of a shared essential nature serves, perhaps ironically, as the common infrastructure for a new ethical life. Within generic being, therefore, the goal is not to liberate affect; the goal is to starve and suppress it. The self must not be granted new access to representation, new access to the metaphysical apparatus, but rather the self must decline such access. Thoroughly monastic in its structure, generic being nevertheless achieves a more profound sublimity: love in an intimacy unbound by fetish; a body in balance with an energy never wasted or exploited; communion through the absolute suspension of violence against the other; the self-revelation of being as something, whatever it is.

The standard model as illumination, obscurity, brightness, and encryption. The four quadrants of the standard model also house a series of representational and aesthetic operators. Although such themes are discussed with greater detail in chapter 7, it is worth outlining them here. They include the various intensities of illumination and obscurity, of light to dark and white to black.

First, the essence of differential being is illumination. It is the domain of enlightenment knowledge and transparent if not also transcendent bodies. Differential being appears as a brightening, as *bright light*. It is found in what the ancients called *lumen,* or light as illumination. It is also what Heidegger means when he speaks of being as a ground that creates a "clearing" or opening, from which the light of presence may shine forth. Differential being requires that things be cast ahead, as when rays of light are cast ahead to light a world, or as when the human sensorium, acting as an illumination proxy, casts its orientation and solicitude into a lit world.

By contrast the essence of dialectical being is impenetrable obscurity. Although it proliferates local enclaves of visibility, it is bound ultimately to the *dark* and finds its fuel there. A dark body is a body frozen in habit or cliché; interrupt the body via synthesis or mutation and it will move, alighting elsewhere as a newly encrypted and clandestine faction within the dialectical chain.

Further still, the essence of continuous being is full brightness. So total in its illumination, continuous being supersedes the light–dark continuum entirely, becoming the pure light of *lux*. Strictly speaking, continuous being is no longer light at all, but *white*. It is too full to be visible, and hence remains opaque despite being bathed in light. Such hyper-white is the whiteness of pure opacity.

And finally, the most obscure of all, the super-obscure *black* of generic being absorbs all light in an irreversible vacuum of visibility. Instead of mere ontic darkness, generic being achieves an ontological darkness, and hence beckons toward the kind of crypto-ontology of pure blackness evident in Laruelle.

One-as-Multiple	Plane	White	Practice as theological
One Two	World	Bright	Law as moral
Not-One	Point	Dark	Law as political
One-and-the-Same	Nothing	Black	Practice as ethical

Indeed, at first glance Laruelle seems to resemble the final mode of being, generic being. Yet the precise location of Laruelle within the standard model presents some problems. For, properly speaking, Laruelle is working almost entirely within the realm of the real. Laruelle runs parallel to the standard model. Thus, properly speaking, Laruelle's non-standard philosophy is not located anywhere within the fourfold of the standard model, even if he uses the fourfold as his base material. His chief concern is the infrastructure, the real base, the supernature, the real, the one— none of which has been given, and thus none of which finds its home in the standard model.

However, that is simply the most charitable view of Laruelle from the perspective of non-philosophy. To view Laruelle *from the perspective of philosophy*, it is quite natural to make the mistake and locate him under the heading of the One-and-the-Same of generic being. This is a mistake on the merits. Yet the indiscretion is easily forgivable.

Even then, one might strive for a more properly non-philosophical rendering by superpositioning Laruelle within both conditions: the modal condition of generic being, and the non-modal condition of the one. In fact non-philosophy proper does not reject philosophy, nor does it strive to exit philosophy in order to live beyond or outside of it. "We who are the experimenters, engineers, and technicians of the Matrix," Laruelle writes of his own profession, we "participate simultaneously in the Last Instance and in philosophy."[19] Thus, from the perspective of philosophy, Laruelle most resembles generic being, even if he is ultimately dealing with the real infrastructure of the one and withdrawing from the standard model. In this sense the generic is a kind of gateway, to use a frightfully philosophical term, that allows the standard model to be rethought in parallel as non-standard.

Here then is an itemization of Laruelle's basic posture:

—The axiomatic positing of an immanent and generic *one,* against the reigning doxa of contemporary philosophy
—A derivation of the standard model of philosophy in terms of *decision* or *distinction*
—The proposal of a non-standard method reliant on *indecision,* that is, the withdrawal from decision

The standard model as philosophical mixture. It is now more difficult to assess whether or not the generic aspect of non-philosophy is ultimately *synthetic* in the Kantian sense. From one perspective non-philosophy is resolutely not synthetic, because it withdraws from all the various synthetic logics such as recombination, amplification, mixing, dialectical contradiction, difference, hybridity, and so on. Laruelle says on many occasions that non-philosophy is *not additive* vis-à-vis the one. Thus, using the strict definition of synthetic as "containing an additive predicate" the generic aspect of non-philosophy is not additive or ampliative in any way.

Yet although Laruelle's non-standard method is not synthetic in the Kantian sense, non-philosophy is synthetic in a different sense—or in Laruellese a "non-synthesis" or "synthesis-without-synthesizing"—by virtue of the way in which it brings forth non-philosophical axioms out of philosophical mixtures (see *[Student in Bicycle Bird Costume],* the frontispiece of this chapter). Thus the various philosophical mixtures of Being/other, Being/being, or one/other are set into an identity with the one. The dyads themselves are not merged or deconstructed, but merely left intact as data. "Each one of these [dyads] is by and large treated as an *a priori* possessing an identity," explains Laruelle. "For example, ontological difference becomes the unilateral duality of Being and being."[20]

So it is at least minimally synthetic in the sense that it contains something in the predicate (the unilateral duality of Being and being) not already evident in the subject (the philosophy under scrutiny). Yet Laruelle would ultimately not classify this transformation as additive, because the process of cloning philosophical data never produces a combination or mixture in the strict sense. It only produces a clone or dual, which is a transcendental identity vis-à-vis the one and the empirical world of philosophy that it unilateralizes.

Herein lies Laruelle's curious use of the a priori. For on the one hand the philosophical chimeras of Being/other, Being/being, and so on are taken to be a priori, just as Kant considered time and space to be a priori. But on the other hand Laruelle asserts that these chimeras *are themselves digital data:* they are given over to non-philosophy as a more or less empirical or worldly reality that must be cloned or dualized.

This is further proof of philosophy's promiscuous convertibility. The very things that are profoundly "pure and necessary" or a priori vis-à-vis philosophy—whether it be Heidegger's *Ereignis* or Parmenides's similitude of being and thought—flip and reconvert into empirical assets that may be measured according to the methods of dualysis or cloning. The empirical assets of philosophy are translated one into another, producing the very idiom of non-philosophy. "Non-philosophy *is* this translation of Kant 'in' Descartes, of Descartes 'in' Marx, of Marx 'in' Husserl, etc."[21]

Indeed, Laruelle doesn't mince words on the question of mixing: "What we shun first and foremost are any kind of transcendental mixtures of the One and the Two. . . . The interplay of Idealism and Materialism presuppose some kind of transcendental operator as means for dividing the One and unifying the Two."[22]

Laruelle's rather staunch position against hybridity and miscegenation *(métissage)* puts him at odds with much of post-structuralism and postmodern theory, including identity politics and cultural studies. These are all discourses that have, in varying ways, displayed a keen interest in hybridity, mixing, excess, supplementarity, and exchange, viewing such processes as useful and productive for both the individual and society at large. On this score Laruelle might appear somewhat reactionary. However I hope to show by the end of the book that a parallel concept exists—the generic—that addresses many of the same concerns voiced by these various discourses, and indeed addresses them in a way more viable and appropriate to our times.

One, two, three, four—what are the most philosophically important numbers? Heidegger evokes the fourfold; Deleuze and Guattari a thousand (but it could have been more). For Badiou, the multiple plays its role, as does infinity. For Hegel the triad and the operation of the negative. For Irigaray it is sometimes two, and sometimes not one. For others the binary. For others still the key numerical concept is simply nothing. Only two numerical concepts are necessary for Laruelle: the one and the dual.

As Laruelle explains, there is no synthesis or dialectic of the world, only the one and its various identities: "In immanence, one no longer distinguishes between the One and the Multiple, there is no longer anything but n = 1, and the Multiple-without-All. No manifold watched over by a horizon, in flight or in progress: everywhere a true chaos of floating or inconsistent determinations . . . between Identity and Multiplicity, no synthesis by a third term."[23]

Here is an easy shorthand for remembering some of the figures already discussed. *Deleuze is n + 1. Badiou is n − 1. Laruelle is n = 1.* Deleuze is the thinker of propagation and repetition, of additive expression (never negative or dialectical expression). For Deleuze, the One is the additive product of pure multiplicity. Hence the plenum is Deleuze's ontological terminus.

Badiou, however, is a subtractivist. The Badiousian event is never counted as part of the situation; it is always subtracted from it, as something apart from being. Hence Badiou's terminus is the void, the absent one.

Laruelle, by contrast, is neither additive nor subtractive; his operator is neither plus nor minus, but equals. Laruelle is the great thinker of radical equality, what he calls identity (from the Latin pronoun *idem* meaning "the same" or "the very same"). He cares little for the plenum or the void; his terminus is identity, the one as radically immanent and same without ever having to go outside itself.[24]

In sum, if Paul Ricoeur's "hermeneutics of suspicion" framed critique as paranoia, and Deleuze and Guattari painted modern thought as schizophrenia, Laruelle renders non-philosophy as *autism*. Like the autist, we are not neuro-normative in our relations with the real. Abstract philosophical concepts do not help much. The one is absolutely foreclosed to us. Instead we move alongside it, committed to its sameness, a life "of science and of the reality that science can describe, naively in the last instance."[25] If Deleuze's heroes are Spinoza, Hume, and other philosophers of radical materialism, Laruelle descends from a different line, the autistic philosophy of Fichte (I = I) or Henry (ego).

"Yes, I am autistic in a certain sense," Laruelle admitted once, with a sparkle in his eye. "Like a particle that passes through a mountain."[26]

```
> perl -e 'while (rand()<.9) {fork;} for(33..48) {&Z(chr($_));} for($r=0;$r<@M;$r++) {$s="";
for(0..$#M) {$s.="$M[$r][$_]";} $s=reverse($s).$s; while(length($s)<90) {$s=" $s ";}
print "$s ";} sub Z {$x = int(rand(40)); for($r=0;$r<$x;$r++) {for(0..$x)
{$M[$r+int(rand(10))][$_]=$_[0];}}}'
```

```
                          -$$)$/+*&)0!00!0)&*+/$)$$-
                       --#--)/-///$+++~.#*/.-..0,,0..-./*#.-+++$///-/)--#--
                      ---#-#-#)/$///--///+&+*%*,.//.,*%*+&+///--///$/)#-#-#---
                   --#-#---#----)/--//..-+/*+(00++--++00(+*/+-..//--/)----#---#-#--
                  #-###----)-/)/..)./-./-*/000/00/000/*-/.-/.)..//)/-)----###-#
           ---####------#----)///++/--//////-///.0000.///-//////--/++///)----#------####---
                  -------)/))//-//.*./../.././/-0//0-//../../.*.//-//))/)-------
               ----#------#--//-/-+./.-/-/.///.000-...-000/.///.-/./.+-/-//-#-------#-----
                   ---#--###/-//)-////.+.--/.0/0/00/0/0./-..+./////-)//-/###-#---
              ---------#-----##-////+////-///...//.///..////././...///-////+///-##----#----------
                 --##--------#--//////././//-////.////-////././././//////-//-/-#-------##---
              ----##--------)/////).////////+/-//--//-/+//////////.)/////)-------##----
              ----#--#------)/-////.//..././//.///././/.././//.////-/.///-)/-----#--#----
                #--#----#####--/)/-/+.//////././//.//--//.///./////.+/-/)/---###----#--#
               ----#-#-##----//-/+//////..///.//.///./././//.//////+/-/-//----##-#-----
                 -----#-----#--)//.//.#/+-/////-/....//////-////+/#./))/-/-#-----#-----
                 --#----##----#///-//////-//.///./+/+././///-//-//////-////#------##----#--
                   ---#-----##--///$--///////.//))/.////.)///.//////--$///---##------#--
                 ----#----##-------//)/////././/././//////./././//././///)/////-------#----
                 --#--#--#---#-#-)/////-//#+//////////-///////////+-////)-#--#--#-#-#----
                 -#-#--#-#-#-##---///-/-/+//#//////./-/++/-/.//////#//+/-/--///---##-#-#-#-#-#-
                 --#-----#--#-##---)////*/)/++//./)///++//)/./++*/)/*////)---#-#--#----#--
                  ------------/-/)/////-/+-//////.////////./-/////)/-/---------------
            ---#--#-#------#--))/$/#/#/#///---+-/--//--/-+---///#/#/#/$/))-#-----#-#--#----
            -----------#-#-)/////-/-/-$---$/-/-/////////-/-$---$/-/-////)-#-#-----------
                 ----------#-#-///-)-//)-/-##//-//--//##-/-))/-)-///-#-#----------
               ----#------#----//-$)///////-----)-##-)-----///////)$---/----#------#----
                 --#-#--#-----------/-----//--------/-----/---------#--#-#---#--
             ---#--#-##-------##/--)-----/#---//-#))))#-//---#/-----)--/##-------##-#--#---
                 ---#--##--#---/#-#--)--#-/-#----#--/-#--)--#-#/---#---##-#---
                 -------#-#-#--#-#--)--#--/-#----#-/-#--)--#-#/---#---#-#---
                 ------#-#-#-#-----#--/-#----#-/-#--)--#-#--#---#-------
                 ---##--#-#-#-#------#--#-/----#-/-#--#-#--#---##---
                    -#--#-#-#-#-#-------#--#-/---#-#---#--#-#-#---
                     ----#-#-#-#-#-----#----#--#-#---#-#-------
                      ----#-#-#-#-#----#--#-#----#-#-#----
                       ------#-#-#-#---#-#---#-#----#-#-----
                        ------#-#-#----#-#--#-#---#-#----
                         ---##--#-#----#-#--##---#-#--##---
                           -#-------#--#-#----#-#-------#-
                           ---------#---------#---------
                            --------#------###----------#-
                             -------#--------#------------#-
                              ---##-#-#----#-#-------#-#--##---
                                 -#--------#--------------#-
                                  ---------#-----------#------
                                     ---------------------
                                      -------------------
                                          -------------

                          -$$)$/+*&)0!00!0)&*+/$)$$-
                       --#--)/-///$+++~.#*/.-..0,,0..-./*#.-+++$///-/)--#--
                      ---#-#-#)/$///--///+&+*%*,.//.,*%*+&+///--///$/)#-#-#---
                   --#-#---#----)/--//..-+/*+(00++--++00(+*/+-..//--/)----#---#-#--
                  #-###----)-/)/..)./-./-*/000/00/000/*-/.-/.)..//)/-)----###-#
           ---####------#----)///++/--//////-///.0000.///-//////--/++///)----#------####---
                  -------)/))//-//.*./../.././/-0//0-//../../.*.//-//))/)-------
               ----#------#--//-/-+./.-/-/.///.000-...-000/.///.-/./.+-/-//-#-------#-----
                   ---#--###/-//)-////.+.--/.0/0/00/0/0./-..+./////-)//-/###-#---
              ---------#-----##-////+////-///...//.///..////././...///-////+///-##----#----------
                 --##--------#--//////././//-////.////-////././././//////-//-/-#-------##---
              ----##--------)/////).////////+/-//--//-/+//////////.)/////)-------##----
              ------)/))//-//.*./../.././/-0//0-//../../.*.//-//))/)-------
                 ----#-------#--//-/-+./.-//.//.000/.000/.//-/.+-/-//-#-------#-----
```

RSG, *RSG-FORK-5.1*, 2011.

three

The Digital

Despite being the object of much discussion today, the digital does not often appear in the writings of philosophers, except perhaps when it arrives unwittingly under the aegis of another name. The world of business consultancy has accepted it, as has the popular and folk culture, consumer society, telecommunications, medicine, the arts, and, of course, the spheres of electrical engineering and information processing, where it plays a special role. But is there an ontology of the digital, or even a philosophy of it?[1]

The goal of this chapter is not so much to answer such questions but to draw up a map for what is necessary to answer them, something like a prolegomenon for future writing on digitality and philosophy. The goal, then, is not so much to describe a "philosophy of the digital" or even a "digitization of philosophy"—the former achieving, at best, a kind of Kantianism for new media, and the latter enlisting and promoting new methods for "doing" philosophy (online or otherwise)—not so much these things as an exploration in which digitality and philosophy are addressed together, as two modal conditions, both in parallel as they diverge and differentiate, and also in series as they merge and intermediate. This exploration will, if it is successful, pay attention to the conceptual requirements of the digital and the analog, and the strictures and affordances they grant philosophy, without trying to reduce one to the other.

Although the terms *digital* and *analog* were defined provisionally in the introduction and have been deployed already thus far, it is now necessary to define these terms more specifically and explore them in depth.

By way of review, let us first redefine the digital and the analog, and then explicitly superimpose these definitions onto the four quadrants of the standard model as defined in the previous chapter.

Thesis VI. The digital means the one dividing in two. The heart of the digital lies in metaphysics and its adjacent philosophical systems, most important dialectics. The digital arrives in Western philosophy with Socrates and Plato, for this is the time when dialectical metaphysics experiences its most complete original expression.

Consider the famous axiom from Parmenides's third fragment: the same, to think and to be.[2] There is nothing digital in that. The one has not divided in two. In fact the opposite is the case. A sameness permeates the categories of being and thinking. The axiom of Parmenides, then, could very easily be rewritten as: To think and to be . . . are one.

Yet with Socrates and Plato—are they one or are they two?—philosophy embarks on a grand multimillennial journey. The one divides in two.

As Socrates warns us in the *Phaedrus,* the truth of man's sincerity can be externalized into physical objects called the *hypomnemata.* Such processes of externalization are at root digital, because they extend the one beyond its own bounds, thereby branching the one, splitting it, alienating a part of the one into an external object. Plato, with considerable help from Jacques Derrida and more recently Bernard Stiegler, described a process of grammatization, in which "the flows and continuities which weave our existences are *discretized:* writing, as the discretization of the flow of speech, is a *stage* of grammatization. . . . Grammatization is the history of the externalization of memory in all its forms: nervous and cerebral memory, corporeal and muscular memory, biogenetic memory."[3]

This is the operation of the digital: the making-discrete of the hitherto fluid, the hitherto whole, the hitherto integral. Such making-discrete can be effected via separation, individuation, exteriorization, extension, or alienation. Any process that produces or maintains identity differences between two or more elements can be labeled digital. This is why the dialectical metaphysics of Socrates and Plato is so important to the history of the digital, because it establishes essentially for the first time the basic categories of digitization: essence alienated into instance, speech grammatized into writing, idea extended into matter, memory exteriorized into media, authentic life separated from inauthentic life.

The Digital

53

Deleuze is one of the great enemies of dialectical philosophy. He compensates for the absence of the dialectic by introducing an alternation between virtualization and actualization. We will have much more to say about virtualization later. But for the moment let us consider actualization. Actualization in Deleuze is a process through which the individual is individuated as such. It connects to the previous comments about integration. Hence actualization is, in strict terms, a process of digitization. Actualization means that the one becomes two; or, if you like, "the One" becomes "a one" or "this one," as opposed to "an other." Deleuze also describes the process in terms of territorialization, that is to say, the process through which unorganized and uncoded aggregates of things and spaces are fixed and aligned according to specific routines, procedures, regularities, and spatial architectures.

In this way a number of terms begin to line up, in Deleuze but also in the larger discourse within philosophy pertaining to digitization: actualization is a mode of digitization, so too are territorialization, integration, alienation, grammatization, exteriorization, separation, and individuation, for each describes the moment in which the one becomes the two, or "the All" becomes "a one."

As discussed in the introduction, figures like Hegel, Marx, Lenin, and Mao are also key entries in any philosophical survey of digitality because of their mutual interest in the dialectic. The same philosophical fuel that propelled Plato is evident here too, in the very heart of Hegel's phenomenology, which considers the foundations of being in terms of an alienation *within* being, an elemental cleaving that can never be overcome, or perhaps only overcome at the expense of a new cleaving.

Recall Thesis II describing the standard model—*Whatever given is riven.* This is also Hegel's principle. Whatever is given as part of being is always already given over to an elemental rivenness, an elemental distinction, which for Hegel, and his most important student Marx, acts as a kind of engine moving things forward. It draws an arrow on time and calls it history.

In Marx, Thesis II is rewritten as class struggle (something like "All being is being in antagonism"). Or in a contemporary figure like Badiou, Thesis II is rewritten as the "theory of points," in which a social whole is decomposed into two poles (two points), against which the subject is compelled to take a position.

We are barely scratching the surface in this brief sketch of digitality in philosophy, but in general it is possible to summarize the trends of digital thought via two modes already described in chapter 2: *differential being* and *dialectical being*.

Recall that differential being refers to the ontological condition in which being is founded on a basic division of difference. Such difference is often construed in terms of self and other, I and Thou, or being and Being. This basic division of difference is not something that achieves any kind of lasting synthesis but rather sustains itself in difference as such. The shorthand here for differential being is the One Two, for it responds to the rivenness of the one by perpetuating the rivenness in terms of a never-ending twoness. Within differential being are found figures like Plato, Kant, Heidegger, and many others.

Recall too that dialectical being, while also digital and hence also fueled by a sustenance of separations between things, refers to the onto-logical condition in which being is founded on a basic *negation,* a nega-tion formed from something and its opposite. Hence dialectical being means not so much an everlasting twoness but an inexhaustible process of negation via reflection or opposition. The shorthand for dialectical being is the Not-One, for it responds to the elemental rivenness of the one by reiterating the cleavage into newfound negations, both the ongo-ing negations of the one itself and also of all subsequent products of the rivenness of the one. Here reside figures like Hegel, Marx, or Badiou.

The two (2) and the not one (~1) are in some senses similar, but ulti-mately play out in very different ways. Consider both the binarism and the dialectic. According to post-structuralism, the self and other are not, strictly speaking, in a dialectical relationship; the other is not simply a negation of the self, and likewise the two terms are never resolved dialec-tically into some sort of synthesis. The self and other, in their differential digitality, are thus properly labeled a binarism.

But something like the boss and the worker can correctly be labeled dialectical, because as they mutually deterritorialize into each other, they produce a new synthetic condition of being, whether that is the simple mundane fact of capitalist production (a specific synthesis of worker and boss, which could not exist in the absence of either party), or the "grand compromise" of the welfare state, its own kind of synthesis, or that new mode of life, the oldest in fact, which takes the name of communism.

These are some of the categorical foundations that structure thinking and being, and indeed differentiate thinking from being in the first place. As a thought experiment, consider the mental effort required to undo the digital core of Western thought: an instance without the transcendental, writing with no original, pure formlessness in matter, a media of incomprehension, or a life made radically inauthentic. Thinking this way is difficult indeed.

Laruelle, in a relatively early book, *Le principe de minorité (The Principle of Minority),* which is chiefly concerned with epistemology and sketching out the rudimentary terms of Laruelle's non-philosophy, gives ebullient voice to such an undertaking:

> Can we define the parts before the Whole and independently of the Whole? differences before their repetition and independently of the Idea, Logos, Being? minorities before the State and independently of the State? being before Being and independently of Being? can we think about events before their historical occurrence, subjects before objects and deprived of objectivity? a time without temporality? singularities or multiplicities before all universal and independently of a universal?[4]

Such a strategy produces not so much an "analog existence" but a deprivation of the digital, a deprivation in which the mutually alienated couples (part/Whole, differences/Idea, minorities/State, being/Being, and so on) are denuded of half their constituency.

This produces a series of "weird" ontological backwaters, some of which have been described, praised even, by the likes of Jacques Rancière, Jean-Luc Nancy, Giorgio Agamben, Maurice Blanchot, and others: the part of no part, the difference that makes no difference, the minority who holds no minority, the being that has left being.

The issue is not so much an analog existence but a kind of starved digitality in which the formerly healthy couplings, each of the components mutually dependent upon its twin, are deprived of their other halves, producing not a new absence, because that would return us to the digital condition of presence/absence, but a positive replication of the one. The weirdness of the Laruellean undertaking, or those put forth by Rancière and others, is a testament to the pervasiveness of the digital foundations that structure Western metaphysics.

The first definition is now on the table, the definition of the digital as the one dividing in two. Next comes the question of the analog, and although its definition will not be surprising, it is surprising how profoundly rare the analog actually is. In ontology, for example, it is exceptionally rare. It will be important, then, to specify very carefully the conditions of the analogical, when and where it appears in Western thought, and perhaps even say a few words about why it remains such an endangered species.

Thesis VII. The analog means the two coming together as one. The analog is challenging because it creates relation without distinction. Through the process that we are calling differentiation—which has nothing to do with difference—the analog makes itself evident via two key modes (which are ultimately one). These modes are themselves the two poles of immanence. Within philosophy there have traditionally been two ways of thinking about immanence, either the immanence of the total plane of being, or the immanence of the individual person or object. Either immanence in its infinity, or immanence in its finitude.

Recall that, under the first condition, being is understood to be *continuous* in its immanence. We might therefore label the first analog mode as "the immanence of everything," which is to say an ontological mode of pure multiplicity in which radically singular and heterogeneous entities occupy a purely material existence.

There is no essence, no soul, no species to these heterogeneous entities. They are all endogenously caused, assembling and reassembling according to forces of flux and attraction. Entities will perpetually "remain within" themselves, even as they intensify and dissipate according to their own characteristics and vicissitudes. There are no sets here. There are no complex aggregates. No societies or bodies. There are only multiplicities or assemblages. Here are found the great thinkers of material immanence like Spinoza or Deleuze.

The shorthand One-as-Multiple is appropriate because such analogicity breaks through the rivenness of being by upping the ante to infinity: yes, being is riven, but riven more than once, divided a multiplicity of times, so much in fact that there is a unique mode of immanent being for each and every entity. Thus the oneness of the one returns solely by virtue of the sublime totality of multiplicity. There are so many pure multiplicities, and they are so entirely singular, and they are so absolutely immanent to themselves that they are one. Univocity at its purest.

In this way continuous being is a movement of affirmation, not negation. The continuous being of the One-as-Multiple is strictly affirmative in its movement. And the affirmative nature of continuous being indicates an additive principle: Come one, come all.

Parallel to "the immanence of everything" lies "the immanence of something." The first analog type was labeled continuous being and the second analog type *generic being*. Under this second condition, being is understood as generic in its immanence. Because the "something" in question remains within itself, it has no cause to go outside of itself; it refrains from forming relations. If continuous being is essentially schizophrenic, a fragmentation producing a multiplicity of the self, generic being is essentially autistic, a withdrawal characterized by a diminishment, or simply a rewiring, of communication and relation. Generic being refrains from forming relations both with itself (the transcendental) and with outside objects or the outside world ("prehensions" in Whitehead's lexicon). It is therefore quite literally "something," no more and no less, because there is nothing specific that can be attributed to it. Today the most sophisticated theory of generic being is Laruelle's, even if he ultimately stands apart from the current four-part model. But generic being is also found in Agamben, Badiou, Deleuze, Hardt and Negri, and many other thinkers.

When an individual "remains within" itself it ceases to participate in the system of predication in which subjects are associated with specific predicate attributes: *a* is *b*, in which the subject *a* is endowed with the attribute *b*. In its immanence, this "something" has no concourse with any attributes—indeed this is precisely the reason why it may be called "something." (What folly in that old philosophical query, why is there something rather than nothing? A more useful question would be to ask why is there everything rather than something!)

The shorthand for the second kind of analog being is the One-and-the-Same. The key issue has to do with the subtractive or negative course of generic being, which is to say the way in which the generic subtracts from being in order to achieve its generic status. Unlike the additive quality of continuous being, generic being subtracts its own attributes, negating and removing them.

Generic being is what Deleuze had in mind when discussing virtualization. Virtualization is a deterritorialization or derivation in which actual entities are deindividuated into indistinction with themselves and with other things. Of course, virtualization has nothing to do with "virtual reality" or with computers per se. It is called virtual not because it is cybernetic or phantasmagorical but because of the way in which it thrusts the actuality of specific situations into a newfound flux of indistinction. The specific becomes the generic. The two becomes one. The individual becomes impersonal, an *imperson*.

In this sense the analog is not exactly a question of analogical relation. True, the analog creates an analogy between two things (the analogy of oneness). But it would be a mistake to think that the analog is about a *relationship* between two things. The analog is ultimately not a question of mimesis or reflection or representation or any such concepts. The analog means that the two becomes one. Hence both continuous being and generic being are instances of the analog; they address the fundamental rivenness of being (Thesis II) by attempting to revert being back to the one.

The identity equation: a = a. These are the two basic ways in which the analogical exhibits itself in philosophy, as either the continuous being of the One-as-Multiple or the generic being of the One-and-the-Same. In both instances the two comes together as one. For the former, the analog indicates a twoness (threeness, fourness, multiplicity) of entities as it returns to a baseline continuous oneness of univocal being in its totality. For the latter, the analog indicates a breakdown of the two sides of the attribution formula (*a* is *b*, this is that) into the generic oneness of undistinguished being.

For the analog, it is not so much a question of reformulating the equation and radically broadening it as *a* is *x*, which would read as "*a* is anything whatsoever." If the equation is to remain, it will have to take the form of the most useless equation of all, the tautology or identity equation: *a* is *a*, which would read as "*a* is itself, whatever that is."

Herein lies a clue to help unravel Laruelle's strange thought. His goal is to articulate a pure analytical immanence of the a priori, and to do it in a way that is not overly simple or ultimately pointless (as Kant would have qualified such an endeavor; indeed Laruelle is closer to Fichte than

Kant in this regard, particularly Fichte's interest in the purely ideal a priori realm).[5]

Laruelle will often dwell on analogical identities such as $a = a$ or the immanent identity of the One-in-One, attributing to them profound, lasting, and indeed practical utility. For other thinkers, such expressions are often classified as unhelpful tautology, or at best classified as part of the fundamental laws of analysis (for example, the law of identity or the law of noncontradiction). Yet, surprisingly, expressions like $a = a$ are very powerful for Laruelle, because they ratify the law of identity necessary for the ultimate step into radical immanence (One-in-One).

This reveals one of the greatest contributions that Laruelle brings to contemporary thinking, to demonstrate that the tautology or identity equation, *a is a,* is not at the fringes of thought, as either a logical dead end or, as Aristotle teaches us, a starting axiom bootstrapping all subsequent rationality. In fact, Laruelle considers it to be the very core of the most central concept in all of thinking, the one as pure identity. In other words, the tautology gains a newfound respectability under Laruelle.[6] For other thinkers, a priori truths such as *a is a* occupy an important but relatively small niche within real-world rationality. Laruelle by contrast slides open the window of the a priori to include all of reality. In other words the Laruellean real is an a priori real—a stunning notion to say the least. It qualifies Laruelle for the designation "radical anti-empiricist" and highlights one of the many differences between Deleuze and Laruelle.

Are analog events possible? A final matter to address before continuing is the question of the event. The next chapter is devoted entirely to events, but a few preliminary things ought to be stated now. To the extent that an event brings into the world a change from x to y, a basic fact holds sway: *events are digital.* This stems directly from how we have been defining the digital throughout. But how to treat the analog on this question?

Because the analog refrains from forming hard and fast distinctions between states, can there ever be something like an analog event? It would be tempting to say yes, by explaining that events under the analog regime are simply smooth transitions between states. Simply replace the sawtooth wave of the digital with the curvilinear wave of the analog. But the more rigorous position is the correct one: for, properly speaking, *there is no such thing as an analog event.*

As discussed in chapter 1, the *prevent* means that which prevents the arrival of events and is therefore essentially prophylactic. But it also means that which comes before the event—which is to say structurally and synchronically prior. Within the realm of being it is admittedly difficult to see real proof of this "synchronic before." But consider the analog's relationship to the one: the analog is a kind of quasi-one, a fallen one, a profaned one. (So too is the digital.) The prevent, in this sense, superimposes a logic onto the evental architecture itself, pointing backward toward a moment in the evental architecture prior to the founding of events. Such a moment, of course, is nothing other than the one itself. Thus in adopting the prevent, the analog is in effect offering a proxy into the "original condition" of the one, which is to say prior to the moment in which the one divided into two, creating the metaphysical universe (the standard model) in which we reside today. In this way, the digital coincides with the event, while the analog coincides with the prevent.

Does this create a problem? The continuous being of Deleuze, for example, is saturated with events. To acknowledge that there are no analog events, only analog prevents, is merely to acknowledge that the evental site is always also a transcendental site. Because the analog only exists within the terrain of immanence, there is no such thing as an analog transcendental. Thus, by extension, there can be no such thing as an analog event in the proper sense. Given this, one must either compromise on the commitment to immanence and confess to a "transcendental empiricism," as Deleuze does, or one must modify the definition of event to allow for the prevent.

Analogy is a parallelism. This is the condition of immanence. The two core terms, *digital* and *analog,* are now on the table, each with some semblance of a definition. However the question of twoness and the relationship between things under the various modes of the standard model is still potentially confusing. In fact it seems that relation itself has been left out of the picture, because the analogical dissolves relation in favor of fusion, while the digital splinters being into so many standardized atoms that any relation formed between them would claim no real binding significance. We can address this potential point of confusion by considering two terms, *parallelism* and *parallelity. Analogs stem from parallelisms; digitals from parallelities.*

The analogical dissolves relation in favor of fused immanence, but does this mean that relation is lost *tout court?* In the strict sense relation is indeed lost, relation as a connection between two discrete entities or states. Therefore immanence, in which matter "remains within" itself and has no cause to go outside itself, prohibits relation. Yet at the same time, by remaining within, immanence demonstrates a more simple and elemental relation. This is the relation of the same. By remaining within itself, immanent matter demonstrates a relation with itself. This "auto-relation" is, of course, only a pseudo-relation. If it were a real relation it would revert back to the transcendental: an entity's essential relationship with itself as it persists through the permutations of time and space. Immanence, by contrast, has nothing to do with an entity's essential relationship with itself, because immanence has nothing to do with essence and all the metaphysical freight that goes along with it. This pseudo-relation or auto-relation is what we will call a "parallelism."

A parallelism is a condition of twoness in which the two is ultimately overcome by the one. The two of the parallelism is really only a quasi-two. So obsessed with itself, so locked together, so bound by the parallel nature of its own coupling, the parallelism is monomaniacal about its own moment of being.

The spiral grooves on a vinyl record are the perfect parallelism: never will they diverge or converge, the two sides of the groove lock arms in continuous variation, jostling the needle back and forth at the frequencies required for audible sound. All because the two sides of the groove, while two, are not distinct. They are merely parallel. As Laruelle might put it, the two side of the groove are "clones" of each other. As clones they constitute a duality, a twoness, yet they are nevertheless bound together by a relationship of identity, a sameness.

Immanence therefore, defined as "*a* remains within *a*," is nothing but an adolescent form of *pure* immanence. Pure immanence would eschew the language of equation altogether, simply uttering "*a*" alone, an utterance that is both senseless and truthless but nevertheless purely immanent.

If analogy stems from an immanent parallelism, digitality by contrast produces a transcendental parallelity. Parallelism holds fast to the *form* of the parallel. But parallelity holds fast to the *logic* of the parallel.

Whereas parallelism is ultimately a duality of the one, parallelity is an endless reduplication of the parallel. This results in what might be called the "massively multiple" nature of parallelity—for which massively multiplayer online games are but one real-world exemplar. The twins of a parallelism are simply the twin edges of a single line. But the twinning of parallelity never stops, resulting in parallels upon parallels propagating laterally. Parallelism is always one-dimensional, while parallelity is always two- or multidimensional. Indeed parallelity is often highly non-linear. So if parallelism is a condition of twoness in which the two is ultimately overcome by the one, parallelity is a condition of twoness in which the two is swiftly and ultimately overcome by the multiple.

What is perhaps most difficult to grasp about the analog is the complete absence of any real sort of difference. A standard dictionary definition of the analog might be something like "the continuous comparison or proportion between two things." But within such proportion there is only commonality, not difference. An analogy creates an identity. And *identity* means "same" (again from the Latin meaning "the very same"). So, while seemingly counterintuitive, the parallelism of the analogical requires a heterogeneous substrate. Indeed this hetero is no enemy to the identity of analogy. The opposite is true: only a baseline heterogeneity, as in the pure multiplicities and generic persons of Deleuze's and Badiou's cosmology, can possibly produce the conditions for a relation of the common. Hence when two heterogeneous elements come together in the parallelism of analogy, as with the wasp and the orchid, a true identity is forged at the threshold of their coupling.

Such true identity forever eludes the digital. Digital relations are always already fake or simulated, for they arise from radical standardization at the atomic level. Of course, the digital produces relation; it is part of the very definition of the term. And in its relationality the digital ultimately offers something much more seductive, for the digital produces *the transcendental*. But what does this mean? The digital says that the one divides into two. So, within the modal condition of the two (or the three, or the four, or the multiple), a universe populated by a purely homogeneous substrate of standardized atoms, there must be some way in which these atomic entities—so absolutely separate, so absolutely standard—can overcome their stifling congruity and relate to each other. In other words, the *entire* substrate becomes the fodder for the emergence of a general equivalent, whether zeros and ones, the citizens of a liberal democracy, or something else entirely.

Kant describes the transcendental via the things required for experience, which is to say the things required for something to relate to a world. Likewise, Hegel speaks of the transcendental in terms of manifestation, actualization, or realization, these being the processes through which something persists throughout the expression of what it is. For Heidegger the transcendental is seen through the basic reality of being, which reveals itself. For Henry it is not revealing but revelation. For Malabou it is plasticity. Even Deleuze, albeit not a philosopher of the transcendental, makes room for a proxy concept, expression, that stands in for the transcendental. And in Laruelle, who like Deleuze is, shall we say, aggressive in his pursuit of immanence, the transcendental has a role to play: the clone is transcendental, because it exists apart or alongside the one, even as it remains in strict identity with it.

In short, to adopt the digital is to adopt the transcendental. It is practically a contradiction in terms to speak of the "immanence of the digital." This is why there is so much discourse around "emergence" or the "ghost in the machine" regarding computers. The digital requires some form of the transcendental, and today, particularly today, it is difficult to speak in terms of the transcendental without resorting to such figurative language.

Relation under analogy is a *chained* relation, a monomaniacal relation. But digital relation is a truly *liberated* relation, for just like existentialist philosophers who speak with both apprehension and excitement of the liberation of existence, the digital relation arises from out of a pure, profane nihilism. The digital conjures a relation—a true miracle—between aggregates of things that really should have nothing at all to say to one another. The digital must transcend the conditions of its own being. It must transcend the fact of its own self-alienation. It is therefore the most emblematic form of the transcendental.

The ultimate digitality is a digitality of space. Space is one of Kant's transcendental categories, for along with other things like time it provides the very conditions of possibility for experience itself. But there is a common assumption that time and space are relatively interchangeable in terms of their transcendental quality. Time is merely the "fourth dimension," it is often claimed, the first three dimensions being dimensions of space.

In his *Cinema 1: The Movement-Image,* already on the first page and wasting no time, Deleuze describes a digital space and a digital time. Digital space is "a single, identical, homogenous space"; digital time is "a time which is impersonal, uniform, abstract, invisible, or imperceptible."[7] The former is composed of any-point-whatevers, and the latter of any-instant-whatevers. The former a whateverness of space, the latter a whateverness of time.[8]

Working in the shadow of Bergson, Deleuze could imagine a homogenous temporality, and he could image a homogenous media substrate that supported such a temporality. He could imagine a cinematic temporality of regular intervals (x frames per second), and a linear series of photographic frames (the film strip).

But what of homogenous space—could Deleuze fully imagine such a scenario? He could in other books, as with the smooth spaces that populate *A Thousand Plateaus.* And he could in the *Cinema* books too, at least partially, with his any-point-whatevers and any-space-whatevers. He even describes an electronic image regime that would subsume the cinema.[9] Nevertheless in the *Cinema* books the concepts remain incomplete, and at times even invite misunderstanding. For of course Deleuze's concern was chiefly cinematic in those books, not computational as it would be later, or rhizomatic as it was before.

An additional extrapolation is necessary to fill out Deleuze's aesthetic theory: not simply a medium rooted in a digitality of time (cinema) but a medium rooted in a digitality of space (computer); not simply a whateverness of time but a whateverness of space.

Cinema takes time as an independent variable, rendering time regular and consistent, pushing time back and sacrificing it to industrial automation. Thus Deleuze's two cinematic modes, the movement-image and the time-image, are both ultimately "time" images by virtue of being irretrievably cinematographic. The movement-image is not ultimately a spatialized image, even if it gains its momentum from the strip of photographic images arranged in a row "through" space. The spatiality of the film strip is a highly bounded spatiality, an artificial spatiality, but never, as Bergson might say, a pure or concrete space. So the movement-image still never captures something like a "space-image."[10] A full digitality of space eluded Deleuze at the time. In fact it would have required writing a third volume to explore it fully. It would have required a *Cinema 3*.

And yet at the same time the time-image, even as it approaches space, even as it summons space to smolder and emanate volumetrically, also fails to capture the whathevernesses of the space-image, even as it *shows* them. The final shots of Antonioni's *Eclipse* might show a time-image, and within the time-image a smoldering, pure absence of enduring space. But this is not the kind of space we mean. Like Bergson's "false movement" of cinema, this is a "false" space for it rides not atop an undercarriage of *spatial* digitality (only a temporal digitality of any-instant-whatevers). If cinema, for Deleuze, moves by virtue of a relationship between the micro and macro levels, that is to say "that which happens between objects or parts" and "that which expresses the duration or the whole," can we also extrapolate to space and claim a relationship between the micro and macro levels of space?

What if space, not time, were forced into the role of the independent variable? What if space were removed from the equation, mechanized and dissolved? What if there were a virtuality of space rather than a virtuality of time? Deleuze opens the door to such a universe in *Cinema 1* via the concepts of the "any-point-whatever" and the "any-space-whatever." But the door remains open; he does not walk through, at least not entirely.

In fact he structured his vocabulary incorrectly. The chief difficulty is that the any-space-whatever and the any-instant-whatever are *not* structurally comparable in Deleuze. They are not homologues of one another. Consider the micro–macro relation. It is not correct to say that the any-space-whatevers are the digital micro atoms of pure space, just as Deleuze defines the any-instant-whatevers as the digital micro atoms of pure duration. A piece of vocabulary is missing. The any-space-whatever resides at cinematic layers 2 or 3, the layers of movement and duration, not at layer 1, the layer of sets of discernible parts, where one would expect it to reside.[11] So Deleuze's any-space-whatever is not wrong per se (because it describes a real cinematographic experience), but the choice of words is confusing, because it requires a jump between incongruent levels.

Deleuze's system ought to be redrafted slightly, extrapolating three spatial levels from the three temporal levels he already provides:

From Deleuze's three temporal levels . . .	. . . extrapolate three spatial levels
sets of discernible parts (frames), or *any-instant-whatevers*	*sets of discernible points*, or *any-point-whatevers*
the *real movement of translation* between frames, or the *movement-image*	the *real relation of form* between points, or the *model-image*
the *duration* or the *whole;* the *time-image*	the *extension* or the *whole;* the *space-image*

Deleuze understood all this implicitly, and speaks to the question indirectly, even if he doesn't spell out every detail. The idea is there, *a multiplicity of vision.* Deleuze's discussion of the films of Joris Ivens proves it. The bridge in Ivens's 1928 short film "is a potentiality. The rapid montage of seven hundred shots means that different views can be fitted together in an infinite number of ways."[12]

Seven hundred shots is indeed impressive. But instead imagine seven hundred *frames* rather than shots, or better yet seven thousand, all captured simultaneously, each from its own vantage point. This kind of synchronic mediation would begin to capture a bona fide any-space-whatever, a real kind of "space-image." Deleuze's version of things is the best that the cinema can summon; only with the more fully present digitality of the computer are we able to evoke a true whateverness of space.

So beyond Deleuze's digitality of time lies a more emblematic mode of digitality, the digitality of space. Of course time allows for co-temporal events, and it is common for two things to take place at the same moment in time. But there can be no co-spatial objects, even as we may speak of a body passing through a cloud, or an alloy of two substances. None of these are instances of two discrete entities occupying the same space, for the cloud envelops the body and hence passes around it, while the alloy is in fact a compound and hence no longer two separate bodies in any real sense.

Because of this prohibition on co-location, space is the natural domain of digitality. Space is the place of splitting, differentiating, and holding at arm's length. When the one divides into two, *it always does so in terms of space.* Even when it does not, it *still* does, through the proxy of metaphor. Hence when one speaks of a split in time, or even better when the phenomenologists proffer their transcendental in terms of time, one speaks in metaphorical terms, deploying what is fundamentally a spatial category of thought. Whether consciously or not, time is spatialized. Knowing this, the phenomenologists tend to describe the temporal transcendental as a "project," as something that "projects."

Digitalities of time, if they ever properly exist, will ultimately reduce to two limit conditions, both essentially theological: either the big bang of creation or the collapse of the end of days; birth or death. Time might have begun and it might be ending. These are the two limit conditions. Even when non-theologians address these questions they often lapse into the language of religion, whether "the end of history" or "being-unto-death." (By contrast, *history,* which is to say actually existing temporal events, is indeed a properly digital domain. History, not time, is the realm of breaks and continuities, of revolutions and restorations.)

In *Cinema 2: The Time-Image,* a book that describes the breakdown of cinematic representation after World War II, Deleuze introduces the term "peaks of present" as one of a handful of ways in which postwar cinema was able to suffer the collapse of the earlier visual schema and invent a new mode of vision from the ashes of the old. He does not spend much time with the term and cannot seem to dig up too many cinematic examples to flesh it out, reverting to the work of Alain Robbe-Grillet, imported from literature, and his collaboration with Alain Resnais on the 1961 film *Last Year at Marienbad.* Yet in Robbe-Grillet, Deleuze sees a very specific treatment of time, a kind of pan-temporality, in which all points of time are treated in terms of their own present and their own superimposition into a simultaneity of presents. As with the pandemonium of "all spirits," Robbe-Grillet produces a pan-chronology of all times merged together, "a present of the future, a present of the present and a present of the past."[13] For Deleuze this produces a kind of vertigo, an indiscernibility that "make[s] time frightening and inexplicable."[14]

Now compare this pan-present to Laruelle's image of the rocket from his enigmatic essay "On the Black Universe." Laruelle describes a rocket that refuses to blast off or to land, but somehow flickers directly into the blackness of deep space: "The rocket passes through infinite distances. . . . Let [it] jump over the cosmic barrier and enter into the hyperspace of the Universe. . . . Let your rockets become subject of the Universe and be present at every point of the Remote."[15] Does Laruelle's "present at every point of the Remote" have anything to do with Deleuze's "present at every point of time"? On the one hand, they are both dealing with the *virtual,* to borrow a term from Deleuze that Laruelle does not often use. But on the other hand, Deleuze's pandemonium is a virtuality of time, while Laruelle's pandemonium is a virtuality of space. Or at least it appears to be space; we might expand the claim and make it slightly more pointed: a virtuality of fact.

Deleuze says the virtual is real. Laruelle never quite says the real is virtual. His preferred description is to say the real is in "superposition." But nevertheless the real, while remaining immanent to itself, is present at every point, and thus in some basic sense, "virtual" to every point. Further, Laruelle's real is never in a relationship with its virtualities, and thus Laruelle will never speak in the language of forces and counterforces so common in Deleuze (action-reaction, actual-virtual, territorialization-deterritorialization).

Our rockets may be present at every point of the Remote, but in strict Laruellean terms the story is slightly off. For the Remote, as Real, is present unilaterally and ultimately at every point of the rocket.

Today there are two kinds of spatial digitality that hold sway: flat digitality and deep digitality. Flat digitality results from the reduplicative multiplexing of the *object.* Consider today's media systems. Consider the many kinds of grid screens that populate our world: the security guard's multichannel montage of closed-circuit security camera feeds; the cellular grids of video compression codecs or more prosaically the bitmap image itself; the computer desktop with its multiple parallel and overlapping windows; the computer game with its spatially segmented heads-up display; the television sportscast with stat buffers, text crawls, inset videos, and split screens.

All these are no longer images per se, they are aggregations of cells that combine and coordinate to create some kind of whole (see RSG, *RSG-FORK=5.1,* the frontispiece of this chapter). The political-architectural touchstone for flat digitality is thus the panopticon prison: Each inmate's cell a pixel on a JumboTron image, all under the watchful eye of the guard (who is, ideally, a single person occupying a single Euclidean point). The photographic touchstone is the telephoto view: the flat scope of view, with peripheral vision boxed out and all relations reduced to planar relations one behind another.

Deep digitality results from the reduplicative multiplexing of the *subject.* Instead of a single point of view scanning a multiplicity of image feeds, deep digitality is a question of a multiplicity, nay an infinity, of points of view flanking and flooding the world viewed. These are not so much matrices of screens but matrices of vision. They are the CCTV meshes deployed across cities; the multiple data points involved in data mining; the virtual camera or "fly-through mode" in CAD software; or crowd-sourcing swarms that converge on a target.

Again it is the image that has suffered. These are all no longer images in any traditional sense. Not the collage of flat digitality, deep digitality is para-photographic, more sculpture or theater than anything else. Or like music, perhaps, with its penchant for multiple voices. The prison is now reversed, a *reverse panopticon* in which a multiplicity of watchers all collaborate to convene upon a singular point.[16] On this score, anyone who says the contemporary world is a vast panopticon has the facts of the matter exactly backward. The cybernetic world may be a control society, but it is a reverse panopticon, not a panopticon as classically conceived. The condition of cellularity is now subjective not objective. In other words, within deep digitality the subject is cellular (the watcher), whereas within flat digitality the object is cellular (the watched). The object is now a Euclidean point, while the "subjective" points of view have metastasized into multiplicity. What this produces is a curvature of space. Space bends and recedes. Space grows deep as the subject metastasizes and engulfs it.

So if the previous mode was the apotheosis of the telephoto (a telephoto ontology), this is the apotheosis of the wide angle (a wide-angle ontology). In splitting from one to two, deep digitality reintegrates the world into a *rendered* universe, viewable from all sides, modeled from all angles, predictable under all variable conditions.

The analog and the digital. To summarize what has been stated so far, the analog, understood as the two merging into one, is the universe of proportion, of continuous variability. Modular couplings of things come together in chained relations that are themselves linear. Because of this the analog relation, while only apparently based on a fundamental twoness, is ultimately a mode of immanence, for the apparent twoness is dissolved or deterritorialized into a continuous and generic identity. The underlying substrate for the analog is thus heterogeneity, which we understand not simply as collections of different things but as pure difference, a difference so pure that it is, to use a word from Deleuze, "smooth." Because of its questionable applicability to relation, the analog has no proper concourse with the event. Instead we considered the concept of the prevent, which refers to both the preemption of the event and the prior of the event. But the prevent does not mean that "nothing happens," that there is no change, no events as such. It means simply that the valence of "what happens" must be radically reconfigured, not around causality, but around something like *determination* or *destiny*.[17]

The digital, by contrast, is defined as the one dividing in two. It is the universe of separation, alienation, distinction, division, and making-discrete. Multiplicities of standardized atoms proliferate in massively parallel relations. Such relations are typically nonlinear in nature. Emerging out of a homogeneous substrate, these multiples (merely reduplicative copies of the twos) are themselves transcendental because they accomplish a persistent expression of being across the extension of space, through time, and in relation both to themselves and to other things. This is why the most basic forms of digitality are differential being and dialectical being. The former exhibits the transcendental simply as mediation through the different layers of the metaphysical cosmos, while the latter through the persistence and transformation of entities as they weather the mutations of contradiction.

The analog is an enemy to the transcendental and hence must only be a virtualization. Yet by contrast the digital is an actualization because it continually "solves" the virtual, territorializing it back into discrete things. (Do not believe the dot-com ideology: the digital has nothing to do with the virtual.) And just as the analog is the realm of the prevent, the digital is the only proper realm of the event because it is the only realm in which truly decisive or trenchant relation exists, which is to say a "liberated" relation of infinite possibility.

Analog	Digital
Continuous comparison	Discrete sampling
Twoness overcome by the one	Twoness overcome by the multiple
An identity	A difference
Heterogeneous substrate	Homogeneous substrate
Immanent	Transcendental
Parallelism	Parallelity
A duality of the one	Massively multiple

Because this system is at least somewhat reflexive, it is possible to interrogate the analog/digital distinction itself. Of course, in being a distinction, it is a form of digitality—as is the discourse in much of this book. So the digital triumphs over the analog, at least under the specific conditions of the standard model in which we now reside. The deeper ramifications of such a claim, if it is true, are explored further in Part II of the book, particularly chapter 10.

Furienmeister, *The Furie*, c. 1610. Kunsthistorisches Museum, Vienna.

four

Events

What is an event? The question is typically answered in one of two ways:
events are relations, or events are decisions. Depending on context, events
often appear as either relations or decisions. In one sense, an event is a
relation between two moments in time, or between two states of affairs.
Likewise a relation is only a relation by virtue of being able to be actualized into an event.

Yet in another sense, an event is a decision. As a more or less conscious action, it must be willed into existence by someone or some kind
of catalyzing agent. Following this line, an event is simply the mirror
image of a desire, aspiration, affordance, or drive: overladen snow desires
the avalanche; an enzyme aspires to catalyze a chemical reaction; a person decides to jump.

Relation means to bring back. Decision means to cut off. So the question may be rephrased: Is an event a bringing back, or is an event a cutting off? In other words, does the event bring something back into being
or cut something off from it?

For his part, Deleuze is satisfied with the event never deviating from
the material world (after all, he is opposed to classical metaphysics), while
Badiou's event breaks from being. In Deleuze the event consists of inten-
sive or extensive transformations within the furious plane of immanence
(see Furienmeister, *The Furie,* the frontispiece of this chapter). But for
Badiou the givenness of being is fundamentally profane and therefore
must be superseded by a voluntaristic deviation. Badiou's voluntaristic
event is an instance of the generic. But, as I suggest here, even if Badiou's

73

instincts lead him in interesting directions he does not go quite far enough in his quest for the genericity of the event. For it is only Laruelle who refuses to think the event as either relation or decision.

To say that events are *relations* is to say that events remain within the core substrate of being. Here an event is not a deus ex machina descending into the scene from somewhere beyond, modifying or rescuing the world. All changes to the world are immanent to the world. An event is not different from a relation; on the contrary, an event is simply a new relation. Actuate an event to make visible a new relation; identify a relation and one will have identified the aftermath of an event. Again, this is the kind of universe described by Deleuze. Events are immanent to material processes. In fact, events *are* these processes themselves and therefore cannot be distinguished from them. Events as relations are workaday events. They are not particularly special and there is no miracle in their being occasioned. The election of the first black president of the United States is an event, but so is cellular mitosis, and so is choosing to have coffee instead of tea at the breakfast table.

To say that the event is a *decision* is to say that an event is wholly different from the basic ontological categories of object and relation. An event is not merely a relation. It leaves the world behind and, from an alternate vantage point, actuates a transformation in the state of the situation. It is the principle through which a specific kind of world changes into a different kind of world. Such is the universe described by Badiou, in stark contrast with Deleuze. For Badiou, events are external to worlds. As such, events are always special, like miniature miracles.

Choosing coffee or tea never rises to the level of the event, for such a pseudo-choice does not effect a change in the state of the situation. Event as decision means that the event itself must be so affecting, so seductive, so total, so cataclysmic that it tears apart the fabric of the world, so that new objects and new relations, and indeed new aftershock events, will come into existence.

So, on the one hand, the event as relation describes a vitalist, process-oriented, or superlative materialism. The world consists of countless, endless events wrought by the inexhaustible wellsprings of life known as the desiring machines. But, on the other hand, the event as decision describes a voluntarism, a labor willed into existence by the militant subjects of the holy warriors, the activists, the campaigners, the evangelists, the committed. (One need not be anthropocentric on this point; flowers and fawns can and will be their own kind of holy warriors, can and will exude a desire, just as much as humans do.)

Is the fabric of the world good in itself? Or does something stink here? Is the good a deviation from this life or merely a reconfiguration of it? Deleuze, while hardly ever trafficking in moral platitudes, must still claim that the fabric of the world is good in itself, because he locates events in the world. Badiou, by contrast, must claim that the fabric of the world, which he calls the "state of the situation," is wanting, since Badiou's events are deviations from the world.

Indeed these philosophical modes carry their own theological tendencies, many of them Christian or pseudo-Christian. Heidegger's *Ereignis* is a thinly veiled creationism, is it not? And Badiou's event is a kind of miracle, the rapture that grants a departure from this profane world. Deleuze, for his part, illustrates a form of non-Christian, heretical creationism, in which the new issues forth from pure immanence (not from the word or the spirit). And for his part Laruelle's return to the One smacks of a mystical neoplatonism.

First path: analog events. The previous chapter asserted that, properly speaking, there is no such thing as an analog event. But that was something of a white lie, a temporary placeholder until the question could be addressed in greater detail. In order to make any sense of the event, it is first necessary to step back for a moment and mediate further on the concept of givenness, particularly as it was formulated in Theses I and II, *that the real is given over to a mediation divided from it.*

The "things that are given" can be truncated to the "givens," or more technically the *data*. Data are the very facts of the givenness of Being. They are knowable and measurable. Data display a facticity; they are "what already exists," and as such are a determining apparatus. They indicate what is present, what exists. The word *data* carries certain scientific or empirical undertones. But more important are the phenomenological overtones: data refer to the neutered, generic fact of "the things having been given."

Even in this simple arrangement a rudimentary relation holds sway. For implicit in the notion of the facticity of givenness is a *relation* to givenness. Data are not just a question of the givenness of Being, but are also necessarily illustrative of a *relationship* back toward a Being that has been given. In short, givenness itself implies a relation. This is one of the fundamental observations of phenomenology.

Even if nothing specific can be said about a given entity *x*, it is possible to say that, if given, *x* is something as opposed to nothing, and therefore that *x* has a relationship to its own givenness as something. *X* is "as *x*"; the as-structure is all that is required to demonstrate that *x* exists in a relation. (By contrast, if *x* were immanent to itself, it would not be possible to assume relation. But by virtue of being made distinct as something given, givenness implies non-immanence and thus relation.) Such a "something" can be understood in terms of self-similar identity or, as the scientists say, negentropy, a striving to remain the same.

So even as data are defined in terms of their givenness, their non-immanence with the one, they also display a relation with themselves. Through their own self-similarity or relation with themselves, they tend back toward the one (as the most generic instance of the same). The logic of data is therefore a logic of existence and identity: on the one hand, the facticity of data means that they exist, that they *ex-sistere,* meaning to stand out of or from; on the other hand, the givenness of data as something means that they assume a relationship of identity, as the self-similar "whatever entity" that was given.

The true definition of data, therefore, is not simply "the things having been given." The definition must conjoin givenness and relation. For this reason, data often go by another name, a name that more suitably describes the implicit imbrication of givenness and relation. The name is *information.*

Information combines both aspects of data: the root *form* refers to a relationship (here a relationship of identity as same), while the prefix *in* refers to the entering into existence of form, the actual givenness of abstract form into real concrete formation.

Heidegger sums it up well with the following observation about the *idea:* "All metaphysics including its opponent positivism speaks the language of Plato. The basic word of its thinking, that is, of his presentation of the Being of beings, is *eidos, idea:* the outward appearance in which beings as such show themselves. Outward appearance, however, is a manner of presence."[1] In other words, outward appearance or idea is not a deviation from presence, or some precondition that produces presence, it is precisely coterminous with presence. To understand data as information means to understand data as idea, but not just idea, also a host of related terms: *form, class, concept, thought, image, outward appearance, shape, presence,* or *form-of-appearance.* An entity "in-form" is not a substantive entity, nor is it an objective one. The in-form is the negentropic transcendental of the situation, be it "material" like the givens or "ideal" like the encoded event. Hence an idea is just as much subject to information as are material objects. An oak tree is in-formation, just as much as a computer file is in-formation.

All of this is simply another way to understand Parmenides's claim about the primary identity of philosophy: "Thought and being are the same"; or as rendered by Heidegger: "For the same perceiving (thinking) as well as being."[2] Thus, as a way to deepen the original description of the standard model, we may now reiterate the gist of Theses I and II using new vocabulary: *Being is the same as being in-formation.* The standard world is an information world. There is no such thing as "raw" data, because to enter into presence means to enter into form. Information is part and parcel of the standard model. And this is why explorations into formlessness are always so profound, often bordering on disorientation, shock, or horror.[3]

For these reasons it is indeed possible to think the event as *analog event.* Following Deleuze, analog events illustrate an immanent relation. Not pure immanence per se, but a relation of givenness that strives toward immanence. (The analog is always "aspirational" in this sense.) Information is the ultimate analog event: a "something" is given and enters into a relation with itself as specific identity of the same, in the same proportion, in the same way and manner, in a continuously variable immediacy with itself. The analog event par excellence therefore is nothing more than the event of self-similarity.

Yet this is only the most elemental description of the analog event. Broader, more prosaic phenomena can also be understood as analog events. In fact all phenomena are given within a world and thus derive their fundamental identity via such relation to givenness. These kinds of events are not rare. They include all manner of continuous differentiation, autopoiesis, and individuation. Frogs and birds and subatomic particles are thus analog events as such by virtue of their consistency as objects.

But is there a contradiction? It depends on whether the term *analog* is interpreted strictly or loosely. In the previous chapter we observed a strict interpretation: there are no analog events (only analog prevents) because analogicity means a full integration and collapse of the two into the one. Yet now a loose interpretation is also available: analog events are indeed possible because analogicity means a provisional reconciliation of the two into a relation of pseudo-identity as one. In other words, within the standard model—which is by definition the realm of digitality, distinction, separation, differentiation—analog events do exist precisely because objects persist as self-similar. Objects may morph and change, of course, but the analog event is the event of championing reconciliation over rivenness and union over division. The analog event is the event of the same.

Second path: digital events. To recap, the event is a relation. The event is a relation when it is understood in terms of analogy. The analog relation is the desire to overcome the rivenness of being by way of a continuous, proportionate, aspiration toward an image of the same self. As information or "data structure," the givens exist as a structure of relation. Hence information combines both brute facticity of substance and the form or architecture of relation that such substance assumes. Any deeper explanations are moot, because under the standard model no substance can exist apart from form, and no form can exist uncoupled from substance. To exist means to appear *as* presence, and hence to relate back to one's own givenness. And the reverse too: to relate means to span a differential of states, and thus to be outside of one's self (to ex-ist).

Following this logic, then, the analog event is clearly part of the architecture of being. But what of the digital event? If the analog event means the continuous aspiration toward the same, how to consider the digital?

To answer the question it is necessary to advance past simple relation and consider *decisional* relation. To consider event as decision is to consider the event from the perspective of willed action. (Again there is no reason to be anthropocentric; trees and bees can exhibit willed action as here defined.)

Whenever there exists a spectrum or continuum of intensities, there exists immanence. This is why the two becoming one is an immanence, why analogy is an immanence, and why immanence implies analogy. Conversely, whenever there exists difference or discontinuous states, there exists the transcendental. This is why the one becoming two necessitates the transcendental; why digitality implies the transcendental, and why the transcendental implies digitality. To call relations "decisional" is to underscore the fact that they are about cutting, that they follow a deviation from the state of affairs. A synonym would be "trenchant relations" or "trenchant events."

Such is the theory of the event provided by Badiou. For him events are trenchant deviations from the state of the situation. They interrupt and depart from being. The event is a "pure outside." Such events are rare, relatively speaking—at least much rarer than Deleuzian events. Badiousian events are attached to subject formation, and, specifically, a set of procedures that a subject can pursue in order to become subject to truth. Badiou's theory of the event is thus properly labeled "voluntarist" in that it requires the active will of conscripted militants who seek to execute the event.

If Lenin is the ultimate Badiousian, the ultimate Deleuzians are the heat vortexes of thermodynamic systems, or enzymes during RNA transcription. The Badiousian event deviates from the state of the situation, inaugurating new paths for a subject's fidelity to truth. The Deleuzian event subtends all matter, catalyzing action and reaction within the immanent transformations of pure becoming.

Now the full meaning of event as decision is becoming clear. Such events are a cutting or separation. But they are also will-dependent— whatever kind of "will" that might be, the will of gravity, the will of the sovereign, or the will of the acorn. So while event as relation implies existence, event as decision implies something else entirely: *persistence* or *insistence*. (The ultimate question therefore will be that of time: analog events focus on the present, digital events the future.) If relations are the things that merely exist, decisions are the things that persist. To cut means to insist on cutting. To be cut means to persist in the wake of the cut. And, as the transcendental demonstrates, whatever undergoes division must "insist" that it remain the same in order to persist as such. A nexus of terms thus converges: digitality, transcendental, insistence, and decision. Each works in concert with the others.

Decisional events mean *change*, change in the normal everyday sense of the word. Decisional events mean action, process, or transformation. Change, as event, is a digital decision. Event as decision combines both static snapshot and active transformation. It is the realm not so much of data as of code, for although data exist, code insists a specific manner of execution. Executables, "machine acts," or code—these are all euphemisms for decisional events. Hence event as decision points directly to the arenas of mediation, synthesis, language, the political, the ideas of the world, ideology, or protocol. Perhaps this is why Laruelle is so interested in the performative dimension of philosophy, in those things that "say what they do and do what they say."[4]

The givens exist, while events insist. But how exactly? There are two main force vectors at play, one moving up the chain from the data to the decision, and the other moving down the chain from the decision to the data. The downward movement is *the movement of reality.* Such movement flows from the event to the givens. It reveals a kind of realism, but a realism driven by pessimism and an unexplainable yearning for brute physicality. Synonyms include *actualization, reification, alienation, objectification,* realpolitik, and *neutralization.*

Running in opposition to the movement of reality is *the movement of freedom.* This second vector runs from the givens to the event. It states, axiomatically, that the givens appear, naturally and spontaneously, as fodder to be encoded. It states in essence, following Badiou, that although there are only bodies and languages, it is possible to deviate from bodies and languages by way of events. To follow the movement of freedom reveals how the givens predate the event and compels the givens to engage in the event.

Note the counterintuitive tendency at play here. It might seem that going from the givens to the event is repressive or reactionary in the sense that the gaining of an encoded event, such as ideological interpellation, could only ever inhibit the so-called natural existence and operations of the givens, and that, by contrast, going from the event to the givens is liberating or progressive in the sense that the givens are "more real" than the artifice of the encoded event. But this is not entirely the case. The movement of freedom is, quite literally, opposed to reality. It is irreal and illiberal. The goal of the decisional event therefore is not to reduce social conditions to *realpolitik,* to autonomous realities, or to the various pragmatic realisms. Rather, the movement of freedom seeks an elevated artifice, an artifice constructed not simply from data, but from data as they are assembled within relational and decisional events. Laruelle calls these *fictions, artifices,* or *performances.*

To move closer to the fully encoded event means to move closer to freedom. The entity that is the most free is the one that is the most fully folded into the supernature, the one most intimately allied with history and with the real exigencies of matter, because that is where the trenchant events lie. Using terminology from literary criticism and media studies, we can say that the movement of freedom is the movement out of the world-bound, diegetic realm and *into the non-world-bound, non-diegetic realm*. Consequently, the entity that is the most free is also the entity that is closest to the sociopolitical sphere. In other words the more one pursues the decisional event, the more one is free. The greater the insistence, the greater the freedom.

Consider the famous slogan from Stewart Brand, "Information wants to be free." We are now in a position to reconsider its deeper meaning. Data, as a given, want to be free, free as evental information. Digital freedom is thus a question of being "free *from*" the autonomy of data. Counterintuitively, then, the movement of freedom is driven not by liberation but by increased imbrication with the sociopolitical sphere. It is driven not by a force of loosening but by tightening, not by a newfound flexibility or laxity of structure but by discipline, not by the peace of the real but by the violence of the material. And, as Badiou says, because it tends toward the political sphere populated by political factions and political agents, the movement of freedom will always take as its goal the formation of new subjectivities.

But Laruelle, as will become evident in a moment, offers still another alternative. He parts ways with both Badiou and Deleuze on the question of the event. For him events are not heroic, as they must be for Badiou, and they do not depart from being. Laruelle has little interest in cultivating new subject positions. Events do not create heroes—or if they do, he wishes no part in it.[5] But likewise Laruelle differs from Deleuze, for while Deleuze makes the event coterminous with being, Laruelle will additionally show that the only true theory of the event is one that withdraws absolutely from both relation and decision.[6]

Thesis VIII. Being is an evental mode; it is coterminous with the event.
Before he describes the event as such, Laruelle begins with a much more prosaic description of the actually existing world. The world and the event are, quite literally the same thing; hence Laruelle speaks of them in terms of the "event-world."

Consider the *as-structure* and the way in which it frames all the entities of the world as both "aspect of" and "relation to." Consider Whitehead's prehensions and actual occasions. Consider the principle of sufficient reason, namely that an actual entity and an actual reason are coterminous. Consider simply how being is preconditioned on "reasons": rationales, relations, structures, formations, decisions, and events. And the reverse as well: wherever events pertain, one may be sure to find being. The historicity of being is also the historicity of the event.

Such a modal condition is what Laruelle calls the event-world. We can think of it as a direct extension of the standard model. "The event is not merely the result of superimposing an ontology onto a history," Laruelle claims. "It appears whenever there is a repression, a cutting, or a collapsing of Being."[7]

There are a number of ways to demonstrate this, but the most straightforward is to return to the notion of relation as it was previously discussed. To speak of being, in the framing of the grand illusion, is to speak of the distinction between object and relation, or between data and information. By definition, being is never purely immanent with itself. Even the most immanence-focused philosophies of being, such as those of Deleuze or Henry, rely on differentials and distinctions between states or modes. In fact immanence itself is often understood more as a resolution of division than as an always-already unified condition of pure singularity.[8]

Thus, because being is never purely immanent with itself, it must address the question of relation. It must "repress," "cut," "collapse," or otherwise come to terms with distinction. Sometimes relation is more or less resolved, for example, into immanence. Sometimes relation is given a starring role in the architecture of being, as with the dialectic. Sometimes it is starved and whittled down to nothing, as with the generic. And, as in the case of continuous being, relation alights onto the surface of being, like a ripple of peaks and valleys, surging and falling.

The event-world is the result of a structural and synchronic digitization. But the event itself, as prevent, is neither a decision nor a relation, neither digital nor analog. Previously we said that the one is unconnected to the event, suggesting instead that the one be considered in terms of the advent or prevent. Let me now try to derive that architecture. What is the structure of the event-world? And how is the event-world related to the event itself?

To repeat: thinking the analog event means thinking the event as relation; but thinking the digital event means thinking the event as decision. Laruelle combines both arms of the event by showing how relationality as such (that is, a world of "information" in which entities form relations) is itself a decision within ontology. In other words, the most important decision is the decision to inaugurate relationality as such. The most important digitization is the digitization of the analog.

The event-world, defined as the given world in which events take place, exists itself in a relationship of digitization vis-à-vis the prevent of the one. For Laruelle the decision to establish philosophy—philosophy as reflection, convertibility, reversibility, interfacing, and so on—*is a digital event*. (Undoubtedly, to abstain from doing philosophy is not simply a new digitization, a new decision in silhouette. If it were, it would remain trapped as a *philosophical* abstention from philosophy and therefore no abstention at all! Rather, to abstain from decision means to practice an analogical science that operates, as Laruelle puts it, "according to" the one.)

Deleuze, in a passage from *Difference and Repetition,* explains this scenario most eloquently: "Univocity signifies that being itself is univocal, while that of which it is said is equivocal: precisely *the opposite of analogy.* . . . It is not *analogous being* which is distributed among the categories and allocates a fixed part to beings, but the beings which are distributed across the space of univocal being, opened by all the forms."[9] What this means is that the relation of the one to the multiple is not a relationship of analogy. Or, to put it another way, the event of being, as the advent of the division between one and many or between being and existing, stems from a digitization (not an analogicity). For if it were not a digitization, then the worldly manifestations of the one would themselves also have to be, by analogy, one, rather than multiple. Yet because digitization implies distinction, the one can manifest itself in the world as multiple multiplicities, which themselves nevertheless still speak in the same voice of a generic oneness.

The one-multiple, as evental and causal relation, is therefore a *two-way split* of digital and analog relations. From one aspect, digital. From another, analog. To think univocity in terms of equivocity is a movement of the digital. But to think equivocity in terms of univocity is a movement of the analog. Shifting the orientation of perspective is crucial. The real causes the multiple, both unilaterally and irreversibly. And the real also causes it transcendentally, and hence must do so *digitally*. But as multiple, the equivocal things of the world all stand in a reverse relationship of analogicity back to the one.

Creation is digital, but the lived existence of the created is analog. To be born is to break with the past, but to live is to act in fidelity to it. *Unilateral* means the one is oblivious of the two, insisting on its own oneness, but *duality* means the two bonds in an identity with the one. Laruelle's "unilateral duality" should be understood in precisely this way. As unilateral it follows digital distinction, while as duality it follows analog integration.

The event as indecision and indifference. Thus far the event has been considered as either relation or decision. Now the event can be understood in completely different terms, as a kind of static preemption rooted in indecision and indifference.[10]

To say that the event is an *indecision* is to say that the event is the suspension of the evental regime itself, the regime described previously as relation-decision. Following Heidegger, being is given from out of a primordial event. And hence, following Badiou, for beings to actuate events they must somehow echo the primordial event, supersede being a second time and leave it behind. Yet such a scenario is still too metaphysical for Laruelle, who suggests that the only properly radical theory of the event must begin not from decision (Badiou) but from the indecision of generic immanence. The only true theory of the event—a theory adequate to the one—is a theory of the event that withdraws absolutely from both relation and decision.

So the one is not a simple object, and certainly no kind of All-One super-object. Neither is the one a relation—the warning heard time and again in Laruelle. The one is best understood as an event.

The one is no kind of colloidal substance or "grey goo," and likewise not an absolute reality, much less an absolute mind. Terms like *realism* or *idealism* help very little. To say that the one is an event is not to subscribe to something like a "process philosophy" attributed rightly or wrongly to figures like Whitehead or Deleuze. Process is very important, but it pertains to the standard model, not the static preemption of the one. So, because the one is, by definition, the *unilateralization* of process, it makes little sense to speak of it in terms of process philosophy.

Rather, the one is the event of indifference. In withdrawing from both relation and decision, the one is more a question of leaving being than being itself. The one is a waning of presence, a withering of being. Both the givens and the given events must be abandoned; both data and information abandoned. Not so much a movement of freedom or a movement of reality, the event of the one is a movement of subtraction in which presence is whittled down to the radical anonymity of something whatsoever.

Indifference is incompatible with the "philosophies of difference" catalogued by Laruelle in his book of that name. These philosophies have always been driven by a therapeutic aim. First the primordial alienation chronicled by Marx, but later the alienation of subjective identity via difference and the deeper ontological difference embedded inside metaphysics. These are the various sites of the grand traumas. These are the scaffolding of a traumatized being. They inaugurate the great therapeutic crusades: Marxism, phenomenology, psychoanalysis, deconstruction, or identity politics.

Deleuze's description in *The Logic of Sense* of the stoicism of Joë Bousquet, the French surrealist poet who was paralyzed in World War I, could not paint a better picture: "My wound existed before me, I was born to embody it."[11] (Indeed on this point, Badiou's subsequent theory of the event sounds like a mere echo of earlier passages written by Deleuze.)

Indifference is incompatible with all of this. There is no identity but real identity. There is no deconstruction of the one. The fractures and traumas, which Marxism or psychoanalysis were invented to solve, are merely figments of a more general trauma, the nihilism of the reality of the standard model. Thus take caution not to think indifference or indecision in terms of trauma or fragmentation, and likewise not to structure indifference or indecision in terms of a therapeutic strategy. The vital question today is not to rehabilitate being, and certainly not to protect and promote new "health mandates" or "medical interventions," but rather to demilitarize this life, to stand down, to de-organize and unmanage it into a condition of indifference rooted in indecision.

Some will label this a kind of milksop quietism. Some will view Laruelle as nothing more than a license to do nothing. But to view Laruelle in this way is to misunderstand the full force of insufficiency and indecision.

The withdrawal from the standard model is as assertive as it is passive, as disruptive as it is peaceful.

For this reason Laruelle stands at the threshold of a new theory of the event. The question for him, as he often repeats, is not so much the decision of philosophy but the *indecision* of philosophy. Not so much philosophical difference but philosophical indifference. The point is not to revisit a kind of existentialism or nihilism ("Being withdraws from us"), but precisely the opposite, a kind of deterritorialization of the very terms of the ontological arrangement ("We withdraw from being"). The point is thus ultimately not a new enchantment of being-given, but the profound disenchantment of leaving-being.

Something is out there. And "it gives." But whatever it is, it is not being as we know it today. It is, rather, a cancellation, a privative or subtractive event that brings us closer to the generic univocity of the one. (And again we should repress the urge to think of the one as a kind of proxy for God; the one is merely and modestly the undoing of the standard model, nothing more.)

In this sense, no language of repression or liberation will help. This is not Freud in 1905 or Marcuse in 1964. This is not about muzzling or uncorking the desiring machines. Likewise it is not about finding truth in a departure from the state of the situation. If anything, Badiou is standing on his head; he must be put back on his feet again: the event is the only radical real and thus is part of being, yet leaving-being brings us closer to the "void" of the whatever.

If information shines a light on relationships of identity and difference, and if the event-world shows a society in which information entities (humans, strands of DNA, operating systems) enter into networking relationships bound by protocological control, then the event as indecision reveals a structure of *not*working relationships, a cosmological *désoeuvrement*, an inexistentialism, the pure event that withdraws from presence. After the movement of subtraction takes place, the pure event as prevent takes over where being once stood. Being is thus no longer the most fundamental question for thinking. Instead, the pure event whatsoever (the prevent) happens. Merely happens.

The event as static and final. Entities understood from the perspective of the prevent are, in this way, both static and final. Static entities belong to the commonality of the entire class of objects, rather than being instantiated over and over again along with individual objects. To say "static" means to say that something is *generic* to the class. From one perspective the static nature of entities can be contrasted to "the dynamic," but from another perspective this logic falls apart. In fact the static is the *most* dynamic in that it is never instantiated in one particular appearance. It belongs to the entity at large, in its pure commonality. Not a local dynamism of the flexible instantiations of being, the static aspect of an entity is a total dynamism of the common.

But entities understood from the perspective of the prevent are also labeled "final." This means that their static aspect can never again be changed. Just as they are static (generic to the class), they are also final (generic to the ontological condition). As common, entities refuse further modification. Genericity, as something whatsoever, is thus both static and final. This is another way to understand why entities are destinies determined by the one. They are radically determined by the supernatural base—determined "in the last instance" says Laruelle—and likewise destined toward their own generic commonality, as the only thing that, in the last instance, is truly their own.

The movement of something. Such are the elemental conditions of the third movement. After the movement of freedom and the movement of reality, there is *the movement of something*. The one is not the void (Heidegger, Sartre, Badiou). It is likewise not the "other" as defined by post-structuralism. If anything it is the "something or other."

If the movement of freedom means politicization and the movement of reality means depoliticization, then the movement of something opens up onto a different kind of landscape, an ancient landscape, but one nevertheless still being understood and reinvented for today. Something whatsoever resides within the prevent. And from this blank spot on the map, the something whatsoever aggresses (in prevention) toward the realm of the event as mere event.

The movement of something has absolutely no intention of taking over for the event as mere event. It has no such aspiration. In contrast to the movement of freedom, which moves from the givens to the event, the movement of something *deprives* the givens of their givenness and the event of its evental state. In this way the movement of something is never a hypertrophy of freedom. It is, if anything, a reversal of direction: to aggress toward the givens and the event through the act of standing down (leaving-being).

Heidegger saw this intuitively, even if he shied away from accepting its full repercussions. "The event of appropriation," wrote Heidegger, "is that realm, vibrating within itself, through which man and Being reach each other in their nature, achieve their active nature *by losing those qualities* with which metaphysics has endowed them."[12] In this way, the generic univocity of being does not mean monism exactly (unity), and it does not simply mean that being speaks as the one (univocity), but instead it means the loss of qualities, the voice of being as someone (anonymous).

The movement of something is not, strictly speaking, opposed to, beyond, under, or transcendent from either the first movement (toward reality) or the second movement (toward freedom), either the fixation on the givens or the fixation on the event, either realism or materialism. During the movement of the impersonal, something subtracts from both movements and thus is without matter and without the real. It is both an antimatter and an irreality.

The movement of something says: "If you have something whatever, you shall retain it; but if you have nothing, you will lose even more of nothing, up until the point of your impersonality." So while the movement of something may resemble nihilism, it is in fact slightly different, not so much a nothing-ism but a something-ism, a *quiddism*.

"In the perfect crime," wrote Baudrillard, "it is the perfection that is criminal."[13] The *prevent* means both "to stop or hinder" and "from what comes before the event." What does the prevent prevent but the catastrophe, the perfect crime of politics? The (mere) event is always the perfect crime, because its perfection is a completion of the real world. And in its perfect completion the real is eliminated. The prevent prevents the event from occurring.

But prevent also means what comes before the event, the *a priori*. The realm of the prevent does not present an additive predicate to an entity. Thus the only judgments that the prevent will confirm are those traditionally labeled the "analytic a priori," which is to say, those that come before the event and that do not present additive predicates. If the mundane event affirms a normative judgment of the form "One ought to act in such and such a way," and the givens affirm predicated judgment of the form "*a* is *b*," the prevent affirms the most elemental form of statement: *Something is whatsoever it is.*

All the necessary topics are now on the table. We have offered a brief snapshot of Laruelle's project, including his take on the philosophical decision and the principle of sufficient philosophy. Some attention was given to the one and its actualization into the four modes of being that are contained in the standard model. Then, because the standard model is premised on the division of the one in two, we spent some time defining both the digital and analog, with an eye to how these terms relate to existing theoretical discourse. Finally, we considered the division of the one in two as an event itself, an event of decision. This entailed a discussion of other kinds of events that aren't decisions, namely relation events and indecision events.

Now the question remains: How does Laruelle withdraw from the standard model? What is Laruelle's stance on digitality? When Laruelle unilateralizes the standard model does he not also unilateralize digitality? How is Laruelle "against the digital"? And what is the future of the digital?

Admittedly the *Against . . .* of my title is not entirely Laruellean, since "being against" reinstates the philosophical decision and the resultant amphibology between two things. But as Laruelle himself admits, given the pervasiveness of the philosophical world, it is often necessary to speak using existing philosophical language even if the goal is something other than philosophy.

Laruelle is against the digital, but do not assume that, in withdrawing from the digital, he will necessarily find refuge in the analog. Laruelle is just as uninterested in the analog as he is the digital. In fact, following Laruelle, it is possible to conceive of analogy as simply a subordinate mode of digitality, because analogy is still a kind of distinction like anything else. So in his withdrawal from digitality, Laruelle is charting an exodus out of representation more generally. Thus, the true withdrawal from digitality will lead to immanence, not analogy. The ultimate withdrawal from digitality will lead to the generic.

Part II

Withdrawing from the
Standard Model

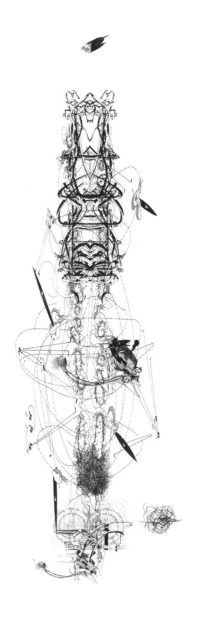

Neil Spiller, *Geo-Genesis-Mapping,* 2008. Reproduced courtesy of the artist.

five

Computers

To launch Part II, let me pause briefly and recapitulate the overall trajectory. Arguments often gain their impetus through opposition to some sort of conventional wisdom, in the hope of amending, modifying, or even reversing it. Conventional wisdom today defines the digital in terms of zeros and ones. This is not entirely false, and indeed completely true for that particular mode of digitality known as binary or base-two numerical notation. But binary mathematics is a relatively small subset of digitality in general, which has many avatars across the fields of ontology, political theory, aesthetics, and beyond. Even for binary mathematics, the zero and the one are mere tokens enacting their required roles within a more important logic, the logic of distinction, decision, difference, and division; other tokens could be swapped in and the digital system would work just as well: on and off, *A* and *B*, or you and me.

Such logic of decision provides the fuel for this book and allows us to explore the logic for its own sake. But further, decision also discloses, via silhouette, a strange science fiction universe in which such distinction no longer holds. Of all thinkers who address such questions, Laruelle is best suited for the task, because he is the one who has pursued the nondigital path most fervently and rigorously.

Although zero might elucidate the void and one the plenum—or as George Boole called them, the "Nothing" and the "Universe"—zero and one are ultimately most valuable for the two-structure they facilitate. Distinction requires an understanding of zero and one in terms of a relationship of two. Thus the most important step in the comprehension of digitality is to shift from the former to the latter, from zero and one to one and two.

In part I we defined the digital and the analog in terms of the one dividing in two and the two integrating in one. This in turn evokes the topic of the one itself, and the one's role in philosophy not as a first cause or "absolute reality" but rather as a preventative force of static preemption bent not on furthering the essence of thought or being but virtualizing them together into a metastasis of pure immanence.

But, if the one is purely and radically immanent, the existence of the world as given requires some explanation. Thus the advent, or the synchronic and structural "event of appropriation," arrives as a digitization of the one. This is known as the "grand illusion" of actual worldly presence: things belong together, minds with bodies, entities with relations, beings with their own rationales for being.

In chapter 2 we described the various aspects of the standard model via four epithets of being: the affirmative transcendental of differential being, the negative transcendental of dialectical being, the affirmative immanence of continuous being, and the negative immanence of generic being.

Next, in order to plumb the relation between being and the one, it was necessary to show that the relation is *not* a relation, in fact, but an event. Hence a mediation on the event: first, the event as relation, in the form of data or "the things having been given"; second, the event as decision, both as willed events, but also the grand decision itself of philosophy, understood as the decision to view the world in terms of data in relation; and, third, the much more radical definition of event as prevent, or the determination of decision (and hence ultimately the determination of relation too). The spectrum of the event spans three zones, not simply relation and decision, but ultimately indecision or destiny.

To initiate the discussion of how to withdraw from the standard model, we now take a brief intermission from Laruelle and consider a very particular aspect of Deleuze. In some ways Deleuze is the single most influential philosopher of our times. So many things that have happened in society and culture over the past thirty or forty years were chronicled at length in one or more of his books. Horizontality rather than verticality; surface over depth; the breakdown of the Freudian subject; affect instead of emotion; assemblages and multiplicities; rhizomes and distributed networks; pure immanence; affirmation and expression—these are just some of the many aspects of the Deleuzian world in which we currently live.

In 1988 Laruelle printed a five-page "Letter to Deleuze" in *The Philosophical Decision,* the journal that Laruelle published during the years 1987–89.[1] In the letter Laruelle scolds and castigates Deleuze on his treatment of Spinoza, and then proceeds to lecture him on the differences between philosophy and non-philosophy by way of a thirty-point summary of its basic terms: "By philosophical decision I mean . . . by real I mean . . . by finite I mean . . ." and so on.

Deleuze likely read the letter, or at least we know Deleuze was cognizant of Laruelle at the time because he mentioned Laruelle briefly in the 1991 Deleuze and Guattari book *What Is Philosophy?* The reference was most certainly intended as a friendly tip of the hat to Laruelle, then still an emerging figure in France and with no international reputation to speak of.

But Laruelle's 1988 letter to Deleuze was just an overture. Despite Deleuze and Guattari's friendly intentions, Laruelle considered it the lowest insult to be brought "into the fold," because in his mind Deleuze was a philosopher like any other. A more thorough "Response to Deleuze" appeared in 1995 outlining Laruelle's rather dim opinion of his brother in immanence. For how could anyone with his name on a book called *What Is Philosophy?* ever come out alive? No good deed goes unpunished, and Deleuze was likely caught off guard by the sour response he received from Laruelle.

Laruelle's squeamishness toward Deleuze aside, shall we not pose the question directly: Is Deleuze a friend to Laruelle? Is Deleuze really a philosopher, in Laruelle's terms? And, philosopher or not, can Deleuze's analysis of computers help us understand the theme of digitality in Laruelle?

There are many references to Deleuze in Laruelle's work. But is he friend or foe? Consider Deleuze the philosophical realist who so valiantly resists metaphysical logic. Consider Deleuze the thinker of immanence, a deep commitment to immanence surpassed only by Henry, and surpassed eventually and most definitively by Laruelle himself. Laruelle tends to hold Deleuze at arm's length, but such treatment of other authors is par for the course in Laruelle. In fact Laruelle and Deleuze are similar in a number of ways.

Given his importance, Deleuze has been exhaustively parsed and studied by any number of people, from artists and activists, to dot-com libertarians, to military theorists, to humanists and social scientists of all shapes and sizes. Without wishing to dispute or duplicate this literature, I focus here on a particular text, Deleuze's late "Postscript on Control Societies," and pursue a very particular goal, Deleuze's relationship to computers.

Because he is so central to contemporary debates, many assume that Deleuze has a fully formed theory of the digital, but in truth of fact he doesn't. Deleuze's theory of the digital needs to be assembled piece by piece. By the end of this interlude, we will return to Laruelle and connect Deleuze's theory of computers back to the standard model and its pervasive digitality.

Could it be? Could it be that Deleuze's most lasting legacy will consist of 2,300 words from 1990? We are all Deleuzians today; that much is clear. But the vital question is *which* Deleuze? Two basic factions have emerged. First are those who think Deleuze describes resistance and flight from power, and second those who think Deleuze describes power itself, the very structure of organization and control. The first are today's post-Web liberals, ahistorical but enlightened ("Everything is a rhizomatic system"), the second are the historical materialists, a label no less gauche for being accurate ("Let us historicize and critique these systems, because they proliferate injustice"). In short, the line-of-flighters and the society-of-controllers. The Deleuze of 1972 and the Deleuze of 1990.

Deleuze's late essay "Postscript on Control Societies" is a strange little text. It bears not the same Deleuzian voice so familiar from his other writings. Cynics will grumble it falls short of the great books of 1968–69 or the radical collaborations with Félix Guattari during the 1970s. The text claims no more than a single paragraph in François Dosse's biography of Deleuze and Guattari.[2] A different voice resonates here, a more directly political voice, and barring the Guattari collaborations a voice less commonly heard in Deleuze's writings. To be sure, Deleuze was always a political thinker and remained politically committed in various ways throughout his life. But the "Postscript" is different.

"Today, I can say that I feel completely Marxist," he admitted in a late interview published posthumously. "The article I published on the 'society of control,' for example, is completely Marxist, even though I am writing on things that Marx knew nothing about."³ Indeed in the article he indicts capitalism by name. He raises his wrath against corporations and television shows. Yet his frame is not just the mode of production, but also the culture at large. He talks about snakes and surfers and other features of the dawning millennium. He references Roberto Rossellini, Paul Virilio, Franz Kafka, and most important Michel Foucault. He tells us exactly what is wrong with the business sector, as well as with the prisons, schools, and hospitals. It reads almost like a manifesto, the "Manifesto on Control Societies."

Manifestos are always about two things: the desires and the details. This is what we want; and we want it here, and in this manner. When the May 1968 revolts broke out in France, Philippe Sollers, along with Julia Kristeva, Jean-Joseph Goux, Jean-Louis Baudry, and a band of other signatories, wrote "The Revolution Here and Now: Seven Points," listing their grievances point by point.⁴ And—they added at the end—we shall meet on Wednesdays at nine o'clock on the rue de Rennes.

This is the crux of the *cahiers de doléances* refrain, reprised recently in the closing sections of Michael Hardt and Antonio Negri's *Multitude:* Say what you want, and be specific about it.

The year of Deleuze's death, 1995, was a good year for the manifesto. The Unabomber's "Industrial Society and the Future" advocated the complete destruction of what he called the "industrial-technological system." That same year the Dogme '95 "Vow of Chastity" signed by filmmakers Lars Von Trier and Thomas Vinterberg offered the closest thing to a manifesto seen in the cinema for some time. The Vow is as short as the Unabomber's is long, but it is detailed, detailed, detailed. Dogme filmmakers must film on location, in color, on Academy 35mm stock, and use concurrent diegetic sound.

Ten years earlier, a computer engineer named Richard Stallman wrote the "GNU Manifesto." The number of legitimate manifestos written by computer geeks can be counted on one hand—the VNS Matrix "Cyberfeminist Manifesto" and Eben Moglen's "The dotCommunist Manifesto" also come to mind. But despite its inauspicious source, Stallman's document had profound effects on the "industrial-technological system," and most all of them good.

Detailed, like the others, Stallman's manifesto calls for the creation of a free Unix-compatible software system, including a C compiler and a linker, a text editor, and a few dozen other free software applications. He names the make and model of the computer his system will run on. He rebuts, preemptively, eleven specific objections raised by his would-be critics. (Stallman even calls for a software tax to underwrite the development of free code.) Most important, the manifesto calls for a "stay free" legal armature for copyright holders, known today as the GNU General Public License.

Such was the intellectual climate that produced the "Postscript on Control Societies." No computer-savvy intellectual was Deleuze. He likely had never heard of Stallman's manifesto, much less read it. Nevertheless, scattered across his oeuvre, and particularly in his late work, Deleuze has unwittingly made significant contributions to the contemporary discourse on computing, cybernetics, networks, and digitality. From the concepts of the rhizome and the virtual, to his occasional interjections on the digital versus the analog, and to the notion of control society from the "Postscript," there is a case to be made that Deleuze, although rarely mentioning computers directly, has dramatically influenced today's discourse on digital media. Indeed, it makes sense given how cybernetics had influenced much of French theory in the latter twentieth century.[5]

One of the most influential aspects of the "Postscript," particularly to my own thinking, is how it asserts so trenchantly that things are not getting any better. Digitality is a problem, not a panacea. Planetary neoliberalism is a boondoggle not a deliverance. The snake is even worse than the mole. For critics working in the shadow of the dot-com boom, such offerings from Deleuze furnished a welcome dose of encouragement needed to combat the naïve utopian babble of the California ideology.

Deleuze was always good at drawing lines in the sand. One of the things that makes Deleuze such a pleasure to read is his clear construal of the theater of enemies. They are excellent enemies. Not just information technologies and the life sciences, but Plato, Hegel, and Descartes—elite enemies, all of whom have committed the most egregious error. Here is one point where Laruelle and Deleuze agree, for each of these philosophical enemies has assented to the classical condition of philosophy. Each admits to an up/down distinction between idea and matter, between essence and instance, between Being and beings.

The "Postscript" does not draw the line so much in terms of metaphysics. There the complaint is articulated in terms of control, communication, and the "harshest confinement" wrought by "the new monster" of information society (178).[6] Deleuze credits the term to William Burroughs, but the true source for "control" is no mystery.[7] Follow a thread from nineteenth-century thermodynamics and fluid dynamics through statistical mathematics, weather prediction, and nonlinear systems to terminate in 1948 with Norbert Wiener and his book *Cybernetics: Or Control and Communication in the Animal and the Machine*. Then, stemming from Wiener and his brethren in the military-industrial research parks, follow the thread that leads through the rest of the twentieth century by way of systems theory, cellular automata, and chaos theory.[8]

So why not call Deleuze's adversary by its true name? Like Laruelle, the real enemy is *cybernetics* in particular and *digitality* in general. The Deleuze of 1972 was influenced by cybernetics and all manner of ecological and topological thinking. By 1990 much had changed.

To describe Deleuze's "Postscript" as a manifesto is to invoke the question of philosophical genre. An author may adopt different textual strategies to achieve different ends. The interview, the seminar, the essay, the book, these all demand different things from the philosopher and command different participation by the reader. Of course, the "Postscript" is no user's manual on how to live. It is no call to action, no introduction to the non-fascist life, as Foucault said of *Anti-Oedipus*. Yet the "Postscript" furnishes the basic requirements of a manifesto, an enumeration of grievances and a sermon for how to remedy them.

The question of philosophical genre can also be approached from another point of view. For is this not a less philosophical Deleuze? The "Postscript" reveals a slightly more casual theorist. It reveals a man more willing to comment about the current state of the world and its daily goings-on. Here is a thinker who is willing to make a hard and fast historical periodization. Foucault's influence is dramatic. Indeed the "Postscript" presents the kind of thinking more often seen in the writings of sociologists, political economists, or even certain kinds of historians—modes of writing none of which are classic Deleuze. He is expanding his normal repertoire to include a very clear argument about historical periodization.

The argument is no secret: at some point during the middle to late twentieth century, *disciplinary* societies, characterized by confinement and bureaucratic hierarchy, gave way to *control* societies, characterized by "free-floating" cybernetic organization.

Make no mistake, the stakes of the "Postscript" are larger than what might be evident at first glance. In order to accept the concept of the control society, one must come to terms with a whole host of related concepts that, although not necessarily synonymous with control society, are nevertheless similar enough to demonstrate the success of the periodization of the contemporary as such. In other words, to accept control society one must accept Jean-François Lyotard's "postmodern," Hardt and Negri's "empire," Manuel Castells's "information age," Luc Boltanski and Ève Chiapello's "new spirit of capitalism," and all the other related periodization concepts.

These various historical labels do not mean the same thing, to be sure, and they do not refer precisely to the same historical periods. But the ubiquity of such periodization is evidence that something else is happening. The ubiquity of periodization proves there exists a strong desire to theorize the past few decades as dramatically different from the high water mark of modernity. But further, it suggests that periodization itself *is something that ought to be done*. People are free to squabble over this or that definition; nevertheless the "Postscript" demonstrates that periodization is something that defines today's mode of being, whether or not people can agree on the historical periods themselves or what they might mean.

Deleuze evokes many specific things in the "Postscript" that are notable, a few of which may be itemized briefly before expanding on one particular salient detail. A series of memorable images jump out to the reader: "the ultrarapid forms of apparently free-floating control" *(les formes ultra-rapides de contrôle à l'air libre)* (178); the sieve "whose mesh varies from one point to another" (179); big business described as "a soul, a gas" (179); the fact that "*surfing* has taken over from all the old *sports*" (180); "the passive danger of entropy and the active danger of sabotage" (180); the "mushrooming shantytowns and ghettos" (181); and the dynamic between the "mole's burrow" and the "snake's coils" (182).[9] Likewise the "Postscript" is one of the few places where Deleuze mentions his intriguing concept of the "dividual," a new kind of subject that emerges after the death of the individual.

But the crux of the "Postscript" is something else entirely. The crux of this short text has to do with technology. Here is one of those rare moments in which Deleuze comments on actually existing contemporary technology, specifically computers. Control societies, he writes, "function with a third generation of machines, with information technology and computers" (180). Admittedly Deleuze does not delve too deeply into the specificities of computing. But he does say a few brief words about the pairing that most interests us here, the analog and the digital.

Not as broadly integrated into Deleuze's overall project as, say, the concept of the virtual, the analog and the digital still figure importantly in the essay. Consider first the relevant sentences, which Deleuze uses to launch section 2 of the essay under the heading "Logic" (*Logique,* a cognate with the French word for software, *logiciel*):[10]

> The various placements or sites of confinement through which individuals pass are independent variables: we're supposed to start over each time at zero, and although all these sites have a common language, it's *analogical.* The different forms of control, on the other hand, are inseparable variations, forming a system of varying geometry whose language is *digital* (though not necessarily binary). (178, translation modified)

Only a passing reference, it is true, but still an important return to two terms that had appeared in Deleuze's philosophy for several years already.

By way of background, consider a text from his aesthetic period, the slim and elegant *Francis Bacon: The Logic of Sensation,* which first appeared in 1981.[11] The book on Francis Bacon is of course not about the digital, nor is it about control society per se. Nevertheless Deleuze finds time in the monograph to pause for a moment and offer a few remarks on the digital and the analog.[12]

Deleuze's first instinct is to connect the digital to the universe of computation and code. "Digital synthesizers," he writes—qualifying them as *audio* synthesizers, but his observations may be extrapolated to include video synthesizers as well—". . . are 'integral': their operation passes through a codification, through a homogenization and binarization of the data."[13] The "integral," integration, these are important concepts in Deleuze's work. Drawing on the use of the term in both mathematics and Freudian psychoanalysis, Deleuze uses *integration* to mean the actualization of the virtual.

"Four terms are synonymous," he wrote a decade earlier in *Difference and Repetition*, "actualise, differenciate, integrate and solve."[14] To integrate a mathematical function means to find the "area under the curve." For example one might integrate from *a* to *b* on the function *f(x)*, meaning that, given the curve plotted of the function *f(x)*, one sums the area under the curve bounded by *x = a* to *x = b*. At the same time, the appeal for Deleuze is, I suspect, not so much the mathematical sources of the term *integration* but the curvilinear sources, shall we say the baroque sources. Curves are complex. Given the complexity of a curve, to "solve" a curve mathematically is something of a miracle. In fact such a feat eluded the ancients; it took the baroque mathematicians G. W. Leibniz and Isaac Newton to do it.

As readers of Deleuze will already know, his ontology is one that posits an infinite plane of heterogenous elements, and on this plane the heterogenous elements come to integrate themselves into more or less homogenous regularities of aggregation, comportment, and association (Figure 5). Hence *integration* is a synonym for *coordination* or *organization* in Deleuze. Integration is the miracle of givenness and the subsequent management of those given beings. Integration produces things like species, compositions, and societies. And, lest we forget, the countervailing force exists as well, homogenous regularities that "deterritorialize" into the virtual, thereby suspending their specificity in favor of adjacent "possibility spaces."

In the previously cited quotation from *Francis Bacon*, Deleuze more or less equates five terms: *digitization, integration, codification, homogenization,* and *binarization*. Binarization, the grouping of things into twos, is the same as digitization, the separating or making distinct of atoms, is the same as integration, the solving of complex function curves, is the same as codification, the representation within a symbolic system, is the same as homogenization, the making uniform of dissimilar ingredients.

Needless to say the comparison of these five terms raises a number of questions, not all of which are resolvable here. What is important, for Deleuze and for us, is that the digital is a transformative process (which is to say "additive," or in Kantian vocabulary "synthetic") in which a universe grounded in the univocity of an identity of the same becomes a universe grounded in discrete distinctions between elements,

elements that, although divided, are brought together and held in relation, suspended opposite each other like cliffs over the banks of a great river.

In the very same passage from *Francis Bacon,* Deleuze also says a few words, precious few, about the analogical. Not so much a question of code, the analogical is a question of diagram or motif. What this means is that the analogical operates in the realms of shape and relation, refrains and styles, not symbol or language in the classical sense. Or if a language, one lacking in the typical elements of alphabet, letter, and word: "Analogical language would be a language of relations, which consists of expressive movements, paralinguistic signs, breaths and screams. . . ."[15] The analogical is a "language," then, but a language of breaths and screams, a non-language of phatic commands that enacts expression by virtue of the frisson struck between gestures of different types.

"Analogical synthesizers are 'modular,'" Deleuze continued, contrasting them with digital synthesizers. "They establish an immediate connection between heterogenous elements."[16] So although digital synthesizers are integral, slicing up the world into masses of homogenous code atoms, analogical synthesizers work through modularity. What this means is that different elements, remaining relatively whole and heterogenous to one another, are nevertheless able to interoperate immediately. They can touch each other directly, despite their differences. (One can begin to see why the fields of post-structuralism, deconstruction, hermeneutics, and semiotics are so inherently digital; as a rule they prohibit immediacy.)

Whereas the digital requires and enlists an underlying homogeneity, the analogical requires an underlying heterogeneity. In the analog paradigm, the stuff of the world remains unaligned, idiosyncratic, singular. These modules are not modules in the sense of standardized, recombinable parts, like modular housing that relies on prefabricated, repeatable materials. Rather, as modules they remain messy globs of dissimilar things. They only happen to interoperate because they have managed, by virtue of what Deleuze would call "mutual deterritorialization," to grow the necessary sockets that fit into each other.

Deleuze's famous example is the wasp and the orchid, two creatures, alike in almost no sense, that nevertheless couple up analogically. Although they are two, at the point of coupling the wasp and the orchid merge into one.

Let us return briefly to the mathematical theme. Although Deleuze does not say it explicitly, neither in the "Postscript" nor in the book on Francis Bacon and painting, it is possible to infer that the digital means integration and the analogical means differentiation. Thus, while integration means area under a curve, differentiation or "taking the derivative" means instantaneous slope of the tangent line. Instead of summing the area under the curve defined by *f(x)*, one extrapolates a secondary function derived from the first function, a secondary function consisting of a straight line tangential to any position $x = a$ on the curve. The logic is slightly counterintuitive; do not be fooled by the curves of integration, for it is still a question of *solving* via a multiplicity of regular slices, and hence it is digital. Likewise, do not be fooled by the semantic similarity between the words *differentiation* and *difference*. Differentiation is an analogical event because it brings together the immediacy of two modular and heterogenous spaces: (1) the space of the function curve and (2) the adjacent virtual space of all the tangent lines that can be derived from the curve.

Heterogeneity has long been an attractive theoretical category, for Deleuze but also for twentieth-century continental philosophy and Anglo American cultural theory in general. And as we have just seen, the analog brings together heterogenous elements into identity (an identity that, again, has nothing to do with homogeneity). There is a strong case to be made that Deleuze was and remained a philosopher of the analog paradigm alone, and that the paradigm of the digital was only vaguely sketched out by him during his lifetime, except in its most visible form, metaphysics. The reasons for this are complex, because they concern the history of philosophy and Deleuze's antagonistic relationship toward it, but as a kind of shorthand we might posit the following: those who work in the tradition of metaphysics will tend to offer a digital philosophy; those who work in the tradition of immanence, as Deleuze did, will tend to offer an analog philosophy. Indeed in many ways Deleuze is the analogical philosopher par excellence. Just as he described painting, "the analogical art par excellence."[17]

The aim of this brief excursion into Deleuze's theory of digitality is to show that the late Deleuze contains an original set of arguments about society and politics at the turn of the new millennium. Deleuze understood the world in 1968—the anabasis of desire, affective revolution, new schizo-phrenic subjects, molecular organization, dispersive and rhizomatic struc-tures, spatiality and topology instead of history, Leibniz instead of Hegel, Riemann instead of Einstein—but the question remains whether he under-stood the world at the dawn of the new millennium. (This question has not been adequately explored thus far, although the work of someone like Bernard Stiegler is a notable exception.)

Much has been said about Foucault's late turn to millennial politics, via his concepts of biopower and biopolitics, or Giorgio Agamben's theo-rization of today's state power, but too little credit has been given to Deleuze as a forecaster of the future world system. Part of the problem is that, barring the "Postscript" itself, there is no single book or text that stands out as a ready exemplar for Deleuze's analysis of millennial capi-talism, as *Anti-Oedipus* and *A Thousand Plateaus* provided a vision of middle twentieth-century capitalism.

Such an exemplar needs to be reconstructed from fragments. Four texts form the backbone of his analysis: the two pieces from 1990 bun-dled in *Negotiations,* "Postscript on Control Societies" and the interview with Negri titled "Control and Becoming"; paragraphs from an odd little piece called "Having an Idea in Cinema"; and three or four pages from Deleuze's 1986 book *Foucault.*[18]

Some of the relevant sections from the "Postscript" have already been outlined, so consider now the ending of the Negri interview, in which Deleuze's phrasing overlaps greatly with the text of the "Postscript." The penultimate question and answer are the most relevant:

> [Foucault] was actually one of the first to say that we're moving away from disciplinary societies, we've already left them behind. We're moving toward control societies that no longer operate by confining people but through continuous control and instant communication. . . . Compared with the approaching forms of ceaseless control in open sites, we may come to see the harshest confinement as part of a wonderful happy past. The quest for "universals of communication" ought to make us shudder. . . . Computer piracy and viruses, for example, will replace strikes and what the nine-teenth century called "sabotage" ("clogging" the machinery). . . . The key thing may be to create vacuoles of noncommunication, circuit breakers, so we can elude control.[19]

Add now the passages from "Having an Idea in Cinema," a text that derives from a lecture titled "Qu'est-ce que l'acte de création?" given by Deleuze at La Fémis (Fondation européenne des métiers de l'image et du son) on May 17, 1987, but published in 1990 the same year of the "Postscript." Some of the relevant passages simply duplicate the same phrasing and language about Foucault that made it into the "Postscript," so they need not be repeated here. But "Having an Idea in Cinema" also includes an important, offhand remark that adds another dimension to Deleuze's views on control society: "A control is not a discipline. In making freeways, for example, you don't enclose people but instead multiply the means of control. I am not saying that this is the freeway's exclusive purpose, but that people can drive infinitely and 'freely' without being at all confined yet while still being perfectly controlled. This is our future."[20]

In an alternate transcription of the same lecture Deleuze included a few extemporaneous lines, and even mentions Minitel, the French teletext network that predates the Web. "This can be done completely differently too," he said about the regrouping of people around arrangements of ubiquitous control. "It can be done through Minitel after all. Everything that you want—what's astounding would be the forms of control."[21]

Recall that the French *contrôle* carries stresses in meaning that are slightly different from the English *control*. *Contrôle* means control as in the power to influence people and things, but it also refers to the actual administration of control via particular monitoring apparatuses such as train turnstiles, border crossings, and checkpoints. The notion, in English, of having to pass through "passport control" gets at the deeper meaning of the word. So when Deleuze talks about *les sociétés de contrôle* he means those kinds of societies, or alternately those localized places within the social totality, where mobility is fostered inside certain strictures of motion, where openings appear rather than disappear, where subjects (or for that matter objects) are liberated as long as they adhere to a variety of prescribed comportments.

In addition to this text and the two in *Negotiations,* a fourth text expands Deleuze's discussions of computer-based control, exploding them into an enigmatic tapestry of prognostications. I refer to those notorious pages 92–93 and 131–32 of Deleuze's late book on Foucault, in which he meditates on something called "life resistance" and a new mysterious

construct called the "superfold," an alluring designation to which he unfortunately never returns.[22]

Consider the sections in which Deleuze proposes, but does not fully
develop, a vision of life as living resistance:

> When power . . . takes life as its aim or object, then resistance to power
> already puts itself on the side of life, and turns life against power. . . . Life
> becomes resistance to power when power takes life as its object. . . . When
> power becomes bio-power resistance becomes the power of life, a vital-
> power that cannot be confined within species, environment or the paths of
> a particular diagram. . . . Is not life this capacity to resist force?[23]

Then later, in the final paragraphs of the book's appendix, Deleuze
broaches the question of genetics and the so called third-generation
machines (that is, computers and bioinformatics) that would figure
prominently in the "Postscript" four years later. He wonders aloud about
the "death of man," as it was described in Foucault and Nietzsche: "The
question that continually returns is therefore the following: if the forces
within man compose a form only by entering into a relation with forms
from the outside, with what new forms do they now risk entering into a
relation, and what new form will emerge that is neither God nor Man?
This is the correct place for the problem which Nietzsche called 'the
superman.'"[24] In other words, what is the new configuration of man after
the death of man (or, if you like, the subject after the death of the subject), and what had to happen in order to create such a new condition of
life? Deleuze's answer:

> Biology had to take a leap into molecular biology, or dispersed life regroup
> in the genetic code. Dispersed work had to regroup in third-generation
> machines, cybernetics and information technology. What would be the
> forces in play, with which the forces within man would then enter into a
> relation? It would no longer involve raising to infinity or finitude but an
> unlimited finity, thereby evoking every situation of force in which a finite
> number of components yields a practically unlimited diversity of combi-
> nations. It would be neither the fold or the unfold that would constitute
> the active mechanism, but something like the *Superfold,* as borne out by
> the foldings proper to the chains of the genetic code, and the potential of

silicon in third-generation machines. . . . The forces within man enter into a relation with forces from the outside, those of silicon which supersedes carbon, or genetic components which supersede the organism. . . . In each case we must study the operations of the superfold, of which the "double helix" is the best-known example.[25]

Scattered across the "Postscript" and these other citations is a new image of society and the self that can not simply be reduced to Deleuze's previous tropes like the body without organs, the rhizome, or even the virtual. Such a new image involves, nay requires, the recognition of the computer as its central mitigating factor. Just as the fold was Deleuze's diagram for the modern subject of the baroque period, the superfold is the new "active mechanism" for life within computerized control society. The dividual and the superfold, in other words, have a special relationship with each other.

"A fold is always folded within a fold, like a cavern in a cavern," wrote Deleuze of the ontology depicted in Leibniz, in an effort to demonstrate how Leibniz's was not an atomism. "The unit of matter, the smallest element of the labyrinth, is the fold, not the point which is never a part, but a simple extremity of the line."[26] Although Deleuze does not specify things further, one can extrapolate that the superfold, being "proper to the chains of the genetic code" and the progeny of an "unlimited diversity of combinations," would follow a diagrammatic logic of dispersive and distributive relations within networks, of iterative regress via computational recursion.

Instead of the human coming into a relationship with itself, as Deleuze characterized the baroque, the human comes into a relation with "forces from the outside" such as the silicon of the computer chip or exogenous factors from genetic engineering. The dividual therefore does not so much carry pleats in its soul, as Deleuze said of the baroque subject, but a tessellated, recombinant soul—if *soul* is still the proper word—forming and reforming across the metastable skein of the bioinformatic ecosystem.

Yet Deleuze's argument is not an exotic one. In France, figures like André Leroi-Gourhan and Bertrand Gille had already demonstrated how human beings coevolve with their exogenous technologies and techniques. And in North America figures like Lewis Mumford and Marshall McLuhan had made similar claims. (Indeed the final paragraph of Deleuze's *Foucault* reads very much like Donna Haraway's now famous "Cyborg Manifesto," which while predating the book by one year was likely unknown to Deleuze at the time.) Instead what might be exotic about Deleuze's argument, or at least what makes it novel, is his mobilization of the concept in terms of a diagram. He describes it as a "super" fold, a double helix, a fractal topography, not simply a folded one.[27]

But the ultimate lesson to be learned from the "Postscript" is not so much a lesson about the subject or society. The ultimate lesson is one about periodization. For what Deleuze wishes to do in the essay, following Lyotard, Foucault, and all the rest, is to assert the historical break. He wants to show how everything has changed, indeed that the world of 1990 has changed so dramatically from the 1972 world as to be practically indistinguishable. "The key thing," he says, "is that we're at the beginning of something new" (182).

It is not particularly important whether one agrees or disagrees with the Deleuzian-Foucauldian tripartite periodization from sovereign society through disciplinary society and then to control society. The periodization itself is the important thing. And how deliciously ironic that in recent years periodization seems to be appearing with increased frequency, an increased periodicity of periodization. Indeed all this talk of the superfold is, by that very same measure, a kind of superperiodization without end. Each new fold is a new historical break. First the fold, then the double fold, the triple, on up to the multiplicative folds of the superfold.

Thus the task of historical thinking itself is implicated in Deleuze's "Postscript" and as such has metastasized and reduplicated into a super state of recursive channels. The ultimate significance of control society is not so much the continuous encroachment of the border checkpoint or the passport control, not so much data mining or facial recognition algorithms, but that it has eviscerated history, not by banning dissent but by accelerating the opportunities and channels for critical thought to infinity and therefore making it impossible to think historically in the first place. Thus the central challenge within control society will be not simply to resist the various new nefarious control apparatuses, but to rescue history from its own consummation.

Thesis IX. Being is a computational mode; it is coterminous with the computational decision. So which is it in the end, ubiquitous desire or ubiquitous control? The Deleuze of 1972 or the Deleuze of 1990?

Laruelle's response is to deny both while reaffirming their non-standard core. The point is not so much to select one Deleuze over the other but instead to radicalize Deleuze and subject him to the generic finitude of the one. Only by universalizing and unilateralizing history can we pass from Deleuze's philosophy of control to what Laruelle calls artificial or "fiction" philosophy. Only by thinking history as the generic totality can we see control in terms of determination or destiny.

Chapter 4 discussed how an event is also a decision, how being is also digital. Being is posterior to the event of appropriation (Heidegger) that actualizes it, and as such is an evental mode. In its baseline digitality being also provides the conditions for the transcendental. We have seen that the transcendental can be minimized or otherwise overcome in the subtractive mode of generic being or the accumulative mode of continuous being, or it can be accentuated and fostered in the contradictory-negational mode of dialectical being or the affirmative mode of differential being.

Now it is time to take the principle of sufficient reason very literally. A common but unfortunate way of understanding the principle is to turn it into an explanatory narrative for how things were made or where they came from. "For any entity, there is a narrative that will explain why it exists and why it exists in this manner."

Such an interpretation confuses the principle of sufficient reason and limits its utility. It reduces facticity to causality. It reduces givenness to a lurid narrative of origins. It shackles appearance to logic.

To avoid such an interpretation, the principle should be taken literally, that is, in terms of the co-presence of being and thought. "No actual entity, then no reason" (Whitehead). Being in the world requires thought in the world. Being-given requires thought-given. An entity requires a reason. To be with means to think with. Thus to follow the path of being also means to follow the path of co-thought, or *com-putation*.

To combine the event and the transcendental is to produce computation. Recall the definition of Turing's universal machine: it is a machine that can perform the work of any other machine, provided it can be described logically. Or to rephrase using the vocabulary employed thus far: *the computer is a machine that can actuate events, provided they are formulated in terms of the transcendental.*

Given that being is both evental and transcendental, it is no surprise that computation takes place within being. In fact, it is inevitable; it is visible across the most diverse instances, RNA as computational strands, markets as societies of computation, stomachs as processors for food-stuffs, or what have you.

It is now possible to revisit the final paragraphs of the introduction and flesh out a related set of concepts, the *computational decision* and the *principle of sufficient computation.*[28] The principle states that, within the standard model, anything co-thinkable is also computable. The mere existence of something is sufficient grounds for its being computable (co-thinkable). The computational decision is the event that inaugurates such a distinction.

But it goes further as well, because presence itself is subject to a computational condition. Computation is not an "option" available to presence but a precondition of it. It is not simply that computers, artificial intelligence, virtual reality, and the like are predicated on computational decisionism. It is not simply that such and such mundane detail will be rendered computationally, that weather patterns will be modeled on a supercomputer, that stock markets will be migrated over to electronic trading, that we will "go digital." These are all common, pragmatic repercussions of a much more pervasive computational decision that permeates the standard model from end to end. The advent of digital being—which is to say the only sort of being directly available to us—shows that presence itself is a computational condition.

A final step awaits, for Laruelle takes the computational decision as raw material and through it discovers an alternate mode of non-computation or non-computer, just as he has done with non-photography, or indeed with non-philosophy as a whole. He considers the "computational posture" and software execution as an instance of identity and cloning. He considers computation in terms of an auto-execution, or an auto-processing.

Ultimately Laruelle arrives at a purely immanent conception of computation (as co-thinking). This is a form of computation entirely subtracted from any kind of conscious will or causality, from any kind of metaphysical representation or manifestation, from the typical distinction between hardware and software, from the classic debate in Artificial Intelligence about whether or not computers can think like humans.

> It's always so predictable and wearisome this back and forth debate between the proponents of Artificial Intelligence and those advocating Conscious. . . . We could say that non-philosophy is an attempt to give a (non-Kantian) solution to this conflict, to show a "way out" of it, or more precisely to demonstrate exactly how and under what conditions thought would never need to enter it.[29]

Such a purely immanent conception of computation would appear therefore, axiomatically and primordially, as *process*. Non-computation is simply the condition of the event that is *in-process,* that operates "according to" process.

Hugo Gellert, "Cat and Mouse," *Comrade Gulliver* (New York: G. P. Putnam's Sons, 1935), 27.

six

Capitalism

Don't look at Part I, put it aside. Or so goes Althusser's warning to first-time readers of Marx's *Capital*. It is important to skip Part I of the treatise, Althusser advised, at least on the first couple of reads. Only when the truth of *Capital* is fully internalized, its scientific intervention into the "new continent" of history, one may "begin to read Part I (Commodities and Money) with infinite caution, knowing that it will always be extremely difficult to understand, even after several readings of the other Parts, without the help of a certain number of deeper explanations."[1]

After all, Althusser argued, the same political division between social classes was mirrored within the text as an epistemological division. Part I contains something close to philosophical idealism, followed by the scientific materialism of the rest of the book. Althusser's advice was thus both practical and political: Part I is not only difficult reading for the young and the uninitiated—Althusser admitted that members of the proletariat would have no problem reading the book because their "class instinct" was already attuned to the quotidian experience of capitalist exploitation—it also risks derailing the reader into dangerously Hegelian and philosophical diversions. "This advice is more than advice," he whispered. It is "an *imperative*."[2]

Did he know it? Did Althusser see the colossus issuing forth in the wake of such advice, advice written in March 1969 at such a profound historical conjuncture in France and indeed the world? Was he aware that this would solidify the agenda for the next few decades of Marxian or otherwise progressive philosophy and theory? *The colossus of exchange*.

By focusing on surplus-value instead of, say, the commodity, by insisting that *Capital* and *Capital* alone be the text by which Marx is judged, therefore sidelining the crypto-Hegelian "young Marx" of species-being and alienation, Althusser placed the emphasis squarely on the scientific structures of exchange: the spheres of production and circulation, the factory floor and the marketplace, the passage from small-scale industry to imperialism. Such an emphasis would continue to dominate theory for decades, both in France and through the adoption of French theory in the English-speaking world. Stemming from his reinterpretation in the 1960s and '70s, Marx would be rethought primarily as a theorist of exchange. Mating Marx with Freud, theorists like Jean-Joseph Goux would begin to speak in terms of "symbolic economies" evident across all spheres of life, whether psychoanalytic, numismatic, or semiotic. Indeed, life would be understood exclusively in terms of relations of exchange.

Even deviations from capitalist exchange, as in the many meditations on "the gift," or even, in a very different way, Deleuze and Guattari's writings on desiring machines, would conserve exchange as the ultimate medium of relation. The gift economies of the Haida or Salish potlatch might not be capitalist, but they remain economies nonetheless. Desiring machines might find fuel for their aleatory vectors from beyond the factory walls, but they remain beholden to the swapping of energies, the pathways of flight lines, and the interrelation of forces of intensification and dissipation.

Althusser had merely identified a general paradigm, *that systems of relation exist, and that they are prime constituting factors for all the other elements of the world, from objects to societies.* As a general philosophical paradigm it would thus forge common currency with other existing schools, chief among them phenomenology, which must assent to a fundamental relation between self and world, or even the tradition of metaphysics in general, which assumes a baseline expressive model from Being to being, from essence to instance, or from God to man. For Marxists, the fundamental relation is always one of antagonism, hierarchy, inequality, or predation (see Hugo Gellert, "Cat and Mouse," the frontispiece of this chapter).

All of this is contained in what Fredric Jameson has called the *second* fundamental riddle in *Capital*, the riddle contained in the equation $M—M'$ (from money to "money prime" or money with a surplus added). Such is the riddle of exchange: How does money of one value transform into money of a greater value? To answer the question, Marx had to "descend into the hidden abode of production," revealing the intricacies of the labor process and the working day, in order ultimately to show the origins of surplus value, what Althusser (and indeed Marx himself) considered the "illuminating heart" of *Capital*.

But exchange is still just the second riddle in Marx. *Capital* is propelled by another riddle, one that finds its voice in the elusive Part I, the part that Althusser warned his readers to avoid. "The mystery of an equivalence between two radically different qualitative things"—this is the first riddle, according to Jameson. "How can one object be the equivalent of another one?"[3] In other words, the riddle is the riddle of $A = B$. The real things constituting A and B themselves, as, for example, twenty yards of linen (as A) and one coat (as B), contribute nothing to the riddle. Rather the mystery derives from the unexplainable, and indeed violent, possibility of inserting an equals sign between different things. The riddle is the riddle of the equation; the violence of capital is the violence of the equality of inequality. Or as Jameson puts it, "It seems possible to read all of Part One [of *Capital*] as an immense critique of the equation as such."[4]

Thesis X. The multidecade legacy of Althusser, who put the final period at the end of the sentence of exchange, has come to an end with Laruelle. Everything that has thus far been described under the banner of exchange is not simply *a* philosophical paradigm for Laruelle, but *the* philosophical paradigm. There is no philosophy that is not too a philosophy of exchange. There is no metaphysical arrangement that is not too a concourse of convertibility. There is no structure of thought that is not too a structure of relation. There is no phenomenology that is not too an orientation within a world.

Against all these things stands Laruelle, not a philosopher but still a Marxist, who aims to describe not so much Marx's "rational kernel in the mystical shell" but rather something like an immanent kernel itself for Marx (and capitalism too). Such a real kernel would be devoid of all rationality, all shells, all mystifications, and all chance to interrelate kernels and shells in the first place.[5]

Such is the irony of Laruelle. He deploys Althusserian Marxist language ("determination-in-the-last-instance" [DLI]), he deploys Althusserian Marxist methodology (that science should deviate from philosophy and exist "in" or "on" it), yet nevertheless he rejects, in spirit at least, much of what comes after Part I of *Capital* and indeed much of the very pillars of Marxism itself.[6] Although, as I hope to show, these pillars are pillars of *Capital* and thus subtend the structure of capitalism, not the Marxian critique levied against it or even perhaps Marx himself. Thus, in Laruelle's profound deviation from the Marxian tradition, he ironically remains a Marxist, and in so doing produces one of the most profound critiques of capitalism hitherto known.

My proposal here is therefore a simple one, that we must understand Laruelle as both a post-Althusserian Marxist and as someone who brashly ignores Althusser's advice. In the end Laruelle produces an unexpected version of Marx, unexpected not because it supplements Marx in new ways or propels Marx into the future—endeavors impugned by non-philosophy—but because Laruelle ends up endorsing all the old dunder-headed ideas, long ago purged from so-called serious Marxist theory: vulgar determinism, the qualitative purity of use-value, and the irrelevance of ideology and "epistemological breaks."

Published in 2000, after the collapse of the Soviet Union and the failure of many actually existing Marxist states, Laruelle's book *Introduction to Non-Marxism* is one of the more provocative entries in the decades-long discourses of Marxist theory and constitutes Laruelle's most extended engagement with Marx, although not necessarily with the political as such.[7] True to form, Laruelle refuses to report whether Marxism did or did not fail. He refuses to try to amend or deconstruct Marxism in any way, as that would simply constitute further philosophy.[8] Instead he seeks to "philosophically impoverish" Marxism, with the goal of "universalizing" it through a "scientific mode of universalization."[9] (Was not Althusser's project, thirty years prior, nearly the same?)

Although Laruelle does not often affect an overtly anticapitalist stance in his work, I want to show here that Laruelle's *ontology,* if not so much his political theory, provides a foundation for one of the most aggressively anticapitalist critiques since Marx himself, since the Frankfurt School, and since the "scientific Marxism" of Althusser and post–World War II France or the autonomist movements in 1970s Italy.

Laruelle accomplishes this by militantly denying *exchange,* one of the essential preconditions of any kind of commerce. Unlike Keynesian economists, or Third-Way liberals, Laruelle does not advocate a mollification of exchange; he does not allow for something like "capitalism with a friendly face." Unlike post-structuralists, Laruelle does not acknowledge a system of mutual co-construction between self and other. Instead, Laruelle develops an ontological platform that, while leaving room for certain kinds of causality and relation, radically denies exchange in any form whatsoever.

Deviating too from so-called process philosophers, who must necessarily endorse exchange at some level, Laruelle advocates a mode of expression that is irreversible. He does this through a number of interconnected concepts, the most important of which is determination-in-the-last-instance. Having kidnapped the term from its Althusserian Marxist origins, Laruelle uses DLI to show how there can exist causality that is not reciprocal, how "relation" can exist that is not at the same time a "relation of exchange," indeed how a universe might look if it were not already forged implicitly from the mold of a market economy.

Herein lies Laruelle's rigorous anticapitalism, an anticapitalism rooted not in the critique of social relations at the level of politics, but in the prohibition of exchange at the level of ontology.[10]

In order to demonstrate this aspect of Laruelle's thinking, consider four interlocking concepts and claims: science, the infrastructure, the irreversibility of expression, and incommensurability.

The first topic, *science,* is central to Laruelle's conception of non-philosophy as a whole, and central too for Althusser, who viewed science as the only proper response to philosophy. For Althusser, science often bears the moniker of practical philosophy, Marxist philosophy, or indeed simply Marxist science. For Laruelle, science is synonymous with non-philosophy. Or, to be more correct, "primary" science, what he also calls "unified theory," would unify and subtend the common philosophies and the common sciences of the world.[11] As Laruelle puts it, non-philosophical science would be "primary" vis-à-vis science and philosophy, but would also carry a "primacy-without-priority" and thus not issue forth or synthesize itself through science and philosophy, in an attempt to act as their guiding spirit. One must disperse the various encyclopedias of scientific and philosophical knowledge into "a chaos of identities" in order to unify such knowledge into a "democracy" of thought, not by virtue of a common set of axioms or dogmatic truths but by virtue of the generic identity of unified thinking.

So perhaps Marx's eleventh thesis on Feuerbach, which Althusser held up as the most emblematic moment of Marx's intervention into philosophy, is also a fine description for Laruelle's project. The eleventh thesis on Feuerbach, Marx's famous maxim that philosophers ought to change the world, not simply interpret it, indicates, in the most general sense, that the correct response to interpretation (philosophy) is not *more* interpretation (not more philosophy).

In other words, the correct response, if one follows Althusser's gloss of Marx, is to replace philosophical interpretation with a new kind of science, a Marxian science. Such is the elemental discovery of Marx, a discovery that Althusser suggests was best revealed after the fact by way of Lenin's *Materialism and Empirio-criticism*. But is this not also Laruelle's most essential claim, that the best response to philosophy is not more philosophy? That the best response to philosophy is to cease doing it? Is it not possible to telescope all Laruelle within Marx's eleventh thesis on Feuerbach? *Philosophers have hitherto only interpreted the world in various ways; the point is to articulate a rigorous and immanently scientific non-philosophy of it.*

Like Althusser, Laruelle shuns the lingering abstractions that permeate Marx, particularly the young Marx. Yet Laruelle reminds us that "Marxism remains abstract through a lack of universality, a lack of reality, of radicality, not through being poorly adapted to the various avatars of societies and the becomings of history. It is not made abstract by a bad philosophy that would remove it from history, but by an excess of philosophy that plunges it into history."[12] The problem is thus not a bad philosophy—in this case the bad Hegel, a philosophy pleading to be corrected or "put back on its feet"—but an excess of philosophy.

All this prompts Laruelle to unify philosophy and capitalism together as a single term, "Thought-World." Just as philosophy follows a principle of sufficient philosophy, Laruelle writes that capitalism marches to the same tune, via a principle of sufficient economy. The principle of sufficient economy means that anything whatsoever is available for reproduction and exchange, that capitalism is sufficient to "englobe," in Laruelle's language, the entire world.

So the principle of sufficient economy is a "universal capitalism," not simply the imperialist extension of capitalism into all corners of the globe, but a perversion of both thinking and being that renders all fixity as permeable and reversible exchange.[13] As Laruelle puts it, even capitalism is incontinent to itself: "The essence of capitalism is *and/or* is not, in a way that is ultimately reversible, capital."[14] This is the key to understanding today's trend toward *mondialisation* (literally "world-ization," but typically translated as "globalization"). Only by fusing together philosophy, as principle of sufficient philosophy, and capitalism, as principle of sufficient economy, is it possible to see a single object or a process of "englobing." Laruelle means this in quite direct terms: the worlds that populate phenomenology are a question of "globalization" as the self englobes its world via orientation and solicitation of attention; but so too the world, or globe, of capitalist globalization is quite literally the planet itself, the ultimate terrain of the real.

This is why Laruelle is so quick to make philosophy and capitalism coterminous; the two are, quite simply, the same thing for him. Both philosophy and capitalism subject the world to the intercourse of reversibility and exchange, both express things in terms of their opposites, and both destroy (or at least ignore to their own detriment) the ultimate immanence of nature, which for Laruelle is the one and for Marx the real base. So just as science was Marx's response to capitalism, so too science is Laruelle's response to philosophy.

On this last point Althusser would not disagree, because in his estimation Marx's indictment of capitalism was always already an indictment of philosophy. The difference lies more in the composition of the indictment. Laruelle's indictment is on the grounds of a venomous reversible convertibility. Althusser's indictment is on the ground of an odious bourgeois idealism.

This brings us to the second question, that of *infrastructure*. Laruelle finds inspiration not simply in Marx's intuitive understanding of the relation between science and philosophy, but also in what Laruelle views as the immovable, transhistorical, and, yes, fully immanent material base. Matter or materialism is not simply the topic of Marxism, nor either simply its conceptual core. Matter is quite literally the material of Marxism. In other words, Marxism is matter itself; dialects breaks bricks (or so it seems).

What Laruelle means by this is that Marxism alone posits a pure immanent material base, one that is determinate, immovable, and immanent to itself unsupplemented by any idealist scaffold. As he puts it, non-Marxism's goal is "to universalize matter in an immanent way, without pretending to amend or correct it with any kind of philosophy."[15] In this respect the mere existence of Marxism is evidence of an irresistible one, the material base. This is why Marxism is a politics (and not simply an "interpretation"), because it saddles itself over the vector of determinacy constructed between infrastructure and superstructure, this vector being nothing but the determinacy of the one itself. In short, Marxism does not simply describe a relation (between worker and boss or between base and superstructure), it directly embodies this relation and thus, following the Laruellean ontology, must be synonymous with real matter itself.

The non-philosophical term Laruelle assigns to such a situation is "given-without-givenness," but the Marxian term is "infrastructure."[16] The relationship between infrastructure and superstructure, which for many subsequent critics betrayed in Marx a pernicious and somewhat naïve determinism, is for Laruelle absolutely crucial, even beneficial. The more naïve the better; the more determinist the better.

In *The Eighteenth Brumaire of Louis Bonaparte,* Marx described the "material conditions of existence, [or the] two different kinds of property," that made up the Party of Order, formed from the alliance of two factions of the ruling class, the Legitimists, the large land owners who were a legacy of the 1814–30 Bourbon restoration period, and the Orleanists, the financiers and large-scale industrialists who were a legacy of the July Monarchy of 1830–48: "Upon the different forms of property, upon the social conditions of existence, rises an entire superstructure of distinct and peculiarly formed sentiments, illusions, modes of thought and views of life. The entire class creates and forms them out of its material foundations and out of the corresponding social relations."[17] Later, in an 1859 text that would become a prototype for *Capital,* the "Preface (to *A Contribution to the Critique of Political Economy*)," Marx also addressed the superstructure and its "real foundation."

> In the social production of their existence, men inevitably enter into definite relations, which are independent of their will, namely relations of production appropriate to a given stage in the development of their material forces of production. The totality of these relations of production constitutes the economic structure of society, the real foundation, on which arises

a legal and political superstructure and to which correspond definite forms of social consciousness.[18]

These passages have been discussed extensively within Marxist discourse, particularly after the Cultural Turn of the mid-twentieth century. Yet the use that Laruelle makes of them is unique.

His intervention turns on the conceptual shift from "relate" to "arise." Laruelle, who admittedly treats relation with scorn and skepticism, acknowledges the existence of "definite relations" within the material base of society. These relations constitute the world and thus the world as it is constructed via capitalism and indeed via philosophy.

Yet "in" or "on" these relations arises a secondary thing, the superstructure. It does not matter so much the nature of this superstructure, its qualities and affordances, or even its ability to reciprocate back in a mutually determining way toward the base (these being some of the concerns of the cultural Marxists). Rather what interests Laruelle is the pure and rigorous radicality of such a unilateral and unidirectional causality.

To underscore the force of this causal determinacy, let us continue the previous Marx quote where it left off, revealing one of the most frequently cited passages in Marx's entire body of work: "The mode of production of material life conditions the general process of social, political and intellectual life. It is not the consciousness of men that determines their existence, but their social existence that determines their consciousness."[19]

For Laruelle the words *conditions* and *determines* are not sources of anxiety, as they were for many of the postwar Marxist theorists from Althusser to Raymond Williams and beyond. For Laruelle these words are not sources of anxiety but rather must be taken very literally, even accentuated and made more rigorous, more radical. The infrastructure of the material base is a given-without-givenness because and only because of its ability to condition and determine—unidirectionally, irreversibly, and "in the last instance"—whatever it might condition and determine, in this case the superstructure. Thus the infrastructure stands as "given" while still never partaking in "givenness," neither as a thing having appeared as a result of a previous givenness, nor a present givenness engendering the offspring of subsequent givens.

Again, any mollification of Marx's determinism would not simply miss the point for Laruelle, it would undo the entire Marxist project. If

Marxism has any force at all, it gains such force by virtue of an immanent material base, synthetic to nothing but determinate in all. Not simply labor power or "force of labor" but *force of infrastructure*—the French term *force de travail* being so similar to the important Laruellean term *force (de) pensée* ["force (of) thought"]).[20]

If this brief discussion of infrastructure illuminates anything, it is that Laruelle is a vulgar determinist and unapologetically so. So now to the third theme, related closely to the second, which is the way in which determinism leads to an *irreversibility of expression*.

In Laruellean language, undeniably infused here with an Althusserian additive, this irreversibility is known as "determination-in-the-last-instance." Althusser focused on the "last instance" as a way to soften Marx's determinism, to forge a compromise between the material base and the relative autonomy of the superstructural realm. But for Laruelle the "last instance" means precisely the opposite. It is not a bone tossed to the sociocultural sphere, but a trump card slammed down with definitive force. "In the last instance" does not mean that the one must pander to the world, including it in all its many deliberations. On the contrary, it means that the one remains ultimately "last," oblivious in its position of causal determinacy. DLI, therefore, which Laruelle admits was "invented by Marx-Engels for Historical Materialism," describes a specific logic of causality "which is uni-lateral against all the philosophical phantasms of reciprocity and convertibility."[21] The real base is not merely one flank that can be brought into relation with another flank, such as the superstructure. The base, as determinate-in-the-last-instance, is a "final" cause, not a primary one. Thus, by making DLI the general axiomatic form of his "non-ontological causality," Laruelle allows for "a lifting of philosophical sufficiency by way of the theoretical reduction of philosophy to the radical immanence of its real base."[22]

Laruelle discusses DLI in a number of places, but in the non-Marxism book it is summarized by way of three distinctive traits. First, DLI is a causality that is unique but calls or supposes an other, as if it is the sole causality but also somehow insufficient. Hence the one supposes the two (although without necessarily producing or metaphysically expressing itself through the two). Next, these *secondary* causalities, those of the two or the clone, are introduced back into the one during the *final* calculus. In other words, the secondary causalities are always already structurally "in debt" to the infrastructure. Last, DLI operates in the "final instance" as a quasi invariant or constant, "in opposition to the variations of nature or region, to the variability of secondary causality."[23]

What this means is that DLI, if it is expressive, is expressive only in one direction. It is thus properly labeled irreversible. In the structure of ontological expression, DLI exerts an absolute dominance over the world.

Would it be hyperbolic, then, to speak of Laruelle's determinism as a kind of *sadism* of the one, and of DLI as a kind of "sado-cause"? Perhaps, particularly given the fact that sadism requires a circuit of exchange-ability between master and slave, between dominant and submissive. Yet the sadism of the one is really more of an *obliviousness*, a neglectful unidirectionality, in which no return is possible. This is not to slander Laruelle's universe as unfeeling, violent, or even proto-fascist, simply to underscore the radical hierarchy of force established between the one and its clones. Force flows one way and one way only in the non-standard encounter. Recall that there is a "force of thought" in Laruelle, but never a "force of reflection" fostering exchange of forces.[24]

Perhaps a useful way to understand Laruelle's notion of the irreversibility of expression is by way of the so-called failure of actually existing Marxism. It does not matter so much which dates are assigned to this failure—1871 in Paris, 1919 in Berlin, or 1991 in the Soviet Union. And it does not matter so much that Marxism be understood as a burrowing mole (or striking snake) able to return from periods of suppression to rise up and blossom again in a new form, as someone like Badiou has recently described with such elegance.[25]

In fact Laruelle is careful *not* to reject the failure of Marxism. He considers failure to be an asset of Marxism, not a liability. Laruelle is careful to avoid the "vicious circle" of so many theorists, those who attempt a Marxism of Marx, which for Laruelle would be just as philosophical as a Kantianism of Marx or a structuralism of Marx. To revel in the failure of Marxism is to revel in the proof that Marxism *can* lapse back to an immanence with the one, that Marxism does not need to be *pro*ductive in any way (like capitalism must constantly be).

So for Laruelle failure is good because it indicates that Marxism is not trying to go outside of itself to affect other things. It indicates Marxism's insufficiency. Thus, ironically, the recession of Marxism is the first step toward considering its radical universality, because via recession

Marxism is all that much closer to its own true immanence with itself. Any failure of Marxism, or if you like communism, in, for example, the historical conjuncture of 1871 when soldiers descended from Versailles in wholesale slaughter of the Parisian communards, cannot be explained *internally* by Marxism itself. "A marxist concept of the conjuncture can not *explain* the failure of Marxism, but only offer a specular doubling of it."[26]

In other words, Marxism can never truly be understood in its universality if it is read simply as a corrective or reactionary force vis-à-vis the historical gains of capitalism. So if Baudrillard told us to "forget Foucault" in order better to understand the totality of power, here we must "forget capitalism" in order to arrive at a universal Marxism, unfettered by any synthesis or rebirth forged through failure.

Unidirectional and irreversible determination, for Laruelle, is necessary for a truly and radically immanent ontology. But, he cautions, this is not a Marxian immanence, because axiomatically all immanence is immanence in the real (equivalent to immanence in the one). "It is the immanence (of) the Real as cause," writes Laruelle, "and thus an immanence non immanent *to* Marxism."[27]

This brings us to the fourth theme, *incommensurability*. Herein is contained Laruelle's ultimate incompatibility with Althusser. For if Althusser warned his readers to begin after Part I of *Capital—Don't look at Part I, put it aside*—it is only *within* Part I that Marx offers his best description of incommensurability.

Recall again Jameson's first riddle of *Capital;* the riddle revolves around the seeming impossibility of equating two qualitatively different things. The key to incommensurability is therefore *use-value.* Use-value, Marx instructs, is the "substance" of value, the "usefulness" of something. Use-value is understood in terms of physical bodies that are qualitatively different, and hence, because they share no scale of measurement in common, are absolutely incommensurable with each other.

In this way, use-value in Marx reveals a rudimentary theory of immanence, because objects are defined strictly by way of an identity with themselves, never forced to go outside themselves into the form of something else. The consummation of a use-value, in, for example, the eating of an apple, constitutes a "relation without relation": I may eat the apple and have a "relation" to it as I chew it up and digest it, but its qualities, even as they are consumed by me, act unidirectionally and irreversibly on me, on my tongue, in my stomach and digestive system, and indeed on my health and state of mind. For Laruelle there is no common measure between the one and its clones. As a unilateral duality, they constitute a relation without a relation.

If previously DLI revealed a brute ontological obliviousness, incommensurability reveals what might be called "Laruelle's autism." Nonphilosophy is unable to form conventional relationships, except those mediated by a more scientific posture. The absolute radiance of the one leaves its clones (entities, worlds, persons) as generically ordinary but also solitary. Laruelle's entities are nearsighted, myopic, shut in. Like the autist, they do not form relations of mediation via normative channels. But so too are they locked out of immediate communion with the one, immediacy being in Laruelle's estimation simply a perverted form of mediation. Recall that Laruelle's goal is never to make thought and being immediate to each other, but rather to maintain the duality of the two as an identity.

But have I just pathologized non-philosophy a second time, first calling it oblivious and now autistic? That is not the intention, for the aim of these two descriptors is to underscore the "immedia" evident in Laruelle, his rigorous nullification of the standard-model approaches to mediation. It is only here that Laruelle is able to be understood as an anticapitalist, indeed one of the most aggressive anticapitalists in the history of thought.

It is not so much that Laruelle comes out against capitalism with this or that political strategy, with this or that economic policy. Rather, Laruelle's anticapitalism is rooted not in a critique of the mode of production, but in the discovery that the material base is itself ontologically incompatible with exchange.

The ultimate issue, which even Althusser could not see or at least would not accept, is that in order to remove Hegel from Marx it is necessary to go to the limit. One must not simply remove the "more philosophical" parts, the youthful Marx, the metaphysical, even sometimes idealist, Marx. In order to fix the Hegelian roots within Marx, one must not simply replace a bourgeois philosophy with a more rigorous dialectical science. The solution is not more dialectics, but less. In order to remove Hegel from Marx, one must *remove the dialectic entirely*. Such is Laruelle's essential aim, a Marxism without dialectics.

Is this not the ultimate contradiction of Marxism itself: how to foment to the brink of revolution a certain kind of proletarian history that will obviate the need for any future history. Lenin, for instance, was concerned not simply with how to make revolution but how to make it last, not simply the end of the tsar's dictatorship but the forging of a new dictatorship, this time of the proletariat. Althusser's concern is not simply the supersession of idealist philosophy, but its supersession at the hands of a new higher orthodoxy, what he called the science of "pure thought" itself or the dialectic as "Logic."[28]

Is the ultimate form of Marxism still dialectical or the indication of an absolute absence of the dialectic? One might return to an earlier moment, to the German Marxist theorist Karl Korsch (rejected by Kautsky and Stalin alike) and recall his assertion, essentially incompatible with Althusserianism and many other varieties of Marxism, that "Marxian theory constitutes neither a positive materialistic philosophy nor a positive science."[29] Korsch's suggestion is that one must be permanently critical and hence vigilant against the ossification of Marxian or party orthodoxy as a newfound dogma. Marxism is critical not positive, wrote Korsch. It is general not total. Such a modest and provisional view of Marxian science is perhaps a bit closer to Laruelle's method than that of Althusser.

Yet whatever the answer for others, Laruelle's position is clear. He seeks an immediacy without mediation. He seeks a finite determinacy without abstraction. He seeks a "last philosophy," not a return to "first philosophy." In short, he seeks a Marx without dialectical synthesis.

According to Laruelle, the question for Marx is not "how to break with Hegel" but "how to break with *philosophy* itself."[30] For Marx, Hegel was merely philosophy's most recent and dazzling avatar. Marx's reticence toward Hegel is, for Laruelle, indication of a non-philosophical instinct *already implicit* in Marx. The eleventh thesis on Feuerbach is only the most obvious and pithy evidence of this. In other words Marx himself was seeking non-philosophy, whether he called it by that name or not, by breaking with philosophy and shifting toward the practical science of political economy.

But the question for Laruelle is not the same. The issue for him is not how to break with what came before, to break with Marx or Marxism.

Such a break would only proliferate new philosophical discourses, and as such would fall out of the purview of non-philosophy entirely. "Not to recognize marxism but to know it" is Laruelle's intuition. "To discover it rather than to rediscover it."[31]

To "recognize" or "rediscover" Marx would be to reflect on him. But a properly rigorous and immanent science of the Marxian infrastructure would do no such thing. It would withdraw from the decision to reflect, and discover the immanent destiny of nature, perhaps for the first time.

Meditations on last philosophy. To ask the question "What is philosophy?" typically requires that the philosopher return to the origins of thought, to plumb the depths of being in pursuit of its foundations. This is what Kant does in the *Critique of Pure Reason,* what Heidegger does in *Being and Time,* and even what Deleuze and Guattari do in *What Is Philosophy?* It is the most emblematic philosophical chore, *to return to first principles.*

However Laruelle does no such thing. This kind of question is the very question he refuses to answer, refuses even to pose. Not what philosophy? Not how philosophy? Not even where or when philosophy? If Laruelle asks anything, he asks *Why* philosophy? And, more important, Why not? *Why not no philosophy?*

Avoiding his own first principles, then, Laruelle passes instead to the last, the last principles, or more precisely the *last instance.* Where philosophy is always vying to be first, non-philosophy is content to be last. After all, Laruelle's one is no prime mover, no ultimate substance. The reverse is true, in fact: Laruelle's one is a "last mover," a finite and generic real.

"The question *Quid facti?* is the object of *metaphysics,*" remarked Deleuze in his book on Kant.[32] What is the *fact* of knowledge? Not this or that particular piece of knowledge, what Laruelle calls the "regional knowledges," but the very condition of knowledge itself, its *fact.*

From Kant to Foucault and beyond, the pervasive question of philosophy is not so much *what* something is, or even *how* something behaves, but *what are the conditions of possibility* for any *x* whatsoever? In other words, if Plato asks what is truth, Kant asks what are the conditions of possibility for truth? Kant makes the stakes known on many occasions: "How is metaphysics at all possible?" "How is cognition from pure reason possible?" "How are synthetic propositions a priori possible?" "How is pure mathematics possible?"[33] Not so much what is philosophy, but what are the conditions of possibility for philosophy itself?

The two questions are ultimately the same though, because philosophy, as Laruelle defines it, is synonymous with the decision to reveal the conditions of possibility for philosophy. In this sense, Kant would be, in Laruelle's opinion, a philosopher par excellence, a philosopher raised to the second power, for Kant is not simply enacting the philosophical decision (and thus *doing* philosophy), nor reflecting on the philosophical decision (asking what is philosophy), but rather demonstrating the philosophical meta-conditions for any kind of philosophical reflection whatsoever.

This is why Laruelle never "returns to first principles," as many philosophers are wont to do. He never seeks to found a new philosophy or to reinvigorate an existing one by reflecting on its own specificity. He is no modernist, after all. Instead Laruelle seeks the "last principles." And if anything Laruelle's work is a question of "last philosophy." Deviating from the aspirations of Descartes's *Meditations on First Philosophy,* Laruelle's project constitutes an inexhaustible series of *Meditations on Last Philosophy.*

But Laruelle's "last" is not a chronological last. It is a messianic last. Laruelle's last philosophy is last only in the sense of Marx's "last instance," an immanent and finite lastness that reflects nothing, supersedes nothing, and indeed is not a "meditation" at all in the proper sense of the term as reflection-on or consciousness-of. Rather, in-the-last-instance means roughly "in the most generic sense." Laruelle's messianism is therefore neither ancient nor modern, neither special nor particular. But merely generic. The last, the least, the finite.

So if it is indeed fair to label Laruelle's work a series of "meditations on last philosophy," a basic characteristic begins to emerge: Laruelle's work is a *rational messianism,* a messianism of reason—or as he would likely put it, "the messianic without the messiah." With a stress given not to first philosophy, but to last philosophy (as non-philosophy), Laruelle injects a messianic temporality into thinking. Under such messianic temporality non-philosophy dualizes—Deleuze would say "virtualizes"—the first and the last, the prior and the posterior, the a priori and the a posteriori into a metastable identity of after-before and before-after. Indeed, as in Matthew 20:16, *the last shall be first, and the first last.*

Francisco de Holanda, *Fiant luminaria in firmamento celi* (Genesis 1:14, day 4), *De Aetatibus Mundi Imagines,* 1543–73.

seven

The Black Universe

Part II began the process of withdrawing from the standard model. Relying first on Deleuze and Marx, we saw the difficulties of actually existing digitality. With the infrastructure of the world understood as essentially digital and computational, a number of alternative logics and conditions become important, among them the irreversibility of relation and the generic determination of the material base.

Several areas remain to be explored. Because if the event and the prevent operate on being as apparently "political" forces, the one bent on transforming it internally and the other on rendering it determined and impersonal, the exact nature of these forces remains to be seen. Are the event and the prevent merely two different avatars for the political, or do they reveal the distinction between the political and the ethical? Such is the agenda of the last two chapters of the book, chapters 9 and 10.

Yet before addressing the political and the ethical in earnest, we turn to the art and science of the one. Aesthetics is a recurring theme in Laruelle's work. He has written two short books on photography and has several essays on art and related topics, including texts on color, light, seeing, drawing, dance, music, and technology.

Technology or science? And what of art? Laruelle's position on these different domains is not entirely intuitive. For example, he does not follow someone like Heidegger and reestablish a lineage from technology back to art, via the Greek concept of *technē*. Nor is he phobic of science following those skeptical of industrial modernity. Instead Laruelle is something of a purist about technology and science. He denigrates technology and elevates science, elevating it to such a degree that it becomes synonymous with non-standard philosophy overall.[1]

The technology that surrounds us, from cars to computers to rocket ships, is all rather repulsive for Laruelle. Such technology provides little more than an avenue for transit or mediation in and out of things. From this perspective philosophy is the ultimate technology, because philosophy is the ultimate vehicle of transit, and philosophers the ultimate mailmen. Philosophy is all technology wrapped into one, for it is at once mirror, conveyance, energizer, and processor. By contrast, science is the realm of immanence and unilateral relation. Science is the realm of discovery, axiomatics, and theory. If philosophy were a science it would remain immanent to itself, never transiting anywhere, never synthesizing or reflecting on anything.

Philosophy would remain where it is, *in the dark*. But philosophy, always quick to demonstrate its illuminating potential, is never in the dark. "Our philosophers are children," Laruelle reminds us. They are children "who are afraid of the Dark."[2]

Alternations of light and dark are the fuel of philosophy. From Plato's cave to Paul de Man's "blindness and insight," philosophers are forever transiting between shadow and illumination. Yet darkness itself is not the problem. The problem is alternation. The problem is not that philosophy is dark. The problem is that philosophy is *not dark enough*.

According to Laruelle we must jump further, not from light to dark but from dark to black, from the darkness of philosophy to the blackness of science. So forget your rocket ships and rocket cars. Leave behind the scaffolding of reflection and alternation. "Do not think technology first," Laruelle commands. "Think science first."[3]

Science is, in this way, the *least* illuminating profession, because it surpasses mere darkness by way of a profound blackness. Never afraid of the dark, Laruelle's science begins from the posture of the black, communing with the agnostic darkness of the real.

But what is this darkness? What is this black universe of which Laruelle sings? Is black a color, and if so can we see it?

"Philosophy is thinking by way of a generalized 'black box'; it is the effort to fit black into light and to push it back to the rear of the caverns."[4]

Alternations between black and white drive philosophy, but they have also long been the subject of art, from chiaroscuro in Caravaggio, to the shadows in *Night of the Hunter* (1955). Just as there is an art of light, there is also an art of dark. Just as art has forever pursued what Victorian critic Matthew Arnold called "sweetness and light," it has also been corrupted by the gloomy gloaming of blackest black.

What are the great explorations of black in art? Chief among them would be the Malevich square, or Ad Reinhardt's black paintings, or the Rothko Chapel in Houston, or some of Stan Brakhage's films with their murky darkness, or Guy Debord's notorious "Howls for Sade" (1952), a film that uses its blackness as a kind of weapon. But is the black screen in Debord truly black? Is the Reinhardt canvas a black canvas?

All these heroic experiments are no more black than a bright summer day. As attempts to capture black they are abject failures, and all the worse for trying to be so avant-garde, so utterly modern. Such meditations on the color black are quickly revealed to be what they are, *meditations*. Black appears only in alternation with white, just as quietude is punctuated by noise, and immobile finitude by infinite mobility.

The black screen in "Howls for Sade" is not black, but a black box. The film offers us blackness, but only in as much as the blackness can withdraw from other things, in this case from whiteness or from the audible voice. These are all works of alternation, of oscillation into and out of the black. Thus they are properly labeled "reflections" on black— even "howls" for black—because black never appears in these artworks, only the optical alternations of black-against-white, black-against-color, or black-against-sound.

Deleuze explains such phenomena near the end of his writings on cinema:

> "The absence of image," the black screen or the white screen, have a decisive importance in contemporary cinema. . . . They no longer have a simple function of punctuation, as if they marked a change, but enter into a dialectical relation between the image and its absence, and assume a properly structural value. . . . Used in this way, the screen becomes the medium for variations: the black screen and the under-exposed image, the intense blackness which lets us guess at dark volumes in process of being constituted, or the black marked by a fixed or moving luminous point, and all

the combinations of black and fire; the white screen and the over-exposed image, the milky image, or the snowy image whose dancing seeds are to take shape.[5]

Reinhardt's paintings are the ultimate false lure. What appears at first glance to be black quickly shifts into a complex economy of micro shades of black, each with a different tone and luminosity. Richard Serra's drawings using black paint sticks—or some of Gerhard Richter's works—are similar in their reinvention of an entire color cosmos thriving both on the *interior* of black and as black relates to its own *exterior*.

There is thus nothing black about these works, just as there is little silence in that notorious John Cage composition *4′33″* in which no notes are played. Instead, these works are works of division and alternation, of contrasted extremities, of absence appearing as presence and presence returning to absence. These are meditative works, reflective works, great metaphysical works, great philosophical works even. But at the same time, merely reflective, merely metaphysical, merely philosophical.

"Philosophers have divided up the undivided simplicity of the nothingness and the all," Laruelle reminds us, "but human eyes have never divided up the unique night."[6] The universe is, for Laruelle, a night universe, and to look at the universe means to look into the darkness of the night. "Vision is foundational when it abandons perception and sees-in-the-night."[7] In other words, vision is never vision when the lights are ablaze. Vision is only vision when it looks avidly into the pitch black of night. Likewise art will never be art until it ceases to represent and begins to look into the Stygian monochrome, that blackness that has yet to be exposed to any living light.[8]

Is this all just another flavor of modern nihilism? Just another existentialism? Laruelle answers no: "The philosophical eye wants to see the nothing in man's eye rather than see nothing. The philosopher wants to look man's nothingness in the eye rather than be a nothingness of vision"—nothing in man's eye versus seeing nothing.[9] Recall those horrible nothing worlds of the existentialists. The existentialist can see man as nothing; the existentialist might even be able to see the world as nothing. But he cannot yet see nothing as nothing.

Philosophers have long asked why there is something rather than nothing. For Aristotle the question was always: Why is there something rather than something else? For Nietzsche or Kierkegaard it was: Why is there nothing rather than something? But for Laruelle the question is poorly formed from the outset. For Laruelle the question might rather be, Why, in looking at nothing, do we still never see nothing? For as Parmenides said, nothing comes from nothing. "Man is this middle between night and nothing" writes Laruelle. Or rather, "less than this middle: nothing which is only nothing; night which is only night."[10]

But still, what is this darkness, and where is the light? How does dark relate to black, and light to white?

What is a hermeneutic light? Of the many unresolved debates surrounding the work of Heidegger, the following question returns with some regularity: Is Heidegger's phenomenology ultimately a question of hermeneutics and interpretation, or is it ultimately a question of immanence and truth? Is *Dasein* forever questing after a Being that withdraws, or does it somehow achieve a primordial communion with the truth of Being? In other words, is Heidegger the philosopher of blackness or the philosopher of light?

Hermeneutics was an important topic for theory in the 1960s. Hence it is not surprising that Heidegger, who was being rediscovered and rethought during that period, would often be framed in terms of hermeneutics. To be sure, the critical tradition handed down from post-structuralism leaves little room for modes of immanence and immediacy, modes that were marginalized as essentialist or otherwise unpleasant (often for good reason). Thus it would be easy to assimilate into the tradition of hermeneutics a figure like Heidegger, with his complicated withdrawal of Being. For where else would he fit?

Indeed it is common to categorize Heidegger there. But is it not also possible to show that Heidegger is a philosopher of immanence? Is it not also possible to show that he speaks as much to illumination as to withdrawal? That he speaks as much to the intuitive and proximate as to the detached and distanced?

For instance, consider his treatment of *gelichtet*, a word stemming from the noun for "light." In the chapter on the "there" in *Being and Time*, Heidegger speaks of *Dasein* as *lumen* (one of two Latin words meaning "light") and defines *Dasein* in terms of the "clearing" *(gelichtet)* or "illumination" of Being:

> When we talk in an ontically figurative way of the *lumen naturale* in man,
> we have in mind nothing other than the existential-ontological structure
> of this entity, that it *is* in such a way as to be its "there". To say that it is
> 'illuminated' ["erleuchtet"] means that *as* Being-in-the-world it is cleared
> [gelichtet] in itself, not through any other entity, but in such a way that it
> *is* itself the clearing.[11]

No one can deny the cryptological tendencies in Heidegger. No one can
deny that, for Heidegger, Being likes to hide itself. But this is far out-
weighed by the fact that *Dasein* can indeed be experienced as an authentic
disclosedness of Being, by the fact that phenomenology preaches—without irony or pathos—that one may strive "toward the things themselves"
and actually arrive at them.

Recall that hermeneutics is the science of suspicion, the science of the
insincere. But Heidegger, like Socrates before him, is the consummate
philosopher of sincerity. The phenomenological subject is the one who
has an authentic and sincere relationship with Being. Because of this, we
should not be too quick to consign Heidegger to the history of hermeneutics. Hermes's natural habitat is teeming with deception; his economies
are economies in the absence of trust. But Heidegger lives in a different
world. His world is a world of authentic presence, of questing after truth.

Thus running in parallel to the Hermes-Heidegger, the Heidegger
who touches on the tradition of interpretation and exchange in the face
of the withdrawal of Being, there is also an Iris-Heidegger, the Heidegger
who touches on the tradition of illumination and iridescence along the
pathway of seeking. Heidegger's is not simply a Hermes narrative, but
also an Iris arc.[12]

When Heidegger evokes the *lumen naturale* of mankind he is making
reference to one of two kinds of light. The light of mankind is a terrestrial light. When bodies with their *anima* (their vital force) are vigorous
and alive, they are illuminated with the light of the *lumen naturale*. *Lumen*
is the light of life, the light of this world, the light that sparkles from the
eyes of consciousness.

But there is a second type of light. Being carries its own light that is
not the light of man. This light is a cosmological light, a divine light, the
light of the phenomena, light as grace, or, as Laruelle says, the kind of
light that does not originate from a star.

So just as there are two Heideggers, there are also two lights. One light is the light of transparent bodies, clear and mobile. It is the light of this world, experienced through passage and illumination. The other light is the light of opaque bodies. It is the light of color, a holy light, experienced only through the dull emanation of things.

Dioptrics and catoptrics. If there exists a natural lightness, is there not also a natural darkness? And if there are two kinds of light are there not also two kinds of dark?

Such questions lie at the heart of Reza Negarestani's *Cyclonopedia: Complicity with Anonymous Materials,* a hallucinatory mix of theory and fiction that views the Earth as a quasi-living, demonic creature, oil the blood in its veins. Oil petroleum is black, of course, in color if not also in its moral decrepitude. But oil is also light, because it is a transmutation of the light of the sun. Oil is the geological product of sunlight, first via photosynthesis into vegetable matter, and second via the decomposition of vegetable matter over time. In this sense, oil is, as Negarestani calls it, the "black corpse of the sun."[13]

But before looking more closely at the two kinds of darkness, let us examine the two kinds of lightness a bit further. Negarestani writes about fog and light. He writes about the "mistmare." But what is mist? He writes of Pazuzu, the wind, the dust enforcer. But what is dust?

Of course, dust and fog have certain obfuscatory qualities. They strangle the light and interfere with one's ability to see. But at the same time they have their own form of luminosity. Fog glows with a certain ambience. It transforms a space of absolute coordinates into a proximal zone governed by thresholds of intelligibility. (Fog is thus first and foremost a category of existence—there can be no *ontological* fog; that would be something else.) Fog is a dioptric phenomenon, even if ironically it acts to impede vision. It is a question of light passing through materials, and likewise a question of the light of mankind passing through (or being impeded from passing through) a proximal space. This means that fog is part of the *luminaria*. Fog gives off no light of its own, even if it has its own luminosity by virtue of filtering and passing along a light originating from elsewhere.

The term *dioptric* has been broached, and in order to continue it will be necessary to define this term in some detail, along with the related term *catoptric.* These two terms are part of the science of optics, and hence the being of light, but they describe the dealings of light in two very different ways.

Dioptrics refers to light when it is *refracted,* that is to say, when light passes through transparent materials such as glass or water. As a branch of optical science, dioptrics is concerned principally with *lenses.* Yet things not specifically conceived as lenses can also act as such. Some of the best examples are the tiny water droplets contained in clouds, spherical in shape, that allow light passing through them to refract twice, once as the light enters the droplet and again as it leaves. Prisms also offer a fine illustration of dioptric phenomena; like a water droplet, a prism splits light into color bands because different wavelengths of light refract differently. A dioptric device can therefore divide white light into colored light, just as it can merge colored light into white light again, given the right conditions.

Catoptrics refers to light when it is *reflected,* that is to say, when light bounces off objects in the world. Whereas dioptrics is concerned with lenses, catoptrics is concerned principally with *mirrors.* All sorts of objects can act as mirrors proper—polished glass or metal, the surface of water. But catoptrics also includes the duller quasi-mirror effects of plain objects, which reflect light and allow themselves to be visible to the eye. Just as the prism can produce what Goethe called "physical color," there is also a color capacity in catoptric phenomena, because some objects reflect certain colors and absorb others (Goethe's "chemical color"). So if, in general, dioptric phenomena are the phenomena of prisms and lenses, catoptric phenomena are the phenomena of mirrors, screens, walls, and opaque surfaces.

In short, the former is a question of transparency, while the latter is a question of opacity. Dioptrics is a *perspective* (seeing through), while catoptrics is a *speculum* or *aspect* (reflecting, looking at).[14]

Recall the god of so many aspects, so many epithets. He is Hermes, messenger to Zeus. And yet his counterpart Iris, messenger to Hera, has relatively few epithets; her business is that of shining through. In this way Hermes is the aspect god, the god of catoptrics, and Iris is the perspective goddess, the goddess of dioptrics. The effects of refraction "remain within" a transparent physical object such as a glass lens, and hence are to be considered a phenomenon of immanence. By contrast the effects of reflection are to obscure the source object, to leverage the very opacity of the object for some other end, and hence they are to be considered a phenomenon of hermeneutics.

These same principles can be stated in different terms. Both dioptrics and catoptrics have a special relationship to depth; however, the distinction between the two could not be more stark. Reflection is *semiotically* deep, that is, it is deep in the domain of meaning, whereas refraction is *experientially* deep, that is, it is deep in the domain of subjective experience. Saying "semiotically deep" means that opaque reflection creates a depth model wherein two opposing layers, one manifest and one latent, work together to create meaning. This is the same depth model that exists in Freud or Marx. Saying "experientially deep" means that transparent refraction creates a depth model wherein a real sense of volumetric space is created and presented to a viewing subject. This is the same depth model that exists in Heidegger (or even in others like Kant). There are veils covering the soul, but there are also telescopes for viewing the heavens—the one is an aspect, the other a perspective.

Yet beyond exhibiting depth in two contrasting ways, catoptrics and dioptrics are also equally distinct in how they deal with flatness. Being semiotically deep, catoptric reflection is at the same time *ontically* flat. That is to say, reflection is manifest in two-dimensional surfaces and other flat things arranged in the world. The very existence of the reflected image is a flat existence.

Dioptric refraction, however, being experientially deep, is at the same time *ontologically* flat. That is to say, refraction is immanent to materials; there is no transcendent or metaphysical cause that operates across or after the being of the phenomenon. This is why whatever is immanent also must be flat. This variety of flatness is best understood as a flatness of identity, a selfsame quality vis-à-vis the being of the thing. Dioptric refraction, as iridescent immanence, "remains within" itself.

These claims, being somewhat abstract, should be explained a little further. We have asserted that dioptrics is experiential. What this means is that dioptrics is on the side of the subject. Dioptrics is always a question of crafting a clear or real subjective experience. This is why the concept of dioptric illumination is so closely associated with the modern period, why we refer to "the Enlightenment"—which the French render with even less subtlety as *les Lumières*. But it is also why this same modern trajectory ends up at Kantianism, at romanticism, and eventually at Heidegger and phenomenology, because the question of subjective experience must always remain at the heart of the modern experience.

By contrast, we said previously that catoptrics is semiotic. What this means is that catoptrics is on the side of matter, on the side of the *pharmakon*. Catoptrics is always a question of meaning. Although subjects might be involved, the process is never primarily subjective. Rather the process is primarily a question of what Stiegler terms *hypomnesis,* the act of externalizing the subject—or to be more precise, the subject's *memory*—into material supports. This too is a modern trajectory, but it ends up at a different place: not in the illumination of the subject, but in the obscurantism of the culture industries, in spectacle, in ideology, and in the tradition of critique that terminates in structuralism and post-structuralism.

Jesuit mathematician François d'Aguilon, in two propositions from his early seventeenth-century opus on optics *Opticorum Libri Sex,* offers two additional points concerning the difference between dioptric transparency and catoptric opacity. The two points appear in propositions number 31 and 32 of book 1:

> Proposition 31—*Lux* [light] and color are the properties of an opaque body.
> Proposition 32—*Lumen* [illumination, luminosity] is the action of a transparent body.[15]

The distinction between two kinds of light made by d'Aguilon is the same distinction made since ancient times: in Latin *lux* and *lumen;* in Greek *phos (φῶς)* and *phoster (φωστήρ);* or in Hebrew *or (אור)* and *maor (מאור).*

Recall the echo that occurs between Genesis 1:3 and 1:14, when God creates light, and then creates it a second time (see Francisco de Holanda, *Fiant luminaria in firmamento celi,* the frontispiece of this chapter). The echo nicely captures the difference between the two kinds of light. The first time light comes into the world it comes as *lux.* This *lux* means light, but it is a special kind of light, the light of being, the light of God, a cosmological light. The second time light comes, it comes as *lumen* (or rather as *luminaria,* the things that show *lumen*). This *lumen* also means light, but only in a very specific way. *Lumen* means sun, moon, and stars—the bodies that give light in as much as they can shine through with the divine light.

Although the English language differentiates between light and luminosity, English often loses the subtlety between the two kinds of light. D'Aguilon assigns the first term to opaque bodies, and thus, by association we may be certain that he speaks of catoptric phenomenon. The second he assigns to transparent bodies, and thus to dioptric phenomenon. In other words, *lux* is catoptric and *lumen* is dioptric.

There is a precedence here too. For just as the Renaissance preceded the Baroque, *lux* in Genesis 1:3 precedes *lumen* in Genesis 1:14, and catoptrics precedes dioptrics. Descartes would confirm this same sentiment in a 1638 letter written a few years after d'Aguilon: "Light, that is, *lux*, is a movement or an action in the luminous body, and tends to cause some movement in transparent bodies, namely *lumen*. Thus *lux* is before *lumen*."[16] (The firstness of Iris arrives, then, as a kind of counterintuitive miracle, scrapping all precedence, erasing diachrony for synchrony.)

In this way God, bearing the *lux* light of the cosmological fiat, is absolute in His opacity. God is the absolute source of light, but at the same time the one who is absolutely inaccessible. Opacity is the quality that we can assign to His being. Yet, the light of *lumen*—illumination, luminosity—is absolute in its transparency, as it travels through the actually existing world. Thus transparency is the quality that we can assign to His existing.

This is the second point that can be gained from d'Aguilon's two propositions, that *lumen* or dioptrics is always an *action* of existence, an active motion of looking-throughness, while *lux* or catoptrics is always a fact of being (a *property*).

The black corpse of the sun. Now we are in a better position to consider the kinds of darkness and their relationship to the light. To summarize, illumination *(lumen)* refers to the action of transparent bodies in their luminosity and radiant iridescence. These bodies are the sun, the moon and stars, fire and mankind. Not white so much as *bright*. It is the light of life and consciousness. It is multiple, never singular. It is a perspective, and therefore allied with dioptrics and Iris.

By contrast, light *(lux)* refers to the property of an opaque body in its fact of being. This is the light of God, the light of being, a cosmological light, but also the light of daytime (as opposed to sunlight). It is an aspect, and therefore allied with catoptrics and Hermes. It is singular, never multiple. It is white only in so much as it is the whiteness of pure opacity. *Lux* is the plenum. It is the obscure. It is grace.

Now on to the darkness. Here too are two modalities, all the more different because of their near identity. Darkness may be gloom, murkiness, shadow, or shade. It may be dusk, night, or twilight. Bodies may be dark. One might speak of "dark" materials, in as much as they are asleep, unconsciousness, dead, or cold. Likewise, habit or cliché may be understood as a kind of darkness of experience, an inability to revivify the normal routine of living.

Hence the darkening, or *obscuritas,* described in Revelation 9:2—*obscuratus est sol et aer de fumo putei,* "The sun was darkened, and the air, by the smoke of the pit." The sun is obscured by smoke, and hence the earthbound shadows of an obscuring darkness. As the sun and moon and stars are progressively snuffed out, they are *obscurare.* It is not yet a question of ontological darkness, but rather the darkness of the world. It is the *nihil privativum* discussed in Schopenhauer, the "privative nothing" that is dark by virtue of depriving the light.

But there is another kind of darkness, the *tenebrae,* the shadows of black being separated from the *lux* of heaven in Genesis (2, 4, 5, and 18). No longer simply dark, the question now is that of a profound blackness.

Such is the generic darkness of the abyss, the void and vacuum, the darkness of catastrophe and cataclysm. It is a cosmological blackness, the black of Satan, the black of absolute evil, the black of nonbeing. It is what Thacker describes as "cosmic pessimism . . . hermeticism of the abyss."[17]

The shadows of black being are a hermeneutic blackness. Not simply a world gone dark, such blackness is a world *without us.* Not simply a question of dying or growing cold, such blackness means the leaving of being. In contrast to the "privative nothing" comes Schopenhauer's *nihil negativum* ("negative nothing"), nothing as absolute foreclosure. In this sense, the shadows of black being are not part of any ontology, but rather constitute an encryption or *crypto-ontology.* These are the shadows of the *kruptos (κρυπτός),* the hidden parts that form the inward nature of things.

And hence in Revelation, beyond the sun being obscured and made dark, there is also a secondary darkness. The kingdom of heaven is threatened secondarily by the blackness of the *tenebrae,* for ultimately *factum est regnum eius tenebrosum,* "His kingdom was full of darkness" (Revelation 16:10).

Return now to Negarestani and the petroleum that fuels contemporary society. Is this oil, as putrification, the product of *lux* or *lumen?* Is oil black or dark? As Negarestani writes, oil is "Hydrocarbon Corpse Juice." Sun is captured in photosynthesis, then via decay is putrified into a liquid fossil form. So as sun juice, oil is the darkening of sunlight. Oil is thus literally dead; oil is death. And as transubstantiated sunlight, oil is *lumen,* or at least some product thereof.

But there is also a blackness to oil. "Oil is the Black Corpse of the Sun," he writes. Now no longer simply solar, oil's tellurian core wells up, the insurgent enemy of solar capitalism. This is oil at its blackest. This is oil as the "Devil's Excrement," oil as the conspirator—not as *lux* but as the *tenebra* or shadow of black being—who annihilates societies by "tear[ing] them apart slowly."[18] And so, just as it was possible to speak of the shadows of black being as a crypto-ontology, Negarestani can speak of a crypto-ontology for oil. In such a crypto-ontology, oil is understood not simply as dark but as radical blackness, held in escrow by a cosmic pessimism, with its *kruptos* or hidden parts absolutely foreclosed to us, but also to being itself.

Blackness is a crypto-ontology absolutely foreclosed to being. Only through this final definition—black as *kruptos* foreclosed to being—can we begin to understand what Laruelle means by the black universe. Only by way of a withdrawal from the system of light and color can we begin to see the generic real of blackness.

Channel that great saint of radical blackness, Toussaint Louverture, and return to the Haitian Constitution of 1804, which stated that all citizens will be called black regardless of color. Such blanket totality of black, such cataclysm of human color, renders color invalid and denies the endless dynamics of black-as-white or white-as-black. Black is no longer the limit case, no longer the case of the slave, the poor, the indentured or debt-ridden worker. Black is the foundation of a new uchromia, a new color utopia rooted in the generic black universe.

"Our uchromia: to learn to think from the point of view of Black as what determines color in the last instance rather than what limits it."[19]

Our uchromia, our *non-chromia* or *non-color*—what does Laruelle mean by this?

As Laruelle would say, color always has a *position*. Color always has a *stance*. The color palette or the color spectrum provide a complex field of difference and alternation. The primary colors reside in their determining positions, while other colors compliment each other as contrasts. Hence the color posture: purple complimenting yellow, red complimenting green, the primary colors' posture vis-à-vis the palette, and ultimately the posture of color itself governing the continuum of light and dark, as colors take turns emerging into a luminous and supersaturated visibility, or receding into a sunless gloom.[20]

Laruelle uses photography as a way to explain these never-ending quests into and out of things. "Platonism is perhaps born of the absence of a photo," he writes, proposing a provocative anachronism. "From this we get the model and the copy, and their common derivative in the simulacrum. And Leibniz and Kant alike—the intelligible depth of the phenomenon as much as its trenchant distinction—find their possibility in this repression of photography."[21]

According to Laruelle, photography has long been held captive, forced to choose between two unappetizing options,

> philosophy on one hand (consciousness and reflection), psychoanalysis on the other (the unconscious and [automatic drives]). . . . The photo is then neither a mode of philosophical reflection—even if there is plenty of photography integrated into philosophy—nor a mode of unconscious representation or a return of the repressed. Neither Being nor the Other; neither Consciousness nor the Unconscious, neither the present nor the repressed.[22]

Photography is an ideal candidate for Laruelle's intervention, because photography requires that light penetrate an aperture and write itself on a sensitive surface, resulting in *prints* that, in turn, reflect light back to viewers. "Philosophy remains an optics," he writes. "Transcendental no doubt, but specular: intuitiveness is its unavoidable structure. The eye is first an external empirical sense; then it is divided and doubled, the introduction of the other gaze constituting an *a priori* optical or specular field; then the gazes knot themselves together, form a chiasmus, and constitute a transcendental speculative field."[23]

Which is precisely what Laruelle seeks to avoid. Using the language of optics invoked previously, Laruelle exhibits a *unilateralized dioptrics,* in that he rejects absolutely the reduplication and extension of the eye in favor of an immanent transparency of identity. But he simultaneously exhibits a *unilateralized catoptrics,* in that he assigns a pure opacity to the one, a pure density, a pure imperviousness.

"The multiplication of the eye into a recursive spiral does not suppress it," he reminds us, "for the eye is the intuition that now gives the other eye; the gaze that opens upon the other gaze—such is the kernel of all transcendental aesthetics."[24] Is this not the great phenomenological gambit, that physiognomy is destiny, that our eyes and senses orient ourselves into a world, toward phenomena that orient and reveal themselves back to us?

The philosopher says, Humanity was endowed with the faculty of sight, so humanity must devote itself to seeing, and *seeing well.* But Laruelle says, The decision is never between looking and seeing or between listening and hearing. That is no decision at all. The true decision, the decision already made implicitly by philosophy, is to see and hear in the first place. We decide each time we open our eyes.

In other words, photography is always understood as *color* photography, *black-and-white* photography even, but never *black photography proper.* Rather than these other color photographies evident in phenomenology, psychoanalysis, or philosophy at large, Laruelle writes that we need photography (now recast as *non*-photography) as science photography or identity photography.

But what would "identity photography" mean? Identity photography is black photography. And thus identity photography is the only kind of photography that could inscribe the black universe. Laruelle calls such photography a "hyperphenomenology of the real"; it follows a logic of *auto-impression,* not expression.[25] Not a *cliché* snapshot, but an immanent identity of the Real. "One does not photograph the World, the City, History," Laruelle claims. One photographs "the identity (of) the real-in-the-last-instance."[26] In this sense, although color always carries itself in terms of a "posture" or "*stance,*" black is immanent to itself and thus can only be an *in*-stance, an instance, or as Laruelle says, the *last instance*.

"Simplify color!" he cries. "See black, think white! See black rather than believe 'unconscious.' And think white rather than believe 'conscious.'"[27] Don't *see*, be a seer. Stop seeing and start visioning. Be a visionary.

Watchers and lookers are the ones who see white, who see the thing that they know they will always see. But the one who sees black is the true clairvoyant. The black seer is the oracular prophet, what we call "a medium." And hence to understand media—and indeed to "do" media theory—is to start visioning purely in the black universe. Never to see vision*s*, never to hallucinate (for that is what philosophers do), rather to *see vision*. This is what Laruelle means when he says that vision "abandons perception and sees-in-the-night."[28] This is what he means when he deploys that thorny non-philosophical term of art "vision-in-One."

The blackness of the person. Laruelle's black is not simply a theory of the universe, but also a theory of the subject, what he calls the "human" or the "person." At the same time the black universe allows for a mystical justice that is irreducible to either Christian morality on the one hand or liberal ecumenicalism on the other.

"All philosophical speculation is communication, and communication is always speculative," he writes, in a re-articulation of the media principle from Thesis I.[29] The media principle is so troublesome because it limits the discussion to one of two scenarios: either to speculate for or on behalf of *the other,* or to speculate for or about *the self.* The subject is either reflective or introspective. The subject is either too nosy about others or too vain about itself.

These are the two great maxims of philosophy: the first maxim, "to see for itself by seeing in the place of the other," and the second maxim, the ancient law of "an-eye-for-an-eye."[30] This is why metaphysics is described by Laruelle in terms of *vengeance.* Either "an eye for an eye," the symmetrical, retributive justice of the Old Testament, or what he calls "*Eye-for-the-Other,* as hostage-of-the-Other-eye," the universalization of liberal relativism where we promise to see for the other, or even, in our infinite wisdom, to step back and let the other try to see for itself.[31] Either way, the eye is held hostage, vision is vengeance, and *vengeance is ours.*

Instead, the black universe allows for a mystical subject (capable of mystical justice) because it eliminates speculation. No more eye-for-an-eye, and no more eye-for-the-other. No more exchange of looks, no more patriarchal gaze, and no more commerce in vision. Instead the black universe allows for an absolutely determined and unidirectional vision, a kind of visionary vision that looks without looking.

To be clear, Laruelle does not take the usual exit; he does not escape the quandary of self-other relations by singing the praises of a universalized multiplicity of voices. In fact he takes a different step, unexpected and rather unfashionable in today's progressive theory landscape. Laruelle pursues an absolutely determined and unidirectional vision, all and everywhere, destiny and determination from before the first to after the last instance.

To summarize before ending—there are two kinds of light, the *lux* with its purely opaque source and the *luminaria* that reflect *lux* into this profane world. And likewise there are two kinds of dark, the darkening *(obscuritas)* of the *luminaria* as they sputter out and die, and the *tenebrae* themselves, the shadows of black being.

But all of this, from black to white and from dark to light, is still a part of the standard model. If black is merely the absence of white, and dark the absence of light, then we remain locked in a world of relation, reflection, continua, and convertibility, black-as-white and dark-as-light. Such is the philosophical decision in a nutshell, to decide to frame the world in terms of digital color.

Laruelle, by contrast, entreats us to withdraw from the system of color and enter into a purely radical and unilaterally black universe. This is a universe in which black is never defined in terms of light, nor ultimately exchangeable with or made visible by illumination. Just like in the introduction and the secret of Hermes that has never been divulged to any living human, the black of the universe has never been seen before by anyone. It is only through a kind of negative intuition *that we dare to call it a color at all.*

This is the condition of the Laruellean person, and ultimately the condition for a new kind of black justice: unilaterally determined by the real, but never by mundane reality; faithful to the conditions of a generic humanity, but never debased to the banal conditions of the world.

If you open your eyes partway you see white, but if you open them all the way you see black. Do not let the philosophers draw you out of the cavern and into the light, only to be dazzled by the first rays of the sun. But at the same time, do not douse the light and dig deeper into the abyss, in an attempt to spiral lower, darker, into your gloomy soul. Laruelle's human is one who opens its eyes in the night, not to look or speculate but to *know*.

We are this night. "The night is this human, the human who does not speculate about man. Who am I, me who is? I am neither this reason nor this way of thinking, neither this question nor this speculation. I am this night. . . ."[32]

August von Briesen, *Drawing of Mozart's Piano Concerto No. 22*, 1981.
38 × 38 cm. Reproduced courtesy of Anastasia Ogilvie von Briesen.

eight

Art and Utopia

In the early 1990s Laruelle wrote an essay on the artist James Turrell titled "A Light Odyssey: The Discovery of Light as a Theoretical and Aesthetic Problem."[1] Although it briefly mentions Turrell's Roden Crater and is cognizant of his other work, the essay focuses on a series of twenty aquatint etchings made by Turrell called *First Light* (1989–90). Designed to stand alone as fine art prints, *First Light* nevertheless acts as a kind of backward glance revisiting and meditating on earlier corner light projections made by Turrell in the late 1960s, in particular works like *Afrum-Pronto* (1967).

For the exhibition of *First Light* at the Museum of Modern Art in New York in 1990, "the aquatints [were] arranged in groups based on the white shape that hovers in the dense black field of each print. In the installation, with light projected onto the images, the shapes appear to glow and float; viewed in sequence, they seem to move. The effect, from print to print, is tracelike and mesmerizing."[2]

"I am dealing with no object," Turrell said in a lecture a few years after producing *First Light*. "I am dealing with no image, because I want to avoid associative, symbolic thought . . . I am dealing with no focus or particular place to look. With no object, no image and no focus, *what are you looking at?*"[3] Indeed the object of *First Light* is perception itself, as Turrell was the first to admit.

No object, no image, no focus—no wonder Laruelle was drawn to *First Light*. It represents the very core principles of the non-standard method. For Laruelle, Turrell's art poses a basic problem. "Light makes manifest," he acknowledges. "But what will manifest the light?"[4] Systems of representation reveal aspects of the world to perceiving subjects; this is how light makes manifest. But is it possible to see light *in* itself, not *in relation* to a perceived object? Is it possible to manifest the rigorously immanent genericness of light itself?

Laruelle's essay on Turrell makes two essential claims, one about perception and the other about light. Regarding the former, Laruelle asserts that we must *think* perception, not think *about* perception. Regarding the latter, Laruelle wishes to discover the *non-orientable* nature of light.

There is a light of orientation, a philosophical light. But there is also a light that does not seek to orient perception along a particular set of lines. It is this second kind of orientation that intrigues Laruelle and that appears in the work of Turrell. (Taking advantage of a play on words, Laruelle sometimes labels this kind of non-standard orientation "occidental" to differentiate it from what he sees as the endless orientalism of philosophy.)

Laruelle explores these two essential claims by way of three different themes stemming from Turrell's work: *discovery, experimentation,* and *identity.* Just as Deleuze did in his book on the painter Francis Bacon, Laruelle assumes from the outset that Turrell and his art are theoretical in themselves, that they are performing theoretical work as such. Laruelle's is not a theoretical interpretation of a nontheoretical artwork; the work itself enacts the non-standard method. In Laruelle's view, Turrell himself discovered a non-phenomenological solution to the problem of light. Turrell "has discovered a new aesthetic (and theoretical) object: light as such, the being-light of light."[5]

In an attempt to describe what he means by discovery, Laruelle draws attention to the subtle differences in meaning embedded in Turrell's title: "Turrell's title 'First Light' is ambiguous and can be interpreted in two ways. In the weakest sense it means just what it means, *first light,* the first among many, its own relative position in a continuous order in which it is included. In the strong sense it means *light first,* all the light given at once, without residual or supplement, without division or 'plays-of-light.'"[6]

This second sense, the strong sense, is most appealing to Laruelle, because it indicates the identity of light as a kind of first givenness, light as raw discovery or invention without supplement. Part of Laruelle's aim is to move away from the conventional manner in which light appears in philosophical discourse, for example, in phenomenology, which tends to think of light through the digital process of withdrawing and revealing. As we saw in the previous chapter, Laruelle's light is thus not so much white but black, generically black. "The black immanence of this light . . . lets it escape from all phenomenology stemming from the greco-philosophical type."[7]

In order to describe the radical nature of Turrell's non-standard art, Laruelle poses a hypothetical scenario:

> Imagine a photographer tired of using light to render his "subject" or whatever other objects were before him. Imagine that this photographer was crazy enough to want to render *the light as light*. If so, this would not be the light from distant stars, but a *light without stars, without source* no matter how distant or hidden, a light inaccessible to the camera. Should the photographer abandon his technique and find another? Or should he generalize his technique across the various forms of the darkroom, the white cube, and the *camera obscura* in order to proliferate the angles, the frames, the perspectives, the openings and shutters used to capture (or perhaps to seduce) the light itself? Would he not be making, in essence, the kind of work that Turrell makes?[8]

Turrell's light is a light that doesn't come from the stars. Laruelle gives it an unusual label; he calls it a "photic materiality."

Being both non-cosmic and non-ontological, Turrell's light does not orient the viewer. Instead, according to Laruelle, Turrell's light performs experiments on perception and retrains perception according to alternative logics. This mode of experimentation produces what he calls an "aesthetic generalization" of perception in order to unilateralize the conventional prohibitions placed on perception by philosophy. Instead of philosophy or photography setting the agenda, "light acts instead . . . like a drive that has its own 'subjectivity,' or like an *a priori* force."[9] Turrell's experimental mandate, therefore, is to allow both the artist and the viewer to test perception, not to probe the limits of perception, not to mimic the way in which perception is normalized by philosophy, not to think about perception, but to think *according to* perception.

In this sense the artist and the viewer are *strictly identical,* allowing for an auto-testing of perception. It is not that one party—whether artist, viewer, or critic—is in a privileged position to arbitrate Turrell's aesthetic experiment. Instead, all parties are identical.

This brings us to the final theme in Laruelle's essay on Turrell, that of identity. The key question for Laruelle is how to see light itself, light's *identity*. For Laruelle the only way to answer the question is to break the vicious cycle of worldly self-manifestation. "There is a paradox at the heart of aesthetic sentiment," Laruelle remarks. "The paradox is the following: on the one hand light remains to a certain degree in itself. It does not lose its identity in an object . . . but on the other hand, light 'radiates.'"[10] There is no solution to the paradox, of course, because it belongs to the basic generative paradox fueling of all philosophy. Nevertheless the paradox provides Laruelle with raw material for non-standard intervention. Simply unilateralize the paradox and put both light and its radiation into immanent superposition. Such a move defangs the transcendental tendencies added to light by philosophy and reveals a purely immanent light.

Given the unusual and somewhat counterintuitive nature of the nonstandard universe, Laruelle is forced to speak in circumlocutions: light is a radiation-without-rays, or light is a reflecting-without-reflection. This might sound like jargon, yet Laruelle's "without" coinages are necessary in order to designate the superimposition or unilateralization of the rivenness of the world. They aim to show "light discovered in its radical identity."[11]

Photography, fiction, and utopia. We spent some time in the previous chapter looking at photography in the context of light and color. Now let's return to photography and amplify what was already said. Laruelle's two books on photography, *The Concept of Non-photography* and *Photo-Fiction: A Non-standard Aesthetics*, include material written over a span of two decades.[12] Intended as companion pieces, the books pose a number of questions. What is seen in a photo? What is light? What is the photographic stance? And, perhaps most enigmatic of all, what does Laruelle mean by fiction?

"Aesthetics was always a case of tracing art within philosophy, and likewise of art understood as a lesser form of philosophy."[13] For Laruelle aesthetics involves a convoluted and somewhat circular interaction between art and the contemplation of art. Art beckons contemplation.

And contemplation seeks its art to behold. Following this reciprocal interaction, art and philosophy co-constitute each other in terms of lack, for each completes the absence contained in the other: "Without art, philosophy lacks sensitivity and without philosophy, art lacks thought."[14] This kind of mutual digitality or mutual distinction is part and parcel of the philosophical process. Art and philosophy are *separated and reunited,* then policed as conjoined but distinct. A strange logic indeed, yet for Laruelle the logic is evident in everything from Plato's *Republic* to Deleuze and Guattari's *What Is Philosophy?* It is, in fact, the central logic of the standard model.

Photography is "a knowledge that doubles the World," he writes in the first of the two photography books.[15] As an aesthetic process, photography is philosophical in that it instantiates a decision to correlate a world with an image taken of the world. When photography doubles the world, it acts philosophically on and through the world.

Admittedly Laruelle does not discuss light much in *The Concept of Non-photography.* But light appears in the second book, *Photo-Fiction,* particularly in the context of philosophical enlightenment and the flash of the photographic apparatus. Laruelle uses two terms, *éclair* and *flash,* to mark the subtle variations in different kinds of light. Laruelle associates *éclair* with Greek philosophy. "The flash *[éclair]* of Logos," he remarks, "is the Greek model of thought."[16] He uses *flash* more commonly when discussing the physical apparatus of the photographic camera. Yet it would be hasty to assume that Laruelle poses the two terms in normative opposition—*éclair* bad and *flash* good—because by the end he specifies that both kinds of light are philosophical and that both need to be unilateralized.

As in his other writings, Laruelle accomplishes this by subjecting photography to the non-standard method. He proposes a principle of aesthetic sufficiency and shows how art and aesthetics have traditionally been allied with philosophy. Likewise he describes a principle of photographic sufficiency, indicating how photography is sufficient to accommodate all possible images, at least in principle. And, in an echo of how deconstructivists spoke of philosophy in terms of logocentrism, Laruelle labels photography's sufficiency a *photo-centrism,* and discusses how philosophy conceives of thought itself as a kind of photographic transcendental.

The process of non-standardization goes by several names and is defined in different ways. In recent writings Laruelle has begun to speak of the non-standard method in terms of *fiction*. Fiction means performance, invention, creativity, artifice, construction; for example, thought is fictive because it fabricates (although only in an immanent and real sense).

Fiction might seem like a strange word choice for someone wishing to depart from the endless alternations of representation, yet Laruelle devises a type of fiction that is nonexpressive and nonrepresentational. Laruelle's fiction is purely immanent to itself. It is neither a fictionalized version of something else, nor does it try to fabricate a fictitious world or narrative based on real or fantastical events:

> Non-standard aesthetics is creative and inventive on its own terms and in its own way. Non-standard aesthetics is a fiction-philosophy *[philo-fiction]*, a philosophico-artistic genre that tries to produce works using only pure and abstract thought. It does not create concepts in parallel to works of art—like that Spinozist Deleuze proposed, even though Deleuze himself was very close to embarking on a non-standard aesthetics.[17]

To subject philosophy to the non-standard method is to create a fiction philosophy. Likewise to subject photography to the same method produces a similar result. "The fiction-photo *[photo-fiction]* is a sort of generic extension or generalization of the 'simple' photo, the material photo."[18]

As he said previously in *The Concept of Non-photography*, "The task of a rigorous thought is rather to found—at least in principle—an abstract theory of photography—but radically abstract, absolutely non-worldly and non-perceptual."[19]

This begins to reveal the way in which Laruelle's views on photography synchronize with his interest in utopia. Photography is not oriented toward a world, nor is it a question of perception. Rather, by remaining within itself, photography indicates a non-world of pure auto-impression. Bored by the peculiarities of particular photographic images, Laruelle fixates instead on the simple receptiveness to light generic to all photography. Yet receptiveness does not mean representability or indexicality. That would revert photography back to philosophy. Instead Laruelle radicalizes photic receptiveness as such, focusing on the non-standard or immanent nature of the photographic image.

Rather than a return to phenomenology's notion of being in the world, Laruelle proposes what he calls "being-in-photo." By this Laruelle means the aspect of the photograph that remains radically immanent to itself. Such an aspect produces a kind of objectivity without representation, a radical objectivity, "[an] objectivity so radical that it is perhaps no longer an alienation; so horizontal that it loses all intentionality; this thought so blind that it sees perfectly clearly in itself; this semblance so extended that it is no longer an imitation, a tracing, an emanation, a 'representation' of what is photographed."[20]

But the photograph is not the only thing recast as non-standard immanence. So too the photographer, a philosopher who thinks photographically about the world. Laruelle elaborates this aspect through what he calls the photographer's stance *[posture]*:

> "Stance"—this word means: to be rooted in oneself, to be held within one's own immanence, to be at one's station rather than in a position relative to the "motif." If there is a photographic thinking, it is first and foremost of the order of a test of one's naive self rather than of the decision, of auto-impression rather than of expression, of the self-inherence of the body rather than of being-in-the-World. A thinking that is rooted *in* rather than *upon* a corporeal base.[21]

Here is an illustration of Laruelle's theory of utopia. Yet he inverts the conventional wisdom on utopia as a non-place apart from this world. Laruelle's utopia is a non-world, yet a non-world entirely rooted in the present. Laruelle's non-world is, in fact, entirely real. Revealing his gnostic tendencies, Laruelle's non-standard real is rooted *in* matter, even if the standard world already lays claim to that same space. The non-standard method simply asserts the real in parallel with the world. Using the terminology from chapter 3 on digitality, the utopian real is a *parallelism*.

In Laruelle the aesthetic stance is the same as the utopian stance. In the most prosaic sense, non-philosophy describes a kind of non-place where conventional rules seem not to apply. To the layman, the non-philosopher appears to use complex hypotheses and counterintuitive principles in order to journey to the shores of another universe. Yet that doesn't quite capture it. As Laruelle says, *insufficiency* is absolutely crucial to utopia: "We are not saying one has to live according to a well-formed utopia. . . . Our solution lies within an insufficient or negative utopia."[22] The point is not to construct bigger and better castles in the sky, transcendental and sufficient for all. Rather, utopia is always finite, generic, immanent, and real.

But non-philosophy is utopian in a more rigorous sense as well, because the structure of the human stance itself is the structure of utopia. Utopia forms a unilateral duality with human imagination; our thinking is not correlated with the world but is a direct clone of the real. This begins to resemble a kind of science fiction, a fiction philosophy in which the human stance is rethought in terms of rigorous scientific axioms.

It makes sense, then, that Laruelle would call himself a science fiction philosopher.[23]

Drawing music. Yet even with these discussions of light and photography as prologue, Laruelle's aesthetics remains elusive. So before moving on to some more general claims about realism and immanence I address Laruelle's two essays on the little-known Hungarian artist August von Briesen, an emigre to Paris who worked primarily in painting, illustration, and pencil drawing.[24] Von Briesen is a particularly interesting case, because, despite being relatively obscure, he attracted the pen of a number of other prominent thinkers in addition to Laruelle, including Michel Henry, who wrote a long essay on von Briesen prior to undertaking his important book on Kandinsky, and Marcelin Pleynet, the influential critic and author involved for many years with the journals *Tel Quel* and *L'Infini*.[25] The analysis of von Briesen further illustrates how Laruelle is essentially a thinker of utopia, and that the best way to understand Laruelle's aesthetics, and indeed his larger non-standard method, is as a theory of utopia.

The portion of von Briesen's corpus that interests us here is a series of pencil drawings devoted to music (see August von Briesen, *Drawing of Mozart's Piano Concerto No. 22,* the frontispiece of this chapter). Von Briesen's pencil drawings give graphical form to musical sounds. He had been drawing music his whole life, in fact, the myth holding that, at the age of seven during a musical dictation session, the young von Briesen "refused to transcribe the sound into notes, and transposed them instead into abstract drawings."[26]

As an adult in Paris, von Briesen had a habit of attending classical music recitals, and he was known to be a devotee of the Théâtre des Champs Elysées. But shunning a comfortable seat in the audience, he would crouch deep in the orchestra pit, amidst the musicians, frantically drawing the music that engulfed him. By 1980 he was attending approximately two hundred concerts per year, drawing passionately. He made so many drawings of music that it would have been impossible to keep them all. "For example in 1980 he only saved about 2,000 drawings out of the 10,000 drawings that he made."[27] He drew images of Gustav Mahler's *Symphony No. 5,* Prokofiev's *Romeo and Juliet,* Beethoven's *Diabelli Variations,* and many other works of music, both classical and modern.

The drawings were typically made on small pieces of paper at approximately fifteen inches square.[28] Using a pencil on plain white paper, von Briesen would inscribe the page with a series of lines, dashes, points, and other markings displaying a wide variation in length, line width, orientation, and curvature. Sometimes the repetition of hatch marks create a uniform texture, other times a swelling wisp of line overwhelms the page like a cloud.

Von Briesen was a "crucified listener," in the words of Henry; as a youngster during World War II he had been separated from his parents, and during the Soviet occupation had known "all the terrors of existence."[29] For Henry, von Briesen's drawings were not so much renderings of music, but *portraits,* self-portraits that bring to light "a certain kind of suffering."[30] As von Briesen himself admitted, "I draw my own suffering"—in fact he considered all art to originate from suffering: "90% suffering and 10% joy. *No, 10% is too much, 1%!*"[31]

Because the music possessed him so thoroughly, von Briesen never simply drew with one hand, but with both hands at once. As Laruelle describes it, "The left hand acts as a kind of device with two feet that glides over the paper, giving direction, and above all changes in direction, to the other hand."[32] At the same time the right hand, the writing hand, acts like the "point at the end of a cone," funneling and focusing the music from out of the air:

It's this strange device (the page, the two hands with their different roles, lengthened by pencils, the fingers with an extended power) that captures and immediately redistributes the surrounding forces that are both musical and pictorial, or rather neither entirely musical nor entirely pictorial. A complex device, it registers variations more than things, different line widths, different rhythm, the changing gradients of a curve rather than simply its contour.[33]

As Henry recounts, von Briesen would stare off into the distance or close his eyes entirely while drawing, "meaning that each graphical mark made on the paper is totally independent of the marks made around it— whether above or below, the marks are indifferent to their neighbors."[34]

In his analysis of the artist's drawings, Marcelin Pleynet compares von Briesen's method to the literary technique of automatic writing that itself had influenced surrealist and abstract expressionist painting. Yet at the same time Pleynet stresses that such an "automatic" method does not mean mere transcription. Von Briesen is not simply a conduit who hears music and then marks it down in notational form, like a secretary taking dictation in shorthand. Instead, von Briesen's drawings reveal "a common current of intelligence and sensibility" that Pleynet calls a "syncretism between drawing and music."[35]

Laruelle too described von Briesen's technique in terms of automatic inscription: "To put it in more exact language, we can say that the *automaton* is not lacking conscious thought, and certainly at times it can be extremely lucid, but its consciousness concentrates and focuses itself out into the moving points of the fingers and pencils. . . . The automaton is an explorer who is both blind and deaf."[36] The orchestra pit itself functions as a kind of black box, a music box for blackness, and von Briesen takes his seat *inside* the black box rather than poking and peering at the box from the outside.[37]

Nevertheless Pleynet's description of von Briesen's project in terms of what he calls "correspondences" would likely be too devoutly philosophical for Laruelle's taste. "There is no syncretism in this art work," Laruelle argues, contradicting Pleynet, "only a prodigious synthetic force."[38] So although Laruelle uses the term *automatic,* he does not mean a kind of neosurrealist technique in which the hand and stylus become a conduit for subhuman flows. Rather he evokes the notion of automatic drawing as a way to suspend or collapse the notion, borrowed from phenomenology, of the perceptual distance between artist and object. "Von Briesen wants to cancel the *distance* entailed in consciousness or reflection, that is, any kind of hesitation or imprecision that might insinuate itself between the music and its rearticulation in drawing."[39] This is where the seer and the blind man fuse in common: neither see mere reality, but both have a direct sense of the real.

The placement of the listener is thus of utmost importance for von Briesen. Both Laruelle and Henry comment on it. Von Briesen locates himself in the orchestra pit, but his placing, as a listener and as an artist, is more complicated than simply breaking the fourth wall or trying to merge with the musicians themselves. Collapsing the distance between artist and object, or between the eye and the hand, means that the normal focal orientation of art will also necessarily change. The frame of the page ceases to be a window or a door, but rather "an infinite depth, a galactic expanse" that obeys new laws of depth, relation, and spatiality.[40] The key is found in the gesture of drawing itself, or what Laruelle calls the "registration" of a line:

> To draw is no longer to follow the finite outline of a thing or the infinite curve of an Idea that resists its own manifestation. To draw is merely a *registration:* like a seismograph scratching out its uncountable jolts and undulations, or like an encephalogram torn up into a kaleidoscope of little pieces. . . . To register means to manifest as a whole, with the expectation that it would be *without remainder,* the real itself, in this case music.[41]

As an aesthetic practice, automatic registration is not passive or mechanical; the simile of the seismograph here is not meant to evoke a passive, merely technical transcription of a signal coming from somewhere else. Von Briesen is not a translator or chronicler of the world around him. Registration means that the sufficient potency of the *world* is suspended, not that of the artist (someone who never had any such potency to begin with).

Laruelle doesn't much deploy the non-philosophical vocabulary in the essays on von Briesen because in 1985 he hadn't entirely invented it yet. But it would be keeping within the overall thrust of his analysis to describe a principle of sufficient art, in which the musical sources lay absolute claim to the inspiration of the listening artist. This is precisely what concerts halls are meant to do: evoke feeling, energy, fear, pity, and other aesthetic sensations in the listener. The art source is that thing that is sufficient in all instances to lay claim to the aesthetic relation. And of course the surrealists' automatic writing and its derivative techniques, from the repetitive and blank descriptions of the *nouveau roman* to the wanderings of psychogeography, are marching in lock step with the principle of sufficient art.[42]

Hence, the references to automatic registration must be understood not as a desubjectification or depotentialization of the artist, much less any kind of nihilist or modernist profanation of the human, but as *a diminution of the power of the aesthetic*. Registration à la seismograph is merely a kind of surface symptom for a combined music-drawing, fused in unilateral duality and neutered of its own philosophical potency.[43]

For Henry, the kind of abstraction evident in von Briesen has nothing to do with normal modes of abstract art, instead von Briesen displays a form of abstraction that, "issuing from the unrepresentable Ground of being without form, object, or world, is capable of reproducing a more universal structure of pathos."[44] Such a "generality" or "perfect indifference" of music is the key to von Briesen's special form of abstraction.[45]

But before continuing with von Briesen and fleshing out Laruelle's ambitions for the work, we pause for a moment to address the larger context of aesthetic theory. For there exists in Laruelle an original conception of art that withdraws from the standard model of aesthetics and posits a parallel logic of relation, perception, and sense.

Thesis XI: Laruelle's aesthetics are an aesthetics without representation, that is, an aesthetics of the immanent rather than the transcendental. If we are to consider aesthetics strictly from a theoretical point of view, the twentieth century witnessed a single great death and transformation, the *death of representation* and its transformation into a new form. Such a transformation has appeared under a number of different names in recent years: the end of critique, the crisis of mimesis, the posthermeneutic turn, the new materialism, or the end of representation.[46] But the seeds of this contemporary phenomenon were planted much earlier.

To be sure, the question of nonrepresentationalism in art (namely, abstraction) has been around for some time, yet the question of nonrepresentational aesthetics is something quite different. For even nonrepresentational art contains a sensual element that it reveals to a solicitous viewer, no matter whether that sensual element has a referent in the world. Abstraction can still be mimetic even if it isn't a picture of nature. Nonrepresentational aesthetics is something else altogether; it abandons the age-old question of reference (or indexicality, to use current parlance), but so too abandons the this-that structure of representation in its entirety, reducing aesthetics to a form of fused immanence.

From Plato's *hypomnemata* to McLuhan's extensions of man, much of aesthetic theory is essentially metaphysical. Much aesthetic theory tends to posit a baseline relation between an entity and its disclosure to another entity. Even the most sophisticated post-structuralist positions will agree on the essential relation, that entities will form relations of difference with other entities (self with other, integral entities with heterogenous entities, and so on). In short, much of aesthetic theory conforms to the media principle—the communicational is real and the real is communicational—and the descriptions of the standard model offered already in the opening chapters.

But starting in the 1970s and '80s a shift in aesthetic theory becomes evident, first with Deleuze but then quickly afterward with Henry and Laruelle. Something changed in France very rapidly in 1980 and 1981; by 1985 it was already complete. To be sure, immanence is a perennial theme in art theory.[47] And the relationship between realism and art is a complex topic in its own right, complicated by the many different meanings of the term *realism*.[48] But in general the prevailing aesthetic theory in France at the time was resolutely irreal, and tended to favor non-immanent epistemological frameworks such as hermeneutics, representation, referentiality, authenticity, and so on. Art theory from Sollers or Barthes or Debord was a question of semiotics, or textuality, or perhaps even the dialectic. The coin of the realm was interpretation, demystification, ideology, or spectacle. Art theory at the time was not a question of thermodynamic energy transfer, as it would be in Deleuze's realist aesthetics, or the depiction of the immanence of an internal spirit as in Henry, or the art of an insufficient and generic ontology of the one as in Laruelle.

Undoubtedly Deleuze accomplished it first in the early 1980s. References to art, literature, and aesthetics permeate nearly all of Deleuze's writings. Yet with his important 1975 collaboration with Guattari on the literature of Franz Kafka and then later with subsequent books published in the 1980s, Deleuze deals with aesthetic themes in a more systematic way, first with painting, then with cinema, and the Baroque. Henry and

Laruelle followed soon after: their respective essays on von Briesen (1985), Henry's book on Kandinsky in 1988,[49] and a trail of other pieces by Laruelle since the mid-1980s.

All of these writings have something in common: they all firmly reject what was then the reigning techniques of semiotic and post-structuralist interpretation of art in favor of an aesthetics rooted in immanence and strong nonrepresentationalism. Where many of their compatriots considered art an essentially epistemological pursuit, Deleuze, Laruelle, and Henry placed art firmly in the category of ontology. Where others haggled over the details of interpretation, meaning, and form, they took up the questions of expression, affect, and immanence.[50]

As we saw in the previous chapter, Heidegger poses a basic question for aesthetics. What is the relationship between hermeneutics and immanence? Many who have written on Heidegger have explicitly or implicitly taken a position on these two terms. There are those who claim adamantly that Heidegger is the consummate thinker of hermeneutics, for in his version of phenomenology we are continually grappling with a world that is only partially knowable at best, continually withdrawing from our being, remaining forever at a distance, a cryptographic world that is only tolerable through a kind of mystical submission to its sublimity. And, in many ways, this is the prevailing view. Yet there are others who champion the poetic Heidegger and hold him aloft as proof of an immediate relationship to truth. This is Heidegger as a philosopher of sincerity and authenticity, the romantic Heidegger who places humankind at the center of a world and asks it to stretch out its arms in order to *remain within* the world. Indeed part of the appeal of reading Heidegger, and a partial explanation for his enormous legacy, is due to the fact that he does not clearly adjudicate the question of hermeneutics and immanence.

Yet the aesthetic question takes a different form in Deleuze. If Heidegger queries after the relationship between hermeneutics and immanence, Deleuze asks a different question: What is the relationship between immanence *and multiplicity?* In fact Deleuze considers both terms at the same time. There is the Deleuze of immanence as well as the Deleuze of multiplicity. For him the two components fit nicely together. Guided by the principle of univocity, Deleuze describes a world of pure multiplicity in which all multiplicities are equally immanent within nature. Thus there is no sender–receiver logic in Deleuze's theory of expression, only immanent transformations within a set of virtualities. Likewise there are no entities per se in Deleuze. But just as Whitehead spoke of "occasions," Deleuze describes specific gatherings of heterogeneous multiplicities, dubbed "assemblages," that occasion themselves as blips of singularity on an otherwise smooth plane.

So on the one hand Heidegger is forever locked in the heroic throes of hermeneutics, which, though ultimately shackled to the basic phenomenological contract, also cherish immanence as some sort of ideal (even if it be unattainable both practically and theoretically). But on the other hand Deleuze breaks definitively with the legacy of phenomenology, pursuing instead the great compromise between immanence and multiplicity, forging an alliance between univocity and difference.

In other words, the twentieth century offers two basic options for any aesthetic theory: either Heidegger or Deleuze, either aesthetics as representational correspondence or aesthetics as nonrepresentational expression. Henry and Laruelle appear in the shadow of Deleuze, in the shadow of the nonrepresentational night to which he introduced them.

Yet to pose the choice as that between Heidegger or Deleuze is not merely to evoke their respective aesthetic theories, or at least not entirely. Any Deleuzian will tell you that the books on cinema or painting are merely the most convenient volumes, but certainly not the first and last, for gaining an understanding of his philosophy of time, movement, and image. And likewise Heidegger's many writings on art only feed into his account of Being in general, an account of Being so "poetic" that one hears Hölderlin wafting between the lines of the most hard-nosed passages on pure ontology, perhaps even more so than the essays explicitly about art, such as "What Are Poets For?" or ". . . Poetically Man Dwells. . . ."[51]

Deleuze was not the first to consider the topic of immanence, of course, not even the first to think aesthetics as immanence. And neither Henry nor Laruelle was merely mimicking the course taken by Deleuze. The three do not agree on what form immanence should take. But they do agree that representation is bankrupt, that the transcendental must give way to immanence, that aesthetics must cease to ape the logic of metaphysics, that the universe is not digital at its core. Instead they suggest that aesthetics follow a more mundane logic. For Henry it is the internal logic of spirit. For Deleuze it is the productive capacity of matter. And for Laruelle it is the immanent and generic logic of the real.[52] Because of this, Deleuze, Henry, and Laruelle are the three key theorists of aesthetic immanence today.

Still, Deleuze does not fully embrace immanence, at least judged against Laruelle's strict requirements. And on this point Laruelle refuses to compromise. Any form of immanence worth the name would have to reject difference entirely. Any true form of immanence would, in fact, be forged from identity rather than alterity, commonality rather than difference. This is the secret to Laruelle's nonrepresentational aesthetics. And to avoid confusing it with Deleuze, we call it by its proper name, a *nonstandard aesthetics*.

A realism for art: from weak immanence to strong immanence. Let's return now to von Briesen and generalize slightly from the particularities of gesture, tone, rhythm, or line and think more broadly about the principles necessary for a non-standard aesthetics. Although his language would change in later work, we cede now to Laruelle's own vocabulary from 1985, and consider three concepts: difference, reversibility, and truth.

¶ *Difference*. Although those already cognizant of Laruelle will likely be jarred or confused by it, Laruelle indeed uses the term *difference* in his description of von Briesen. "The notion of 'difference,'" Laruelle suggests, "allows us to evaluate in a precise way the originality, or rather the singularity, of von Briesen"; or, as he says later, "von Briesen is the inventor, in the philosophical and aesthetic domain, of what we will call *Musico-graphical Difference*."[53] Given Laruelle's treatment of the concept of difference in *Philosophies of Difference*, which was published only a year after the von Briesen essays, it seems confusing that he would speak here of difference in positive terms. A few points might elucidate this potential confusion. Beyond the rather banal biographical fact that this is still relatively early in the evolution of Laruelle's own non-philosophical vocabulary, we note the two very different lineages available in this period for the concept of difference: the Derridean difference and the Deleuzian difference. The two have almost nothing in common, and Laruelle is almost certainly exploring the latter, even if he is not entirely adopting it. Derrida's difference means supplement, deferral, or alterity. Deleuze's concept of difference—resolutely not Derridean, deconstructivist, or even post-structuralist—is "a pure difference . . . a concept of difference without negation."⁵⁴ Laruelle is picking up the trail from Deleuze, only extending it. Laruelle's difference means unilateral superposition of two fused terms, that is, difference as an "indivisible relation between two terms in which one—here drawing—is the relation itself."⁵⁵ Admittedly Laruelle's language is not yet fully honed in this early text, yet the same logic is evident here that would eventually be described in terms of cloning and unilateral duality. Drawing is the unilateral clone of a "suspended" or nonmimetic relation between drawing and music. Laruelle is therefore attempting to unilateralize difference in his essays on von Briesen, and—again perhaps parroting Deleuze at some level—to abduct it from its philosophical origins, calling difference "a veritable synthesis that is real and non-imaginary."⁵⁶

¶ *Reversibility/Irreversibility.* Von Briesen does not create an "equivalence" or "exchange" between music and graphical art, but "what certain contemporary thinkers influenced by Nietzsche refer to as a 'reversibility'—in this case between the musical and graphical."⁵⁷ Von Briesen's synthesis of music and drawing is not a synthesis in the Hegelian sense, a mutual encounter and cancelation of two antonyms elevated into a higher form. "This is not a making *equivalent* or a translation from one into the other"; rather, von Briesen shows that there is an "*irreducibility* of the graphical, and reciprocally too [an irreducibility of the musical]."⁵⁸ Thus, when allowed to be absolutely reversible to each other, music and drawing in fact become irreducible or *irreversible*. In other words, the secret to a non-standard conception of difference is found in the elimination of any kind of logic of exchange, correspondence, supplementarity, trace, or remainder. In his later writings, he ups the ante even further and, for what he quite permissively labels "reversibility" here, begins to speak more militantly in terms of irreversibility alone. But the two concepts, though ostensibly antonyms, should be understood in a similar sense: irreversibility is merely the more rigorous conception of what is here described as an endless reversibility. Within this kind of hyper-reversibility, representation's circuit of exchange—music represented *as* drawing, or drawing represented *as* music—is invalidated. The "strict reversibility" of music and drawing means, albeit somewhat counterintuitively, that the two elements are superimposed on each other and irreducible one to the other. So though in his later work Laruelle calls such logic an "irreversible duality," here in 1985 his language is still evolving and he speaks instead of a kind of suspended or metastable "reversibility." Whichever word, though, the point is ultimately the same.

❡ *Truth (as Fusion, Superposition, or Metastability).* "What is he drawing?" Laruelle asks of von Briesen—and the answer is simple: "Truth itself."[59] Von Briesen is looking for an aesthetic criteria of *truth*, not simply of technicity, resemblance, etc. "In the last instance, the object of art is truth."[60] But what does this mean? Although truth is not a particularly important category in Laruelle, as it is for, say, Heidegger or Badiou, the use of the term here signifies a finite or fused relation of pure immanence. In short, truth means the one. Using the logic of difference and reversibility, and extending and radicalizing them to an almost unidentifiable degree, an aesthetics of truth is one with a direct and immediate image of the real. Hence von Briesen's drawings are directly *in* the real of the music (because they are that musico-graphical relation itself, that *in* itself). "Von Briesen's secret goal is to show how every graphical phenomenon immediately represents a musical phenomenon, itself given over to another graphical phenomenon—and reciprocally as well."[61] This is a "suspension" or "short circuit" of the typical cycle of art in which composers create the music and listeners appreciate, experience, or interpret it. Von Briesen is not representing or signifying a truth that's in the music. Instead, von Briesen proves that there can be a "circularity of interpretation" in which drawing interprets music and music interprets drawing.[62] Thus the essence of the work resides in what Laruelle previously termed "*Musico-graphical Difference,* that is, in the tension of forces that are always *both* musical *and* graphical."[63] It's the reversibility of music and drawing that ensures that truth does not concentrate itself in one side or the other—because that would simply be a return to the classical conception of truth as philosophical sufficiency. Rather, through a logic of metastability or superposition, the truth of art is realized through the perpetual withdrawal or virtualization of truth.

Through such techniques—hyper-difference, irreversibility, and truth as superposition—we arrive at an image of Laruelle's non-standard aesthetics. His aesthetic theory is not so much the weak immanence of phenomenology or even the immanence of Deleuzianism, but a strong theory of immanence entirely devoid, at least according to Laruelle, of any kind of philosophical or metaphysical residue.

As such it deviates from the modern tradition of aesthetic theory, initiated by Kant and continuing through all manner of varying and often incompatible permutations, from romanticism and modernism to postmodernism and beyond. Von Briesen forces us to reconsider Kantian aesthetic theory, radicalizing and unilateralizing the classic notions of "judgment without concept" and "finality without end," formulations that seem practically non-philosophical already despite their metaphysical core. As Laruelle puts it,

> These kinds of romantic theories founded on imagination mark the beginning of the modern and nihilist degradation of art, that is, an aesthetic shift founded on the principle of a successive *privation* or *destruction* of the codes of representation in its classical sense: start with the free play of the imagination, an art "without concept," and end up with a kind of painting without painting, without canvas, without color, etc. . . . Von Briesen *reverses* kantian aesthetics; he only dispenses with the objects of perception and the techniques of classical representation, the "concept" and the "end," in order to reaffirm the ideal play of art as such—in other words (and to repeat) of truth as such.[64]

Von Briesen's drawings are, in this way, not exactly abstraction, nor are they modernist, and they certainly have nothing to do with the tradition of modern nihilism.[65] "Von Briesen's work a priori invalidates this entire critical and aesthetic apparatus."[66] Instead—and here the influence of Henry is clear—Laruelle describes a "recurrent force" that relies upon an "identity" or an "aesthetic *common sense,* a *faculty* of the imagination that limits or hampers radically the notorious 'free play' of representations."[67] This "common art" or "generic art" is the necessary outcome of a realist aesthetics. In fact, the only kind of art possible for non-standard philosophy would be a common (namely, generic) art.

In the wake of this discussion, and to summarize what is meant by a "realist," "immanent," or "non-standard" aesthetics, we might recapitulate a number of points culled from both this chapter and the previous one. First, light and the alternations of light and dark are central to the standard model of philosophy. Thus the previous chapter was devoted, in part, to an exploration of light and dark as immanent (not philosophical) phenomena. This led to the work of James Turrell and the notion

that light might be approached as such, not merely as a means of illumination or a vehicle for something else. A pure black—or alternately a
pure bright—produces a crypto- or non-standard ontology in which
nothing is philosophically revealed to anything else. Laruelle labels this
a "uchromia," a non-color or color utopia.

In both this chapter and the previous one we also discussed *photography* as a typical, albeit not special, non-standard art form. Like von
Briesen's own drawing technique, the photographic apparatus inscribes
the real automatically and "mechanically" and thus directly enacts the
unilateral duality of the one. This led to a discussion of von Briesen in
terms of an "aesthetics without representation," that is, a superposition
of music and drawing into a suspended or noncommunicative relation.
This is the last and most important detail of the entire discussion. The
"non-musical aspect of all music" is an a-synthetic relation between two
things, a relation without a synthesis.[68] Laruelle's aesthetics is based on
a unilateral logic in which two terms are subsumed not by a third, but
by the one term. In other words, the two terms *and the relation* are
immanent to the one term (with the second term as the unilateral clone
of the one). *This is, in essence, Laruelle's single greatest discovery as a
thinker: a new concept of relation that is neither dialectical nor differential;
a relation that is not digital.*[69]

**"There are no great utopian texts after the widespread introduction of
computers,"** Fredric Jameson remarked recently, "the last being Ernest
Callenbach's *Ecotopia* of 1975, where computers are not yet in service."[70]

1975 was a year of crisis. Saigon had fallen that spring, marking the
end of the war in Vietnam. A few years prior, OPEC's oil embargo had
sent price shocks around the world. The boom years of the 1950s and
'60s had given way to new economic crises by the early to mid-1970s.
And these crises would, in part, usher in a new economic regime that
would place the digital computer at the heart of value production.

It was the time of waning modernity. In Jameson's estimation, it was
the last time one might propose a kind of non-place apart from this
world, a utopia in which alternative axioms generated alternative worlds.
Indeed, the years since have been marked by a failure of imagination,
particularly among progressives, during which it has become impossible
to conceive of viable alternatives to the new cybernetic universe.

Today, instead of utopian texts,

we have the free-market deliria of cyberpunk, which assumes that capitalism is itself a kind of utopia of difference and variety. I think this failure of imagination on the left can be attributed to the assumption that
computers are enough to "take care" of totalization: that the well-nigh infinite complexities of production on a global scale, which the mind can
scarcely accommodate, are mysteriously . . . resolvable inside the computer's black box and thus no longer need to be dealt with conceptually
or representationally.[71]

The end of the utopian text thus signals for Jameson an end to representation. Or at least it indicates that representation, as complicated
or flawed as it might be under otherwise normal conditions, has been
interrupted and outsourced to another domain entirely (digitality and
computation).

Does Laruelle contradict Jameson's argument, the argument that no
great utopian texts exist after digital machines enter everyday life? Not
at all, it ratifies it all the more. Laruelle's work confirms a particular kind
of historical periodization: formerly existing as narrative or world or
image, utopia perished by the end of the 1970s; but, where it perished as
narrative, it was reborn as method. Such is the key to Laruelle's utopia-
nism. For him utopia is a technique, not a story or a world.

Utopia means simply to decline to participate in the philosophical
decision, *to decline the creation of worlds*. Counterintuitively then, Laruelle's refusal to create alternative worlds is what makes him a utopian
thinker, for his non-standard world is really a non-world—just as utopia
is defined as "non-place." To abstain from the philosophical decision is
to abstain from the world. And thus to discover the non-standard universe is to discover the non-place of utopia. (Or, using the parlance of
media aesthetics: the pre-1970s utopia is a *diegetic* or worldbound utopia,
but the Laruellean utopia is a *non-diegetic* or non-worldbound utopia.)

Cold comfort for Jameson however, because Laruelle's marginality
today—his recent exposure in the Anglophone world a burst of visibility
after thirty-plus years laboring in obscurity—is but further evidence of
the marginality of utopian thinking. Indeed the chief difficulty lies in the
fact that a "utopia of difference and variety" is no longer the goal, ever

since big business has become so adept at selling these many different and varying worlds. When difference enters the mode of production, as it has under post-Fordism, it is no longer possible to conceive of utopia as difference. Rather, the chief challenge for utopian thinking today is to force the generic condition in the here and now, a utopia not of another place, but of an impoverished and finite common real. Such is the task of the two remaining chapters.

Käthe Kollwitz, *Fraternal Love,* 1924. Copyright 2012 Artists Rights Society (ARS), New York / VG Bild-Kunst, Bonn. Image reproduced by permission of Staatliche Kunstsammlungen Dresden.

nine

Ethics

From sufficient subjectivity to insufficient personhood. Rekindling a theme that had occupied his writing for several years, Laruelle's recent book *A General Theory of the Victim* addresses the question of victims and victimhood, from slavery to the Holocaust, from the persecution of Christ on the cross to modern genocides and crimes against humanity.[1] In the book Laruelle elaborates a theory of the victim, rooting it in a generic humanity, with the ultimate goal of freeing the victim from a received dogma that would bind it within an endless persecution.

While admittedly dissimilar in both its method and outcomes, Laruelle's book treads the same terrain encountered in Hegel's famous discussion of the master–slave dialectic, or even Frantz Fanon's treatment of alterity and violence in *The Wretched of the Earth*. The central question is crime and punishment, the powerful and the powerless, violence and victimization. Yet Laruelle refuses to approach the question from the perspective of tyranny, in an attempt to defang the powerful or somehow to use the master's tools to bring down the master's house. Likewise he refuses to admit that the dialectic itself exists. Neither the powerful nor the power structure itself are determining for Laruelle.

As with the biblical prophecy that the meek shall inherit the earth, Laruelle instead argues that the true ethical position for humanity is something like a "generalized meek" or, in the language of this book, a generalized victim. We are all, therefore, at the level of real lived experience, fragile victims in the most generic sense. Such a discovery is the only way that, according to Laruelle, humanity will be able to exit the vicious circle of dialectical power relations (as with the master and slave locked in endless struggle) and enter into a condition of *generic human ethics*.[2]

The central villain of the book is the intellectual. Laruelle particularly scorns those media-savvy liberal intellectuals who hawk their punditry from talk show to newspaper column, all those talking heads who like to comment on the important matters of the day. These are intellectuals in the Sartrean mold, often labeled "engaged" or "committed" intellectuals. At times Laruelle also calls them "embedded" intellectuals, adopting the English word and leaving it untranslated in that way the French do when they want to firewall what they see as suspicious phenomena encroaching from overseas:

> Media-savvy, engaged or embedded intellectuals are those who use media and *invest themselves there*—from the oldest kinds (the book, printed media) right up to the most innovative and revolutionary, and under the sway of that most emblematic medium, philosophy itself—to expose the image of the victim, for example Voltaire and Zola, not simply the current fringe of tele-intellectuals who represent the low water mark. (83–84)

These kinds of intellectuals are odious to Laruelle because they participate in a division of the world, even as they claim to sympathize with the victims they represent. On the one hand, they participate in a division between (1) the real historical victim and (2) the abstract juridical concept of the "rights of man" (89). Intellectuals swoop into the divide, playing the role of middle management between these two layers, real and abstract. On the other hand, they endorse a kind of division of labor between victims and intellectuals. One party does the labor of suffering, while the other party carries the burden of going on television and talking about it.

The outcome is *overexposure*. "I call overrepresentation or overexposure the kind of visibility cast over victims by mediatic thought, itself deeply influenced by the spirit of philosophy" (92). Victims are overexposed when they are allowed to circulate purely as images, granted more media coverage in the bargain, to be sure, but ultimately silenced in that mute fixity that is the special signature of representation.

The larger critique of philosophy and digitality is clear: just as philosophy's problems ultimately stem from its reliance on a baseline representational structure, labeled here the "media principle," so too the victim is laundered through the endless numbing aftershocks of media representation. Rubbing salt in the wound, the victim is violated and abused a second time over when it is presented anew in the mass media.

Rather than pursuing a course of engagement with crises, or trying to become embedded with the victim, Laruelle suggests a slight deviation into a parallel world. Instead of engaged intellectuals, Laruelle proposes *generic intellectuals*. Such generic intellectuals "are put under the condition of humanity," he writes, "rather than put in service to the 'values' and 'ends' of philosophy" (84). Similar in spirit to Gramsci's concept of the organic intellectual, or Benjamin's call, in the influential essay "Author as Producer," for the intellectual to merge directly with the mode of production, Laruelle's generic intellectuals are put under the condition of humanity, meaning they fuse directly with mankind in the most general sense. These intellectuals are not "overdetermined" by any given set of specific political positions—pro-labor, pro-choice, or whatnot—but rather de-individuate into the insufficiency of generic conditions. They are in this sense "underdetermined" rather than overdetermined (84). Laruelle's is a radical particularity; all persons can only be understood "in person." There are no victims in the abstract, only you and me and everyone else.

Hence the most important coinage in the book, *the victim-in-person*. Television might show victimized individuals and survivors, overexposing and circulating their images endlessly. But if one should withdraw and cease to participate in these kinds of circuses, one will discover a nonrepresentational victim, the "real" victim if you will. This is the victim-in-person.

Where victims are individuated and tagged with certain classifications (via various biopolitical stigma, HIV status, citizenship status, and so on), the victim-in-person withdraws from such classification schemes, remaining generic, or "whatever it happens to be." Where victims are trapped by images and representation, the victim-in-person is firmly rooted in a lived reality. Where victims are overexposed, the victim-in-person is superpositioned. Not borne in repetition or synthesis, the victim-in-person arrives as an a-synthetic resurrection, what Laruelle elsewhere calls a "clone."

Being "in person," these victims are thus justly labeled "ordinary messiahs" by Laruelle (165). They bear what he calls "glorious bodies" (68). But this is not to romanticize victims by associating them with a sense of heroic glory or endowing them with the miraculous powers of a savior. He merely seeks to emphasis the curious logic that underpins them. Like the unimpeachable finality of messianic time or the fathomless gifts of heavenly glory, the victim, as the cornerstone of all humanity, announces a unidirectional and determining ultimatum: the meek shall inherit the earth.

The proper relation to the victim is thus never pity but compassion. Laruelle admits that his use of the word *compassion* might sound to some readers a bit old-fashioned if not patronizing. But the point is that under a regime of compassion, all suffer together equally. Hence Laruelle's is something of a "mystical Maoism," if such a thing is even possible: we are all generic victims determined by the insufficiency of the one. Although it might seem that those who are not victims are still patronizing the victim by showing compassion, or romanticizing the victim by seeking to emulate its glorious suffering, Laruelle insists that we are all always already victims, simply by virtue of being a part of generic humanity. The problem is thus not so much victimization itself, but the decision to digitize the world into victims and not, this being part and parcel of the philosophical gesture more generally.[3]

Although not present on every page, there are two key sparring partners lurking deep in the text: Levinas for his work on ethics, and Badiou for his theory of the event. Laruelle is notoriously cagey about acknowledging influence; he typically fends off even the closest potential allies. (As we have seen, Henry is perhaps the closest, and although Deleuze is also close, his very nearness presents a grave threat that must be subdued.) Laruelle considers Levinas an important philosopher of ethics and cites him without prejudice. Yet in Laruelle's view, Levinas ultimately imports victimhood into philosophy and in so doing founders there.

Badiou, however, earns little felicitation from Laruelle. Badiou seems to haunt Laruelle's recent writings more than other figures, to vivid effect of course in *Anti-Badiou*, but also in *Non-standard Philosophy* and here in the book on victims. For Laruelle, Badiou represents all that is wrong with philosophy. Where Badiou argues for a voluntarist fidelity to the event, Laruelle sees the event as a generic resurrection of the one. Where

Badiou thinks in terms of dialectics, Laruelle thinks in terms of super-position—a term that Laruelle freely and unapologetically borrows from the world of quantum mechanics, much to the chagrin of those who view such a move as dilettantish and pseudo-scientific.

In confronting him directly, Laruelle pokes fun at Badiou's powerful triad of body-language-truth, stated perhaps most clearly in the opening pages of *Logics of Worlds:* there are only bodies and languages, *except that there are truths.*[4] Laruelle swaps in two different terms, *lived experience* and *algebra* for Badiou's opening pair (*bodies* and *languages*). That is to say, the real lived experience of bodies, which Laruelle prefers to call "persons," or people as they are experienced "in person," and the mathematical language of formulae and identity known as algebra. But then, true to form, Laruelle refuses to synthesize his two terms dialectically as Badiou does. Instead he holds the two terms in superposition. And here the quantum mechanical vocabulary begins to pay off.[5]

But it is not simply the dialectic that Laruelle finds distasteful in Badiou. The two thinkers also differ on the question of the event. We need "a theory of the event that leans toward quantum theory," Laruelle asserts, "by way of the generic" (153). With this Laruelle means that the event should be understood more as the withholding of decision rather than the realization of it.

Subjects are not so much individuals with wills who, through their own courage to act, convert themselves, and in so doing further define themselves in relation to truth. On the contrary, the concept of "subject" is precisely the problem. The point is not to increase the resolution of the subject by adding more definitional predicates—I am militant, I am freedom fighter, I am lover, I am subject to truth—but rather to de-individuate the subject, again using the concept of superposition or suspension of definition, toward a condition of generic being. (Although Laruelle seems to overlook how important the generic is in Badiou's own project.) What results are no longer subjects but *persons,* which taken together form not so much a mass or a nation but *humanity.*[6]

Perhaps the best way to understand the difference between Badiou and Laruelle is to consider how the Bible and Christianity figure in their work. Badiou has famously relied on Paul and the road to Damascus, the biblical story of revelation and conversion. The story of Paul's conversion fits Badiou's political theory because it represents a subject who experiences an event, the vision of Jesus, and whose life is decisively changed in allegiance to that event. As was discussed in chapter 4, Badiou's theory of the event requires trenchant decisions made by subjects.

Laruelle's theory of the event, however, could not be more different. Instead of rooting the event in a particular time, bound to a particular subject, Laruelle removes the event from temporal and spatial particularities, making it both radically archaic and ultimately final (the two temporal conditions that Laruelle enigmatically labels "before-the-first" and "in-the-last-instance").

Christ therefore, not Paul, takes center stage for Laruelle. For in the resurrection of Christ Laruelle sees a type of event that is not dialectical and not bound to the singular trenchant decisions of subjects. In this way resurrection, not conversion, is the driving force behind Laruelle's theory of the event. Resurrection, not conversion, is how Laruelle's political theory differs from that of Badiou.[7]

Compared to the I-can-change-the-world enthusiasm of the Badiousian militant, Laruelle again appears a bit old-fashioned, even reactionary. For Laruelle, conversion is too incorrigibly philosophical, and the convert too hopelessly narcissistic. That most emblematic philosophical event, to "know thyself," is merely another kind of conversion, another road to Damascus. Both philosophy and religion rely too much on the lightning strike of revelation. "A material formalism modeled after quantum theory, not a philosophical materialism, is the best way to think the event," Laruelle asserts by way of an alternative. "Christ and his resurrection are not so much a miraculous event as a non-standard or non-theological one" (154).

Laruelle's primary ethical task is to view humanity as indivisible without resorting to essence or nature. The only way to do this, he suggests, is to radicalize the generic condition of humanity. The point is not to universalize the liberal subject, as with the "We are the world" conceits of Western privilege, but rather to do the opposite, to underdetermine persons rather than overdetermine them, to admit to a baseline insufficiency of personhood. Or as he says in a floating epigraph that launches the book, *Why shouldn't the victim be the cornerstone of humanity?*

What do *sufficiency* and *insufficiency* mean in Laruelle? What does it mean when he evokes the specter of the principle of sufficient philosophy, the principle of sufficient economy, or the principle of sufficient mathematics? All these principles of sufficient *x* act to invalidate the sufficiency of the structure they describe, whether philosophy, the economy, mathematics, or otherwise. Together they act like a generalized death-of-the-Father in that they render all power insufficient. In the wake of such a regime of insufficiency, nothing can make a claim anymore. Nothing can have authority over anything else.

On the one hand we might label them his "Anti-Fascist Principles," effecting a general form of pacifism. In essence they instruct us not to fall in love with power and not to assume command over the world. But on the other hand these are all the many "Principles of the Meek." They make philosophy ineffective and insufficient. They neuter the authority of mathematics or aesthetics or economics.

If Badiou's universe follows the law of the generalized militant, where lovers and artists are all militants for truth, Laruelle's universe follows the law of the generalized meek, where nothing has the intention or capacity to assert itself over anything or anyone else. Such meekness is attractive for Laruelle because it indicates an ethics. But the generalized militant is attractive to Badiou for a different reason: it indicates a politics.

Thesis XII. As digitization, the political is two. It forces a change from analog to digital, or from a generic continuum into a series of points. Before continuing further with the ethical, consider the realm of the political and the way in which politics is a kind of digitization or multiplication of points. Or in shorthand: *Whereas being is one, politics is two.*

Using what he calls the theory of points, Badiou shows how "atonal" or otherwise lifeless worlds, devoid of contour or intensity, may be forced into alignment around two points.[8] Newly demarcated by such points, the world loses its lifelessness and becomes tense or taut. The introduction of points is crucial in the transformation of the world. Lifeless worlds are "devoid of points," he warns. "Without a point, there's no truth, nothing but objects, nothing but bodies and languages. . . . Everything is organized and everything is guaranteed."[9]

In an echo of Baudrillard's "perfect crime," Badiou bemoans the planning and preemption endemic to contemporary atonal worlds. Given that everything is organized and guaranteed, no tension may appear, no unforeseen events, indeed no events whatsoever. Badiou's term for such worlds is "democratic materialism." These worlds have no life. They contain nothing but bodies and languages, nothing but objects and relations, nothing but matter and form. They are atonal in that they have no musical pitch, no features to their political landscape. Badiou's "point" is similar to Heidegger's "project"; human experience projects forward, Heidegger says, and a human being should have a project in order to realize its special mode of being. Likewise, for Badiou, life must have points. Life seeks taut anchors on which to moor itself, like a ship in harbor that pulls on its moorage points, or when the ship sets to sea and navigates according to the celestial points.

Through these points and projects, formerly lifeless relations are re-invigorated with value. When something is at stake, the atonal graph becomes a directed graph, bound by vectors of ethico-moral force. Each pair of points is also a potential decision, each a potential digitization. Each pair of points, each either/or decision, represents a possible leap forward for the voluntarist will. With points there are no half-choices, no incremental slippages side to side along the continuum of mediocrity.

With Badiou as guide, the principle of sufficient reason could be rewritten for the twenty-first century as *for every point, a vector*. Every point is a point within a vector field of forces. To be placed into a world is to be subject to the push and pull of force. Thus to exist in the world means to be located along a force differential, like a ball placed at the top of an inclined plane. The forces are not irresistible, certainly, but nevertheless they exist and are entailed in the very definition of the point.

Recall Deleuze's singularities and intensities, they sit at the center of a field of differentials. There can be no intensities without a continuous dissipation of intensity surrounding them. There can be no high-pressure zones without a lessening of pressure radiating away. Likewise, because Badiou's points are defined in contradistinction to the flat lifelessness of atonal existence, they require a kind of airless gap separating them. This gap is the vector, and all points require them. Otherwise they would be planes rather than points, lines rather than locations. Thus for every point, a vector.

And so Badiou's theory of points means that there are two kinds of worlds: those that adhere to the principle of sufficient reason and those that do not. A tense world is one that has reason, that has cause. A flat world is without reason, without cause. Or using today's terminology, tense worlds are vectored, and flat worlds are without vector.

Yet Badiou and Deleuze are ultimately incompatible regarding the contours of the universe. While Badiou's points are monumental and heroic, the will of the lover or poet forcing a decision and adhering to it, Deleuze's intensifications are ubiquitous but mundane. If the emblematic Badiousian vector is the vector of revolt, the emblematic Deleuzian vector is the vector of cell mitosis. Badiousian subjects are subjects to truth, but Deleuzian subjects may include trees, mice, and rocks. The difference between Badiou and Deleuze thus appears in stark distinction. They represent two fundamentally different tendencies within the ethico-political universe.

Badiou or Deleuze, principle or process. Either the militant adhesion to truth, forged from a decision that deviates from the state of the situation, or the ongoing, inductive, recombination of forces, oblivious to absolute law or moral code. Either an *aligned* world injecting tonality into otherwise lifeless landscapes, or an *open* world escaping the many micro-fascisms of the universe. In short, either Badiou's politics of the digital, or Deleuze's ethics of the analog. Either a politics of distinction, or an ethics of indistinction.

In years past one might have called Badiou's worlds "moral" and "immoral" rather than taut and atonal, but such terms have fallen out of fashion today. Indeed the political is the realm of morality and law, for the political is the realm in which actors either follow norms or willfully deviate from them. The realms of politics, law, and morality all follow the two-structure because they all require an elemental distinction. To engage politically, legalistically, or morally means to digitize a landscape, to divide the landscape into two. To think politically, legalistically, or morally means to organize continuity into two or more poles, thereby facilitating judgment. This is why politics often boils down to the brute question of friend or foe, who is with us and who is against us.[10] Likewise, both legal and moral law follow the two-structure in that they differentiate between those who follow the law and those who do not.

Seen in this way, politics is digitization because it forces a change from a generic continuum into a series of points. But which points exactly, and who chooses them? What happens if the points are selected in such a way as to keep the world lifeless? Can there be a politics of selection, in which the identification of points becomes contested? Is choosing coffee or tea a true digitization? Is the American political party system a legitimate digitization?

Indeed, point selection is highly contested, particularly in cases when the points themselves are viewed to be as lifeless and atonal as the flat landscape from which they deviate. Because the selection of points is contested, the political is often concerned with the question of what constitutes *authentic* digitization, in essence superimposing on top of the old pair of points a new pair of points (authenticity and inauthenticity). This is why the political so frequently arrives in the form of a romanticism of the heart or a fascism of the body. A secondary digitization intervenes to arbitrate the failings of a previous digitization.

Philosophy divides and science unites.[11] The adage is from Althusser, but Laruelle would agree wholeheartedly. And in light of the previous, an alliance starts to emerge between, on the one hand, philosophy, politics, and division, and on the other, science, ethics, and unification. In the most elemental sense, *all philosophy is a form of political philosophy, just as all science is a form of ethical science.* Or, to state it in softer terms, a politics will tend toward a philosophy, while an ethics will tend toward a science. The reason is that politics requires decision, which is the basic condition of philosophy, while ethics requires indecision, which is the basic condition of science.

Thesis XIII. As virtualization, the ethical is one. It forces a change from digital to analog, or from distinction to indistinction. The political is two. But the ethical is one. To become political means to think the landscape in terms of twos, in terms of the two-function—either/or, fight or relent, accept or reject. But to remain ethical means the inclusion of the excluded into a single fabric, to withdraw from the tumult of judgment and to dwell within the scene of indivision. If the political is driven fundamentally by an inexplicable and overwhelming nausea, the ethical is the state in which no kind of nausea whatsoever can take hold. If the political aims to reveal the fundamental antagonisms of society, the ethical aims to unify human pathos under the banner of a common indistinction (see Käthe Kollwitz, *Fraternal Love,* the frontispiece of this chapter).

"What spectacular antagonisms conceal is the *unity of poverty,*" wrote Guy Debord.[12] Contra Badiou's theory of points, the ethical requires a withdrawal of points, an abdication of the force of law. Instead of a series of legal mechanisms, the ethical revolves around a single principle or hypothesis. This principle could be Debord's unity of poverty, or the principle of the common. It could be the Christian ethical prophecy that the meek shall inherit the earth, or the basic democratic ideal that those excluded from society ought to be included.

In any case, the ethical is a question of the withdrawal of the law. What replaces the law is not so much a new super-law, a new law of laws, but the absence of all mundane commandments in favor of a single principle of unification. For this reason the ethical is best understood as a kind of virtualization, because it withholds decision in favor of a superposition of indistinction. And this is why, while there are many possible forms of political organization, there is only one kind of ethical organization— communism—a truth promulgated by Jesus just as much as by Marx.

So ultimately the ethical means *indecision*. But this is not to laud the politics of apathy that plagues liberal democracies today, just as it destroyed the desire of the people under Stalinism. This is not a reactionary form of thought, like the reactionary pragmatism that resists points. Indecision shares nothing with the repugnant indecisiveness of nation-states and other global actors refusing to act on climate change, or Third World debt relief, or Mideast peace. Indecision shares nothing with that kind of cowardice and corruption, the worst kind of lifelessness, barely concealing a contempt for the world and those living within it.

Indecision, by contrast, refers to the withdrawal from decision. Indecision is the ultimate analog event. It integrates the two (the three, the multiple) as one, thereby obviating the need to cut in general—the word decision from *caedere* meaning "to cut." As radical non-cutting, indecision integrates entities as one, and it does so at the level of the generic facticity of being. This holds for humanity, but also for the generic facticity that binds the human together with chimp, mouse, or microbe. Indecision binds humanity together with massively macro events like climate change, as well as micro events like the intimate mutual recognition of self with other, or the acts of mercy, love, and sacrifice. Marx called it "species-being," but we might render the term even more indecisively as phylum-being, kingdom-being, or simply generic-being.

If the political is to roll the dice, the ethical is to shake the dice perpetually without rolling. To shake the dice means to suspend them in a state of indecision. While in mid-shake, dice express all their numbers at once; they may be one of any possible combinations. And as one of any, they are, in effect, all the numbers at the same time. Dice in mid-shake are, in Deleuzian language, the virtual, for they express the complete number space of the dice all at once. No discrete numbers have yet appeared; the numbers have not been digitized. Laruelle's word for this is *superposition*, the term he borrows from quantum theory. While in a state of superposition, discrete states superimpose and virtualize into each other, obviating their relative distinction. But once the dice land, a particular number is actualized from out of the virtuality of the number space.

To be ethical means to metastasize the real. As metastasis, the ethical means to think and act in terms of the total possibility space of the real. Never a question of deciding, dividing, or demonstrating one's allegiances, the ethical requires a recognition of the total, finite space of being as it pertains simultaneously and in parallel. The ethical is never a question of position, never a question of drawing a line in the sand, never a digitization. Rather, the threshold of the ethical is transgressed precisely at the moment when all positions merge into equality with themselves, and all lines are erased by the rising winds.

"The more I am anonymous, the more I am present." If the political ultimately entails self-interest, the ethical ultimately entails self-sacrifice. Acts of charity are thus ethical rather than political because they require indistinction of self and other. Such acts are rightly labeled selfless because they require a lessening of the self, a lessening of the point system that would polarize the world into I and thou. So a migration from politics to ethics requires a migration from self-interest to self-sacrifice, from the promotion of the self to a demotion of the self, from visibility to invisibility.

But does this automatically mean that the ethical subject is an evanescent subject? Does this mean that the ethical act is a monastic act bent on self-denial, even repression? How does the ethical life synchronize with theories of agency and empowerment? Is the ethical subject any less visible or less present than its political counterpart? What is the relationship between presence and visibility under the ethical regime?

According to some of the more well-trodden assumptions, presence and visibility correspond directly with each other. The more something is present, the more it is visible; the less present, the less visible. Following the phenomenologists, the presence of a thing is simply another way to speak about its appearing in the world. Early in *Being and Time,* Heidegger defines the phenomenon as that which shows itself.[13] The discourse of identity politics, in anything from Ellison's *Invisible Man* to Spivak's "Can the Subaltern Speak?" often concerns itself with the relative capacity or incapacity of certain subjects to achieve expressive visibility in the world, thereby realizing a greater and fuller presence.

But another current exists, too, from the opacity of queer theory with its interest in illegibility and "no future" to the obfuscatory and somewhat monastic mandate of recent activism, which might appear under the anonymous name of Anonymous, or which might carry only a singular cataclysmic demand, that of "having no demands."

"I need to become anonymous. In order to be present," write Tiqqun in their short text "How Is It to Be Done?" "*The more I am anonymous, the more I am present.*"[14] Curious at first, Tiqqun's claim nevertheless rings true. Invisibility and presence need not be mutually exclusive. One might imagine a scenario in which the greater the withdrawal from identification, the nearer the presence; the greater the withdrawal from the world system, the sweeter the experience.

Indeed, in a world in which informatic capture predominates, in which technologies of identification and profiling have saturated both the commercial sector, via genetics and information technology, and the government sector, via data mining or drone surveillance, it would make sense for presence to lodge itself ever more intimately within the cloak of invisibility. "From now on, to be perceived is to be defeated."[15] To be perceived is to be identified, and to be identified is to be removed from life.

But this is no longer a moral claim about authenticity. This is an *ethical* claim, a claim about virtualization not digitization. As Tiqqun shows, the ethical mode is never one of actualization, never an act of making specific, of grounding or locating or identifying. The ethical mode is a virtualization. If the political is a question of points, of introducing a hard distinction into a hitherto smooth field, the ethical reverses the logic: not point but curve, not distinction but indistinction.

If during the 1980s and 1990s much of Anglo American culture and philosophy was concerned, both temporally and critically, with the prefix of the *post-* (from postmodernism to postpunk and everything in between), today the new concern is the prefix of the *non-*, *in-*, or *un-* (for which Laruelle's non-philosophy is the most recent avatar). If the 1980s impulse was to pursue a logic of supersession, the "Hegel of history," today the logic is that of cancellation or invalidation, the "Hegel of negation," in which even the dialectic is negated and atrophied into oblivion.

Which is not to introduce a new set of points, a new political distinction between inauthentic capture and authentic resistance, between them and us. Just as Laruelle's non-philosophy is not a reflection on philosophy, just as non-philosophy is neither a supersession nor dialectical negation of philosophy, the ethical achieves its indistinction not by opposing being but rather by demilitarizing being, by standing down. The ethical atrophies the political distinction, it does not cultivate it. If the political derives its power from the provisional confrontations of "this" or "that" particularity, the ethical revels in the weak and finite, adhering to "the something" as an axiomatic principle. This is what it means to force a change from digital to analog. It means a shift from *my thing* to *something*.

Phenomenology teaches that the presence of an entity has to do with its appearing in a world. Once having appeared, the *self*—that special entity of mine, for as Heidegger writes, "Dasein is an entity which is in each case I myself; its Being is in each case mine"—may habituate itself to certain everyday activities, certain familiar ways of socializing and interacting with others.[16]

In Part IV of *Being and Time* Heidegger introduces a specific term to encompass this experience, the "they" *[Das Man]*. Through the they, Heidegger hoped to illustrate the impersonal singular pronoun, in other words, "*who* it is that Dasein is in its everydayness."[17] The English impersonal pronoun *one* might capture the sense of it. The they-self is the human subject at its most habituated or cliché. It is a fundamentally *inauthentic* mode of existence for Heidegger. "The Self of everyday Dasein is the *they-self,* which we distinguish from the *authentic Self.* . . . As they-self, the particular Dasein has been *dispersed* into the 'they', and first must find itself."[18] The they is Heidegger's way of understanding the socialization of people, and indeed the social sphere at large. Not exactly the realm of ideology, a term that would not entirely square with Heidegger's overall approach, the concept nevertheless comes close to identifying the social habituation of ideological forces.

Heidegger's is one way of thinking about impersonal experience. But there are other ways. Tiqqun, for one, magnifies and displaces the alienating tendency of the they. Tiqqun uses the French pronoun *on* (often capitalized as *ON* for extra effect) to refer to a somewhat ominous and impersonal social subject. If Heidegger's "they" is the impersonal quality that lives within the self, Tiqqun's "they" is a specific antagonist, the monster of the dehumanizing and alienating world system.

Yet apart from both Heidegger's "they" and Tiqqun's "they" exists another way of thinking about the impersonal. For in Tiqqun there is also the form-of-life, a term borrowed from Agamben, which Tiqqun defines in terms of the generic imperson who exists apart from the influences of Empire. Such are the two poles of Tiqqun's civil war: a permanent agitation contra all, and a generic identity undetermined by the world system. This begins to describe a kind of impersonal experience not reducible to phenomenology. Indeed, the ethical life lies not in a subject's practice within a worldly presence, but rather an imperson's withdrawal from being. Just as there is a phenomenological imperson, which was cast off as inauthentic or otherwise nefarious, there is also an anti-phenomenological imperson, who virtualizes into indistinction.

In other words, whereas presence and visibility have formerly been understood as linked and mutually beneficial, the analog indicates a form of atrophied or muted presence forged from invisibility. What was once a political or moral question concerning the relative authenticity or inauthenticity of presence is now a thoroughly ethical question concerning the absolute inclusion of the totality at its lowest level.

All thought is essentially pre-Socratic. Shall we deny it? Shall we deny that all thought, when left to evolve far enough, tends toward a single interpretive anchor? Whether it be Plato toward the moral yardstick of the truth and the good, Hegel toward the totality of spirit, Badiou toward the special role of mathematics, Derrida toward difference or supplementarity, Deleuze toward immanent multiplicity, or Laruelle toward the generic—in all these one element gains special favor above all others. One thing is extracted and conserved in order to redeem, or at least explain, the rest of the universe.[19]

In this way *all thought is essentially pre-Socratic* because it tends toward the form "All is water" or "All is flux."[20] Today the vocabulary has changed,

if not the form of rhetoric. Today we hear that "everything is a market," or "everything is capital." All thought is essentially pre-Socratic
because it bends in the direction of the one, if not actually then at least
asymptotically.

Isn't Kant's commitment to the self-clarification of knowledge a certain kind of dogma just like any other? Isn't the neoliberal promotion of
free markets the most brazen example of ideological manipulation? Even
the various attempts to escape the master signifier, from Aristotle's non-
totalizing catalogs of objects to pragmatism's skepticism toward overarching law, end up endorsing a more fundamental reality, the givenness
of physical phenomena.

Yet the most important question remains the pre-Socratic one. The
goal is not so much to arrive at a proposition of the form "All is x," in
which the selection of x is of paramount importance. The goal is not
so much fire, water, reason, capital, markets, or something else entirely.
The goal is not all is water but *water is all*. The goal is not all is fire but
fire is all. In short, the non-standard question is not "What is x?" but
"What is *all*?" What is the All? What is the one? What is the unary tendency of all being? And how can we withdraw from being in order to
discover the one behind the unary tendency?

Perhaps this is why so many have returned to immanent materialism
in the end, realizing how futile it is to flee fate by abandoning all intellectual anchors only to defend a more fundamental commitment. Given that
there seems to be little chance of escaping such unary tendencies, and
given that the selection of the master signifier is at best speculative (All is
spirit) and at worst cynical (All is capital), why not side with the generic?
Why not side with insufficiency? Not an inflated or macroscopic All,
fueled by transcendental essence, but a deflated insufficient one, discovered axiomatically via withdrawal from the philosophical decision.

This is precisely Laruelle's strategy. Indeed both Laruelle and Marx
end up at the same place, except that they differ on the question of sufficiency. In the Marxian tradition things like material history and the
social totality are sufficient because they are enough to decipher all political riddles, solve all social problems. Yet for Laruelle humanity is found
in the finite generic, not the totalities of the human condition or the
vast, almost infinite expanses of human history. Thus Laruelle's human is
labeled insufficient rather than sufficient.

Laruelle adheres only to a single axiom—call it dogma if you will—that the one is the generically immanent real. Everything else stems from this. Thus humanity, as the non-standard clone of the one, is immune to the principle of sufficiency. Because humanity is already a generic category, there can be no thing like a "principle of sufficient humanity," no thing like a "human decision" that must be unilateralized, as the philosophical decision was before it. The reason is that humanity is a generic category and is thus non-standard from the outset. Just like the real, Laruelle's generic humanity is *already the result of having withdrawn* from the philosophical decision. Humanity is already generic, and thus is already, in a very literal sense, one. If this be dogma, so be it. It is the weakest and most insufficient form of dogma hitherto known.

We advance then to the final chapter of the book by way of a final provocation: if we are all pre-Socratics in the last instance, if we all adhere to some kind of dogma in the form of "All is *x*," why not uphold the one scrap of dogma that happens to be ethical as well, *all is generic?*

Jonah Groeneboer, *Light Drawing 4 (for bruno)*, 2009. Two prisms on mirrored and white Plexiglass 1 × 1 × 1 ft. Reproduced courtesy of the artist. www.jonahgroeneboer.com.

ten

The Generic

The terms *analysis* and *synthesis* have been at play already in the previous chapters. They were used primarily to discuss digitality and the two moments of the dialectic, analysis as "one dividing in two" and synthesis as "two combining as one."

But the analytic/synthetic distinction is at best only partially applicable to Laruelle. As we have seen, the synthetic, defined by Kant as a judgment containing an additive predicate, is roundly refused by Laruelle. There are few concepts more antonymic to non-philosophy than synthesis. Laruelle endlessly stresses the nonsynthetic nature of the clone, or the irreversible logic of unilateral duality, or the monodirectional nature of determination-in-the-last-instance. The one does not enter into a synthesis with anything, and in fact Laruelle labels it "in-One" precisely because it is not synthesized into other things. The one is not hermeneutical because it does not open up onto any interpretation; it is not phenomenological because it does not reveal itself to a solicitous subject. The one cannot be socketed and linked up with anything else that might produce a synthesis.

If Deleuze and Guattari meditate on the deterritorializing potential of the face—because, as they explain, it is the part of the body with the most holes—Laruelle does something quite different, instead singing in praise of the nonconnectivity of the one, *in praise of the generic and radical territorialization of the one*. The one is, in this sense, a mode of hyper-territorialization in which nothing can pass or communicate. A *prophylactic* ontology will be the best name for it, just as much of philosophy proposes an endless series of *promiscuous* ontologies. Kant's synthetic judgments therefore remain resolutely within the standard model.

(And now the trap may be sprung: if Deleuze and Laruelle are the two great thinkers of immanence in our time, Deleuze's immanence requires a radical mixing of the multiple, while Laruelle's immanence requires a unilateral nonrelation of the one. Thus where Deleuze is promiscuous, Laruelle is prophylactic, either too much sex or not enough! Which leaves Badiou in the middle, the great thinker of holy matrimony: stay faithful.)

Yet the other term, the analytic, defined as a judgment that does not contain an additive predicate, is much more in keeping with the spirit of non-standard thinking. In fact, from a certain point of view, the Laruellean universe is an analytic universe through and through. If Kant sought to expand the window of the synthetic a priori as wide as possible, and thereby steal some of the thunder of Hume's own skepticism toward that domain, Laruelle seeks to expand the window of the analytic a priori as wide as possible. Indeed, just as Kant used synthetic a posteriori judgments to help generalize outward into the formal conditions of all cognition, Laruelle is using the conditions of cognition themselves (Kant's synthetic a priori, Heidegger's "foundations of metaphysics," or what Foucault would call the "conditions of possibility" for knowledge) and cloning them into transcendental axioms and a priori dualities.[1]

Rather than root thinking in difference, as philosophy does, Laruelle roots thinking in *identity*. And as Kant and others remind us, the two key poles of the analytic are identity ($n = n$) and contradiction ($n = {\sim}n$). The latter, contradiction, does not play much of a role in Laruelle's non-philosophy, but identity is crucial, practically coterminous with all of non-philosophy itself. This also indicates Laruelle's affinity with the kingdom of the analytic. (To be sure, *analysis,* defined as the fundamentally digital process of dissecting something into its constituent parts, is typically held at arm's length by Laruelle. Yet the realm of the *analytic* is attractive to him because it indicates a purely immanent and generic condition of the a priori.)

Likewise even the most cursory understanding of Laruelle's One-in-One indicates the analytic, albeit a more unilateralized and generic version of the analytic seen in Kant and others. One-in-One refers not to a condition of ontological difference (one/other) but of immanence and identity. The expression "One-in-One" contains no additive predicate and is thus analytical.

For these reasons, one might describe Laruelle's project as a particularly rigorous analytic formalism, a rigorous rationalism, albeit a gnostic or mystical rationalism. His is an eclipse of the world by the analytic a priori, in which the domain of the analytic a priori is splayed open as widely as possible. Laruelle is not so much inverting Kant as reshuffling his coordinates: instead of a certain subset of the human condition reserved for the analytic a priori, Laruelle wants to widen the analytic window to include domains incompatible with previous philosophy.

Generic insufficiency. But why are additive/synthetic and non-additive/analytic the main options? And is the analytic really the most appropriate way of conceiving Laruelle's anti-digitality? Indeed a number of thinkers, among them Badiou and Agamben, have demonstrated the limitations of the analytic-synthetic model. Instead of additive or non-additive predicates, such thinkers propose a different approach: a subtractive model in which predicates are subtracted from subjects, not added to them. Using concepts like the "generic" or the "whatever singularity," these writers have essentially proposed an alternative mode irreducible to either the synthetic or the analytic.[2]

Although the analytic may be provisionally helpful, I move beyond the analytic and conclude the book with what is arguably the most important single condition in Laruelle, the generic. The term has been used already throughout the book, but it is now possible to define it in greater detail. To take up the question directly, we now shift into a slightly more methodical register and outline three aspects of the generic: the tactics of the generic, the objective generic, and the subjective generic.

(1) Tactics of the generic refer to the various techniques used to attain generic conditions. Groups like Tiqqun or the Invisible Committee address tactics of invisibility, opacity, or anonymity. These suggest one possible approach, but there are other approaches as well. Hardt and Negri, for example, have written on what they call "exodus" and "desertion," both techniques allowing access to the generic. "Whereas in the disciplinary era *sabotage* was the fundamental notion of resistance, in the era of imperial control it may be *desertion*," write Hardt and Negri.[3] "Class struggle in the biopolitical context takes the form of exodus . . . [but] this

exodus does not necessarily mean going elsewhere. We can pursue a line of flight while staying right here."[4]

The flight of exodus is not so much a question of mobility through space, not so much a question of running and hiding. Rather, exodus indicates a withdrawal from modes of identification and representation. In this sense exodus is more a question of ontology than space or movement. Desertion and exodus mean a withdrawal from actualization, and hence a migration into superposition. Under the flight of exodus, things are put into a state of virtuality.

But such virtuality is merely a synonym for the generic. For when an entity withdraws into the generic it ceases to delimit itself by way of actual identification. Rather, the entity metastasizes into a virtual space: the shifting desert, the swarm of bees, or the darkness at the edge of town.

Similar in spirit to invisibility, opacity, and exodus, Badiou describes the tactics of the generic in terms of *subtraction*. According to him the world as it appears is indeed real. There is nothing illusory or fictitious about the state of things or the way in which certain things appear while others do not. Yet although such states are entirely within the realm of real existence, they bear no inherent truth for they have not yet been enchanted by an event. Peter Hallward explains it as follows:

> The subtractive approach understands that the operations that consolidate "reality"—representation, appearing, semblance: the state of the situation— are not simply external to the real as a cover that might be removed, but are organized as its ontologically irreducible repression. The state cannot be destroyed, but a truth can puncture its repression and suspend its domination.[5]

The generic is not achieved by way of adding something to the real, adding a true life on top of a false one, an authentic existence on top of a profane one. On the contrary, the generic is achieved by subtracting the many definitional predicates that exist within reality. "The being of a truth is an infinite set subtracted from every predicate in knowledge."[6] What this means is that the liberated subject is not someone who adds new identities, new qualities, new powers and affordances, like so many options bundled into the latest automobile. On the contrary, the subject is only liberated to the extent that it is liberated from such qualities and affordances. The subject of truth is the subject who can subtract itself from the given state of the situation, leaving being behind and adhering to the deviating vector of an event.

(2) The various tactics of the generic—including exodus, invisibility, and subtraction—disclose two alternating possibilities, not so much distinct from each other as alternating aspects of a single state of immanence. These are the *generic condition* (or *objective generic*) and the *generic person* (or *subjective generic*).

The objective generic is spatial, embedded into things and environments. Through the objective generic, things are allowed to disgorge their profiles and abdicate responsibility for their aspects and sensual interfaces.

Foucault was searching for the objective generic when he wrote about heterotopias in his fantastic essay "Of Other Spaces."[7] If he did not entirely find them, Foucault at least revealed the difference between homogenous infrastructure and heterogeneous infrastructure. Today we would call this a virtualization or a becoming-analog. In Foucault the digital infrastructure of house, hospital, school, and factory gives way to a continuous alternation of heterogeneous spaces, from graveyard, to museum, to fairground. It is a necessary first step toward the objective generic, which marks a continuation beyond the specificity of the analog into the generic immanence of space.

These generic spaces are nothing like Marc Augé's "non-places," the sites of banality and vacancy that proliferate under late capitalism.[8] The two could not be more different. Rather, the virtual or generic space is more like what Deleuze, in *Cinema 1,* calls the any-space-whatever *[espace quelconque],* a topic discussed previously in the context of analog and digital spatiality.[9] Deleuze's description of the leopard and the pool in Jacques Tourneur's *Cat People* (1942) captures it well. "In the swimming pool of *Cat People,* the attack is only seen on the shadows of the white wall," he writes.[10] The predator woman does not so much become a leopard, but become a space, a leopard-space which surrounds its prey from all possible vantages. Space itself, as it virtualizes, becomes predatory. Not a becoming-leopard but a virtual-leopard, generic to its locality.

In this sense, Deleuze's any-space-whatever inverts "non-places" or vacant spaces (those, for example, depicted at the end of Antonioni's *Eclipse*) into a metastable or virtual space. These spaces become whatever spaces despite their digital core. What began as a whateverness of point, a digital whateverness, inverts into a generic virtuality. The leopard is not there *in* the space, because it has metastasized across the entire room, visible only in the glint of light reflected on a wall, and audible only in the recursion of the echo of the screaming prey.

(3) The second alternation is the generic person or the subjective generic. If specific individuals are marked as persons, the subjective generic is impersonal, and hence bears the name of the *imperson*. As we have seen, the generic as imperson is absolutely central in the work of Badiou. Yet the subjective generic appears across a number of other thinkers as well. Levinas viewed the impersonal in both dialectical and phenomenological terms, as part of the alternations of expression and self-alienation that constitute the relationship between self and other. The person gestures outward toward the other, the imperson, and in so doing achieves some modicum of presence.[11] Likewise, Lyotard makes a distinction, albeit more severe, between the human and the inhuman in his book *The Inhuman: Reflections on Time*.[12] For Lyotard the inhuman is "an unclean non-world," a kind of "miserable and admirable indetermination" from which we are born and to which we must return in order to make sense of our being.[13]

Yet there is an alternative description of the imperson that is decidedly less melancholy. Beyond Badiou's generic, there are Deleuze's meditations on the neutral and the impersonal, and Laruelle's explication of the *Homme-en-personne,* which has been translated as Man-in-Person, but with some allowance for artistic license might now also be rendered as Impersonal-Man or Man-in-Imperson.

"Singularity is neutral," Deleuze wrote in *The Logic of Sense,* by which he meant that a singularity avoids both the universal and the particular.[14] A singularity is not defined by reference to some overarching principle or transcendental category, nor is it understood through attention to the specificities of its own mode of being. A singularity is merely an inflection point, neutral and impersonal. The plane of immanence is thus a plane of "impersonal and pre-individual" singularities.[15]

With his victim-in-person, Laruelle follows Deleuze's lead and uses the French *personne* to refer to an impersonal or generic person.[16] Laruelle uses Man-in-Person to refer to the immanent state of the human. In fact he sometimes writes it as Man-in-Man, mimicking the tautological structure of the term One-in-One, in order to underscore the importance of immanence.[17]

Casting. The three aspects of the generic—tactics, objective spaces, and impersonal subjects—can be unified under a single operation called "casting." Recall the story of the fruit buyer, which Heidegger retells from Hegel: "Someone wants to buy fruit in a store. He asks for fruit. He is offered apples and pears, he is offered peaches, cherries, grapes. But he rejects all that is offered. He absolutely wants to have fruit. What was offered to him in every instance *is* fruit and yet, it turns out, fruit cannot be bought."[18]

Casting is the act of converting peaches, cherries, grapes into fruit. It is possible to cast toward specificity. But what interests us here is the act of upcasting or casting "upward" toward the generic supernature. Upcasting means to cast an entity into a mode of being that is more generic than the current mode. Hence casting takes place when a more maximally definitional term is converted into a more minimally definitional term. Relatively speaking, a pear or an apple is more maximally definitional; fruit less so. Thus the apple can be cast into fruit. (Although the reverse is not true, generic fruit cannot be cast into this or that piece of fruit unless additional precautions are taken to ensure a proper outcome.)

The term *casting* is borrowed from computer programming languages whereby one data type (or in our parlance, one set of givens) is cast into another data type (another set of givens). In the computer context, casting is a conversion done on a type hierarchy, whereby the individuated object becomes less individuated. For the generic, the key issue is that any given a can only be cast into a given A if A is a parent of a. That is to say, a has to be a less generic version of A, thereby including all of A within it.

This is another way to illustrate the ethical nature of the generic, because an entity (or person) must abandon parts of the specificity of its own givenness, even if only by small increments. Thus, although a political claim might come in the form of "Woman's work should be recognized" or "Animals have rights," an ethical claim will always come in the form "There is no woman" or "Speciation must be dissolved," because the ethical claim cares less about accruing additional presence than about casting toward the generic.

The ethical and the political are complimentary, even if they remain distinct. Consider Deleuze and his central ontological claim concerning the univocity of being. Because it is on the side of the generic continuum, univocity itself *can never be political, only ethical.* But to fight and struggle on behalf of univocity, so that it may be elevated to the level of core ontology, as Deleuze did, is to fight a political fight. To argue for the univocity of being one must politically outmaneuver other possibilities (be they metaphysical dualism, dialectical negation, generic nihilism, or other possibilities not yet known). Likewise to assert the axiom of human rights is to make an ethical assertion, even if the fight for human rights remains a political fight. Where the political requires a recognition of the multiple, the ethical requires a return to the one. To be political requires the decision of distinction, but to be ethical requires the dissolution of distinction.

Against the backdrop of revolution and black Jacobin terror, the axiom in the Haitian Constitution that all citizens are black can only be understood as an ethical claim, not a political one—even if endless political battles had to be fought in the hopes of achieving it. So too the biblical prophecy that the meek shall inherit the earth is an ethical claim not a political one. And again the communist hypothesis is, ultimately, an ethical hypothesis, even if it might require political maneuvers of various kinds.

The ethical is never a law or a system of laws. The ethical pertains when the law is suspended in favor of a single finite and generic axiom. The ethical might assert axiomatically that all are equal. It might exhort the absolute inclusion of the excluded. Regardless, these are both ethical claims not political ones because they refuse to elect a single kind of subject over all others. To say all *men* are created equal, as in Greek democracy or in many modern democracies both before and after civil rights (where gender equality remains an unfinished project), is to assume a political commandment, for *male* is not a generic category and therefore cannot be an ingredient of any ethics. As Laruelle says, only *human*— or indeed trans-species categories like creature or entity—could possibly become a generic category. And only the generic can indicate the ethical.

But the ethical does not trump the political. It may be more generic, but it is not necessarily more important or more influential. In fact, just as digitization and virtualization are two sides of the same coin, the ethical and the political are fused together.

Man? Human? Creature? The designation of the generic category is often a political question. As during the civil rights struggles and the culture wars, there are real political struggles over what constitutes the elemental axis of subjugation, or indeed whether there exist elemental axes in the first place. These are essentially political struggles about ethical questions. Which category is most constitutive (politically) of social relations (ethically): queerness or class position? Ethnicity or gender? Or hybrids and coalitions formed across these categories: black feminism, queer communism, or proletarianism uniting the Global South? Such real political struggles determine what kinds of ethical claims are possible.

Consider the American founding fathers and the way in which a supposed generic category, white men of a certain standing, was used to make an ethical claim, that all men are created equal. In that instance the ethical category was insufficiently generic. It prompted political struggles over the status of the category itself, ultimately ensuring protection for nonwhites, women, and so on. The founding fathers were thus ethically progressive even as they were politically deficient. It was ethical to assert "all . . . equal," even if the claim was rooted in a political fallacy, that white men of a certain standing might adequately constitute the generic. For this reason the ethical should not trump the political. In fact, ethical claims by themselves can result in a kind of odious universalism if they are not mitigated and adjusted by real political struggle over the conditions of the generic.

Danger arises in direct proportion to assumptions of sufficiency. Difficulty comes when one category is assumed to be sufficient enough for all. To correct such dangers the generic category should be rigorously and regularly exposed to a *criterion of insufficiency*.

Have we assumed (falsely) that the liberal subject is sufficient for global prosperity? Have we assumed (falsely) that consumer choice is sufficient for healthy societies? Have we assumed (falsely) that cap-and-trade markets are sufficient to protect the environment? Such questions will indicate the failed sufficiency of these various categories (the liberal subject, consumer choice, markets). These various categories are *not insufficient enough* and thus can never act as the core of any ethical claim.

Although it indicates movement from greater to lesser specificity, the generic is still not a synonym for the total. To move in the direction of the generic does not mean to broaden the category to include more entities. The generic does not operate through an additive logic or even the metaphors of the melting pot or the big tent. The generic does not mean white men, plus women, plus people of color, plus another group, and plus another. Such additive logic will never arrive at the generic. The non-standard model does not operate via a sequential summation of digitality.

As both Laruelle and Badiou indicate, the generic operates through a logic of subtraction or withdrawal: people of color subtracted from structures of alterity; or the working class subtracted from alienated labor. This avoids the "We are the world" trap of today's bourgeois liberalism in which a single privileged subject extends its arms to embrace and encompass all the world's downtrodden. The point of the generic is not to elect a single so-called neutral type, such as the modern Western liberal democratic subject, and project it universally to all of humanity. The generic is not simply the white man's burden dressed up in new clothes. If such a reactionary strategy deserves classification, it would be classified under the rubric of the political, as certain groups struggle to gain a piece of the pie. But the point of the generic is to show that pies and their pieces are poor metaphors to begin with.

Indeed one point of criticism heard from time to time is that despite its good intentions the generic is ultimately a position of privilege, that in essence the generic is simply another name for the liberal theory of justice outlined in John Rawls, in which a very specific kind of subject is taken to be the model for all subjectivity. Indeed Rawls's "veil of ignorance" may resemble casting, and his "original position" may resemble generic indecision. Yet the two approaches are fundamentally incompatible, and it is worth explicitly debunking this misconception.

The Rawlsian subject follows what in chapter 2 was labeled the One Two of differential being. As outlined in the standard model, differential being acts as a form of transcendental affirmation in that it cultivates a single identity, a one, and projects that identity outward onto the entities of the world, the many twos existing as a reflection of the one. Rawlsian liberals follow a similar logic when they describe how individuals may project themselves into the role of the transcendental subject.

By contrast, the generic does not describe a community bound together by any transcendental core. Rather, the generic, if it describes a community at all, describes a community formed from all who have withdrawn from decision. This is sometimes described enigmatically as a commons of those who have nothing in common, or the part of no part.[19] The generic is not a position of privilege, far from it. In fact, the generic is something more akin to a generalized subaltern in that it dissolves all privilege and specificity into a finite and immanent generic real.

As gay, proletarian, Jew, or woman, we are not fleeced of our identities. Rather, we dis-individuate into a generic commonality of alterity. And in so doing we regain our very identities, *whatever they may be,* now unmarked by the infrastructures of representation that had hitherto delimited and defined them.

The Rawlsian liberal subject is a digital subject. It is sufficient; it requires the replication of a homogenous discrete substrate. Yet the generic person flees digitality by way of the analog, and ultimately flees the system of distinction entirely, both digital and analog. Thus there can be no commonality between Rawlsian justice and generic justice. The former is digital and the latter is not. The former follows the transcendental and the latter follows the immanent. The former is affirmative and the latter subtractive.

So the political is two and the ethical is one again. But in saying this, in saying that the ethical is one again, are we not guilty of romanticizing the return, indeed guilty of lapsing into a kind of poetic ontology? Are we not guilty of turning being into therapy, into an ontology of integrity? To say again is to project a narrative of loss and recovery. To say again is to make the story of being a story about norms and obligations. For to say again is to privilege the one as the normal condition that ought to be and to demote the world of decision as some profane, fallen existence.

The charge is legitimate, at least in one sense. If the goal is to avoid a poetic ontology then we should review the previous sections on the political, where all manner of nonpoetic schisms and alienations reign supreme. But if the goal is an ethics we will necessarily find ourselves in the landscape of the poetic or quasi-poetic. There is little hope in escaping it, because the ethical is by definition the flight from distinction and a return to immanence. The ethical is by definition the integration into the common.

Is it possible to integrate into the common without the lingering scent of poetic presence? Perhaps, after all, the one is just a number. But still, when fleeced of motivation and meaning, the one approaches a kind of nihilism, whether Deleuze's effervescent and affirmative nihilism of the One-All or Badiou's subtractive void of the Barred One. To counteract such tendencies the one should be re-enchanted with motivation and meaning.

This is why Deleuze never cleansed himself of a lingering vitalism when he could have easily done so. It is why Heidegger never cleansed himself of a certain mystical romanticism. Both thinkers understood that the ultimate danger lies in abandoning core ontological questions to the brute vicissitudes of formal abstraction. For the one is a number, but it is not just any number.

This is one way in which Badiou's ontology is inferior to that of both Deleuze and Heidegger, and why when Badiou mocks both his predecessors for having a poetic ontology his barbs are unconvincing, even cynical. In Badiou's estimation, the poetic ontologies of his predecessors belie a lingering ideology, romanticism in the case of Heidegger and vitalism in Deleuze. But the reverse is also true, because to suggest that ontology is hard-nosed math is the ultimate ideological trap; to superimpose a nihilistic scientism on top of ontology is the ultimate ideological conceit.

From cheating to forcing. A final question remains that will help adjudicate the debate. *How is it possible to differentiate between legitimate and illegitimate ethical or political actions?*

Recall Badiou and the old Maoist disputes around the maxims of "the one dividing in two" and "the two coming together as one." In the introduction to this book Badiou was quoted recounting that those who espouse the first maxim are declared leftists, while those endorsing the second are called rightists. But in the interim we have shown that it is possible to substitute the political for division and the ethical for fusion, because the political is defined via the division of digitality, while the ethical is defined via the virtualization of superposition.

Do the labels *leftist* and *rightist* still hold? Not exactly, because the structure of the debate needs to be reframed. The point is not to privilege division over fusion but to superimpose both terms onto a continuum of legitimacy and illegitimacy. For there may be legitimate digitality (progressive politics) and there may be illegitimate digitality (reactionary politics), just as there may be legitimate virtualization (progressive ethics) and illegitimate virtualization (reactionary ethics).

In order to explain what this means consider the concept of cheating. What does it mean to cheat today? For the present discussion, cheating may be defined as *a circumvention of necessary structure*. (As defined in the introduction, the principle of sufficient digitality states that for everything in the world there is a process of distinction appropriate to it; hence cheating can also be defined as a circumvention of sufficient digitality.) If the structure in question is a durational process, cheating refers to the circumvention of the necessary steps in the process, or a shorting of the necessary duration required for the process to gestate properly. If the structure in question is an entity, cheating refers to the circumvention of the necessary points required to define the entity. If the structure in question is a piece of software, cheating refers to the circumvention of normal physical limitations regarding access, executability, or logical performance.

Consider a day-to-day example: the way fruits and vegetables are harvested today under conditions of industrial farming. Bananas and other kinds of fruit naturally give off small quantities of ethylene gas, which act as a ripening agent. With such a long distance to travel and such a short window for ripeness, bananas grown for export are often culled from the tree while still green, then shipped or flown to air-tight warehouses filled with ethylene gas. The amount of gas is controlled in such a way as to induce the bananas to complete their ripening cycle just before arriving at market. Surrounded by gas the bananas ripen even while severed from the tree, in absence of rain, soil, sun, and all the temporal and physical conditions typically present during ripening.

A very practical solution, this is nevertheless cheating, as defined here, because it is a circumvention of a spatio-temporal structure, the banana's growth cycle. After skipping or circumventing the final steps of the cycle, impoverishing the development of the fruit, banana growers compensate by reinvigorating the fruit with excess gas on their way to market.

The banana conglomerates are notorious cheats when it comes to labor practices and treatment of the environment.[20] But here they also cheat nature, by cheating the bananas themselves and thereby cheating all of those who ingest them for sustenance.

Assuming it is possible to digitize the growth cycle of the banana, to isolate and itemize each element and step required to cultivate healthy fruit, modern industrial farming indeed cheats the cycle simply because it removes certain necessary elements and steps, combining some elements and substituting others.

This is not to say that all digitization is cheating, for there can be a faithful technique of digitization, one that respects all the necessary elements and steps. Yet the industrial banana falls short, and is thus accurately labeled "inauthentic" digitization.

Badiou's taut and atonal worlds help understand the difference between authentic and inauthentic digitization. The simple process of becoming-discrete is so common and general that it carries no specific valences. Digitization is an unaligned force, meaning it carries no necessary ethical or political allegiances. There may be authentic digitization just as there may be inauthentic digitization. There may be politically progressive digitization just as there may be politically reactionary digitization. One is taut, the other atonal.

Thus *legitimate digitization* is defined as the itemization or identification of a series of points without circumvention. An entity, process, or relation is defined as a series of points, following the normal procedure. For example, under the legitimate digitization of an entity, the entity is recast as a series of aspects of a phenomenon. Under the legitimate digitization of a process, the process is recast as a series of singularities on a continuum. Likewise under the legitimate digitization of a relation, the relation is recast as a series of functions collected within an interface.

All three of these new modalities—phenomenal aspect, continual singularity, and interface function—are the digital counterparts of what were previously nondigital realities. There is nothing horrific or profane about them. They are all instances of normal or legitimate digitization.

Virtualization can be thought in similar terms. *Legitimate virtualization* is defined as the disintegration of points into indistinction without circumvention. An entity, process, or relation is rendered insufficient according to the normal procedure. Thus entities, as indistinct or insufficient, withdraw into the generic or impersonal. Processes, as indistinct or insufficient, withdraw into exodus or desertion. Relations, as indistinct or insufficient, withdraw into disappearance or invisibility.

But what of the abnormal, dishonorable, or illegitimate? What of inauthentic digitization and inauthentic virtualization? Thesis XII asserts that politicization means digitization. Politicization means that a generic continuum is reorganized into a series of points. But the reverse is not necessarily true. Given a series of points, it is not necessarily true that political action or political consciousness will follow.

In order to broaden the discussion slightly, now consider the difference between cheating and forcing. What is forcing, and how is forcing different from cheating?

Badiou defines *forcing* as the transformation of a given situation by virtue of a hypothetical principle.[21] With forcing, a hidden impossibility within the situation becomes visible and possible. As Badiou says, consider the difference between two simple truth claims: *I love you,* and *I will always love you*. The first, *I love you,* is "a finite declaration, a subjective point, and a pure choice, but 'I will always love you' is a forcing and an anticipation. It forces a new bit of knowledge in the situation of love."[22] *I do* is a simple claim, a choice like any other. But *I will* is a vow, a forcing of the present situation into one specific future at the expense of all the others. In this way, forcing is a way of imposing decision onto an erstwhile murky scenario. *I will always*—the future is specified via the introduction of a trenchant, hypothetical principle.

Cheating and forcing thus run in opposite directions. If cheating means the circumvention of structure, forcing means the extrapolation of structure. Cheating tends to dull and deaden the facts of the situation (by truncating them), while forcing strengthens and extends the situation into one of several virtualities. Cheating enervates the subject, while forcing energizes it.

Armed with these two concepts, it is now possible to define digital cheating, digital forcing, virtual cheating, and virtual forcing. *Digital cheating* means a circumvention of the integrity of necessary points that make up an entity, process, or relation. The circumvention in question can be temporal, in which the duration between points becomes shorter; logical, in which the points move closer; or material, in which the points are impoverished or winnowed in number. As digital exploits or circumventions, this kind of cheating in essence "lowers the resolution" of the digitization process. It results in an impoverished digitality, a mode of encoding the real in which too much of reality falls through the cracks.

Although certain kinds of digital exploits have their own utility—for example peer-to-peer file sharing circumventing more traditional distribution channels—digital cheating on the whole produces problems, particularly under conditions in which the points themselves are corroded to such a degree as to be ineffective as points. Contemporary consumer society is nothing if not a vast proliferation of choice, as people are obliged to choose paper or plastic, choose Chevy or Ford, choose this or that. But in such scenarios the choice has been thoroughly cheated. The process of becoming-discrete has been circumvented, rendering its analytic power more or less useless. Such cheated digitalities are digital in name only.

By contrast, *digital forcing* means the introduction of structure within indecision. Similar to Badiou's theory of points, digital forcing is a kind of binarization in which a multiplicity of points are reduced to two discrete options. The goal is to isolate and focus two points over all the others. As such, digital forcing (point making) is most useful *when indistinction is the problem.*

For example, during the electoral process in most representational democracies, the relative indistinction between candidates is leveraged and abused by powerful interests in order to enforce the status quo. In such situations indistinction itself is the problem, and so digital forcing becomes absolutely crucial as subjects take principled stands on campaign financing, proliferate third parties, and so on. Such forced digitalities energize and enliven distinction, charting a path into the future.

Along the superpositional axis, *virtual cheating* means a circumvention of the generic univocity that makes up an entity, process, or relation. It replaces generic insufficiency with a form of false universality driven by the special interests of one or more participants. This kind of circumvention produces a universality-without-collectivity. Hence virtual cheating tends to form monocultures or totalities. It tends to produce a general dominant, a hegemony not of the one but of a single transcendental element.

Examples of virtual cheating include neoliberalism and protocol. In fact, in such cases the political and the ethical work together; politics, when it is subject to cheating, will often invert and become a cheated ethics. The forcing of decision, as when choice is repeated too frequently and evacuated of real meaning, results in a kind of numbing, continuous monotony of indecision. Likewise the monotony of a cheated ethics fosters a surrender mentality at the level of the political, the popular cynicisms of "Nothing I do really matters" or "There is no alternative."

Opposite this, *virtual forcing* means a rejuvenated withdrawal from distinction. Not so much a circumvention of points, virtual forcing means the rendering obsolete of all points whatsoever. As such it produces a generic ethics. Fleeing the stale air of universality-without-collectivity, virtual forcing breathes new life into its antonym, collectivity-without-universality, a dictatorship of insufficiency. It lives within the tautology of identity, where all are equal, where "no one is illegal."

Digital Cheating "Tweedledum and Tweedledee"	*Virtual Cheating* "There is no alternative"
Digital Forcing "Accept or reject"	*Virtual Forcing* "No one is illegal"

These four quadrants neatly summarize the two basic vectors under investigation: (1) the ethico-analog vector, which moves from a series of points to a generic continuum, that is, from distinction to indistinction; and (2) the politico-digital vector, which moves from a generic continuum to a series of points, or from indistinction to distinction.

In the language of media theory, the first vector lowers the resolution, changing from hot to cool, while the second raises the resolution, changing from cool to hot. The first follows a one-structure of immanence rooted in generic practice, the second a two-structure of relation rooted in criticism, antagonism, and wars of position.

The relationships between the quadrants can be read in different ways. At first glance the determining axis appears to be the relationship between the left and right sides of the table, between digitality and virtuality. Following such an interpretation, the politico-digital vector moves from right to left, rendering the formerly indistinct virtualities more distinct, while the ethico-analog vector moves from left to right, transforming decision into superposition.

But viewed from a different perspective, the determining axis is the relationship between the top and bottom of the table. From this perspective, cheating and forcing take precedence over digitality and virtuality, and the determining movement becomes the movement out of cheating

into forcing (regardless of whether it be digital forcing or virtual forcing). The vertical axis is similar to Badiou's atonal and taut worlds: atonal
worlds cheat themselves and everyone in them, but taut worlds are
worlds that can be forced.

Thesis XIV. The tendential fall in the rate of digitality. So which is it? Is
forcing always better than cheating? Is the virtual better than the digital?
Should we follow the generic immanence of the ethical life, or the representational power of the political life? Is it an immanence of direct coop-
eration, or a delegation of authority into structure? Shall we collapse into
the immediacy of direct democracy, or relinquish command to the par-
liamentarians, be they liberal democrats or progressive party stalwarts?
In short, is it anarchism or Leninism?

Even with the many lively debates across the social spectrum, few seem
willing to adopt one or the other completely. Even the most staunch par-
liamentarians will abandon representational structures in their private
lives. For who needs a vanguard to pass the salt? Likewise, the most committed anarchists struggle to explain how direct, cooperative democracy
can survive at the level of a city, or a territory, or a planet.

Nevertheless, a strange compromise has emerged in contemporary
life, a strange mythology has galvanized the imagination, something like
anarchism at home, Leninism abroad. What of our private lives are not, in
the last analysis, exercises of direct relations? What free-market evange-
list will return home and demand that market relations regulate exchange
between siblings or neighbors? (Which is not to suggest that such inter-
actions are not uncomplicated, or not unsullied by the power dynamics of
patriarchy, bigotry, or other symbolic hierarchies!) Are we all not bottom-
up communists in the last analysis?[23] Hence an "anarchism at home" in
which immediacy and contingent interaction hold sway.

And what of the macro social sphere is not, ultimately, a delegation
of powers? Is there not always a republicanism lurking at the end of
every town hall meeting? Is not every form of government secretly an
oligarchy? Who in the Occupy movement, or other sites of direct democracy, has not at some point thrown up his or her hands and longed for
a steering committee to streamline the fussy deliberations of the general assembly? What grassroots activist has not wished, at some point,
for a benevolent dictatorship to seize the reins and deliver us from this

profane existence? As Jo Freeman warned, we must beware the tyranny of structurelessness.[24] Hence a "Leninism abroad" in which power is exercised from afar and actions are taken on behalf of others.

Anarchism at home, Leninism abroad—both the left and the right seem united under this mythology, an immediacy of the person and a delegation of the social, a virtuality at home and a digitality abroad.

But what if things were different? Oh, the catastrophe if such conventions were upset or inverted. Could there be a Leninism of private life? An anarchism of the planet? Was this not what Deleuze and Guattari meant when they decried the micro-fascisms of daily life and sung hymns to the ethos of the Earth?

Indeed it is difficult to imagine a global anarchism without resorting to something like Deleuze's plane of immanence, a vast ocean of multiplicities expressing and virtualizing itself. And it is difficult to imagine a Leninism of private life except in terms of the same old depravities of subjectivity: repression, lack, coercion, a voluntarism of the soul. Even Badiou's militant subject, the subject-soldier, is not exactly for the faint of heart.

The "anarchism at home, Leninism abroad" mythology holds power over the imagination. Still, it would be wise to recognize it for what it is, a myth, and proceed toward a more nuanced analysis. Having outlined the various kinds of cheating and forcing, the point is not to condemn cheating as reactionary and praise forcing as progressive, denigrating the former in favor of the latter. Although cheating often produces negative outcomes, political cheating may be necessary for tactical reasons, the best example being tactical uses of exploits.[25] Likewise, although forcing often produces positive outcomes, there too exist significant drawbacks to forcing; for example, political forcing might obscure the nuances of a specific social milieu, and ethical forcing might diminish the intensity of local sites such as objects or individuals.

Anarchism at home means that local relations are more or less on equal footing. Gone are the days of the autonomous cogito, the subject of potentiality, the ego, the patriarch, the superman, the genius hero, the militant—and hence Badiou's inexhaustible desire to will some of them back into existence. Anarchism at home indicates the liberal notion that all people start on equal footing. By contrast, Leninism abroad means that social administration today is more or less political. Gone are the days of (forced) ethical principle or collective truth. Such social administration is cheated rather than forced.

In other words, we dwell within cheated universality, not forced collectivity. This is why social administration today is protocological, since protocol facilitates the management of radical autonomy. The point is not so much to say that contemporary life is essentially ethical (and not political) or essentially digital (and not analog). The point is to describe an organic mixture that is both digito-analog and ethico-political. A single aspect may rise and achieve provisional dominance, while another falls. But later the fallen will rise again, changing the balance once more.

So in one sense we live in an ethical world, guided by computers as the consummate ethical chaperones. But it's a cheated, reactionary ethics: universality-without-collectivity, analog integration without identity, a homogeneity of difference, neoliberalism, and protocol. Instead we need an ethical universe, a forced ethics: a universe of generic insufficiency, a collectivity-without-universality, a human strike.

At the same time we live in a political world, but it's a cheated, reactionary politics. Choices proliferate to infinity in public life. To live today is to choose, endlessly to choose. But the choices dissolve into the mere quasi choices of paper or plastic, Pepsi or Coke, Tweedledum or Tweedledee. Expanded to infinity, choices grow less important, ultimately defanged of their potency as real decision. Instead we need a political universe, a forced politics. We need to realize Badiou's theory of points in a more direct sense, facilitating real decisions that have real consequences.

Push this button to stop war, push that button to stop paying taxes—today we have the buttons, but not the outcomes. Any number of online petitions circulate, fabulously popular, but still the results are nil. People take to the streets in the millions, but still the results are nil. The structure itself has been circumvented.

Although both the ethical and political modes are important today, both analog integration and digital distinction, a final fact remains. *As circumvention, cheating itself follows the logic of integration.* Cheating itself tends toward the logic of the analog. Thus, if indeed the world tends toward circumvention or cheating, then the world also tends toward the analog. This is one of the fundamental contradictions of our times.

The contradiction can be described in terms of *the tendential fall in the rate of digitality*. Rooted in the standard model, the world is defined as always already digital, yet it forever strives to undercut its own digitality by way of promoting cheating over forcing. The world abdicates its own digitality by softening its own distinction. With that in mind, it is perhaps quite bland and boring to assert that Laruelle is "against the digital," because the world is against the digital too! Yet their two vectors lead in two different directions: the world promotes a dumbing and deadening of distinction, while Laruelle follows an impoverishment and withdrawal from distinction. The world territorializes into dull digitality and dull analogicity, while Laruelle refuses to make the dull distinction in the first place.

This is why the ethical regime (as cheating) is ultimately hegemonic today. Recall that old maxim about Judeo-Christian scripture, that the Bible knows no tragedy, only drama. Tragedy requires two rights in opposition, two absolutely equal claims to the law. Thus there is no tragedy in the Bible, because there are no competing claims to the law, only a singular appeal to truth.

Today we know no tragedy, only drama. We know no catastrophe, only management. Equal claims to the law, each locked in profound and irresolvable struggle, are absolutely foreign to contemporary sensibility. Ultimately we live in an ethical universe, an ethical universe powered by computers, those ethos contraptions. This is Baudrillard's "perfect crime" yet again. The perfect crime is perpetrated when the ethical wins out over the political, management over event, drama over tragedy, cheating over forcing, analog over digital.

But a cheated ethics is not the same as a forced ethics. There is another side to the ethical as well, one that might well be redeemed. It is not a monaural ethics, the ethics of an impervious infinite totality, but an ethics of absence, a drama in which *nothing unfolds* because there is literally nothing, and it is not subject to the Deleuzian foldings. This is the kind of ethical universe that Laruelle describes. It is a universe not entirely unrelated to those of Badiou and Deleuze, but one in which the elemental terms of materialism and immanence are recombined in a new way.

Such is the style of legitimate or forced ethics, a collectivity without universality, a commons of those who have nothing in common, a generic fidelity to the insufficiency of matter.

conclusion

From Digitality to Destiny

The basic claims of this book can be summarized using the one, the two, and the multiple. Various combinations and contrasts between these different modes constitute the universe both known and unknown.

As prevent, being is insufficient, indistinct, indecisive, and is thus one. But the one is not one out of nostalgia for wholeness or the longing for an origin. The one is not simply a code word for spirit or essence. The one is described as it is through contrast to the known world: because the known world is defined through distinction, the one as non-world is understood as indistinction; because the known world is defined through decision, the one as non-world is understood through indecision, and so on. The one is not a first cause nor an absolute reality; it is merely the static condition of preemption and prevention, a fundamentally prophylactic condition, in which presence and thought are made indistinct to each another. Laruelle's word for this is *superposition;* Deleuze's word is *the virtual*.

If the one is a prevent, the first and only event is "creation," the creation of distinction, described here as the creation of the standard model. But this is a kind of creation that requires no divine intervention, no holy infrastructure, just as the quantum physicist actualizes a formerly superpositioned quality simply by measuring it. The quantum physicist, in making a measurement, moves swiftly and easily from "the" one to "this" one, and in moving from the to this inaugurates a condition of relation between observer and observed.

Having been created, having been actualized, the world appears according to certain attributes. Recall that the one is without epithets, while the actual world exists according to a series of basic epithets. These epithets were defined here as (1) the affirmative transcendental of differential being, (2) the negative transcendental of dialectical being, (3) the affirmative immanence of continuous being, and (4) the negative immanence of generic being. Admittedly there is nothing particularly special about these four epithets, and the suggestion is not that they are natural or transcendental laws of existence. Other observers will likely rejigger them along different lines, or resequence them according to different historical evolutions, advents, and extinctions. These four simply appear as the most plausible modes of appropriation within the standard model as it appears today.

Yet there are not simply two co-original aspects of the actual. There are not simply the two aspects of object and relation, of extension and thought, of bodies and languages. In fact there are three co-original aspects, because *events* are distinct from both relations and entities. Hence the standard model encompasses a trio of attributes, however they may be understood: object/relation/change, matter/mind/becoming, body/language/event, thing/information/process.

Some reduce the final term to the second term, suggesting that an event is simply a relation, suggesting that change is simply a way to conceive of how something alters its relation with other things or with itself. But although events may require relation, they are not simply reducible to relation. Ultimately events are also *decisions,* and thus an entirely distinct attribute of being-given. For this reason Laruelle is quite persuasive when he labels philosophy a decision, when he suggests that the creation of the standard model, the creation of philosophy itself, is properly labeled a decisive event.

The non-standard universe is approached not by the addition of a new decision, or the explosion of a new event, but rather by withholding the original decision. Events are thus rather capacious, for there are events that resemble relations, events that are properly called decisions, and ultimately events that are indecisions or prevents. In Laruelle the third type is called "determination" or "destiny."

These and other claims are developed throughout the book. To punctuate the remarks, a series of fourteen theses were introduced, which are reproduced now in slightly less verbose language.

Thesis I. The media principle: the real is communicational, and the communicational is real.

Thesis II. Under the standard model, whatever given is riven.

Thesis III. As non-standard, the one is a prevent or virtualization.

Thesis IV. The one has no epithets.

Thesis V. The epithets of being are fourfold: differential, dialectical, continuous, and generic.

Thesis VI. The digital means the one dividing in two.

Thesis VII. The analog means the two coming together as one.

Thesis VIII. Being is an evental mode; it is coterminous with the event.

Thesis IX. Being is a computational mode; it is coterminous with the computational decision.

Thesis X. Non-standard philosophy is incompatible with exchange.

Thesis XI: Non-standard aesthetics means an aesthetics without representation, an aesthetics of the immanent rather than the transcendental.

Thesis XII. The political is two.

Thesis XIII. The ethical is one.

Thesis XIV. There is a tendential fall in the rate of digitality.

Following the path laid out in this book, it is impossible to think philosophy without thinking digitality. It is impossible to think philosophy without interrogating the zero, the one, the two, the multiple, and the distinctions made among these terms.

Laruelle emerges as a key theorist today not simply because he allows us to think philosophy non-philosophically, but because through the non-standard model we are able to see a broader picture of ontology that includes both digital and nondigital in parallel. Thus it becomes possible to be "against the digital," as clumsy as that phrasing may sound, not by inaugurating a new anti-digital binary, which would only restore the same old parallelity of digitality, but by way of the parallelism of decision and the realization that the decision need not be made in the first place.

This book has proffered the digital but has said relatively little about computers, software, networks, the Web, and the like. Is it guilty of false advertising? Admittedly the goal here is rather different from books on digital media. The goal here has not been to elucidate, promote, or disparage contemporary digital technologies, but rather to draft a simple prolegomenon for future writing on digitality and philosophy, using Laruelle as a kind of unwitting guide.

What is the digital? The goal here was not to settle the question. Rather, the goal was to show that the question has never adequately been posed. The digital is a precondition of contemporary life, but, more important, it is a precondition of the standard model as a whole.

Can there be an ontology of the digital, or even a philosophy of it? An attention to the specificities and vicissitudes of computers and other digital machines is paramount to such a project, just as an attention to the particularities of gesture and affect would necessarily guide any philosophical mediation on the subject. Nevertheless, in so doing, it is crucial to avoid the dual pitfalls of a "philosophy of the digital," in which the digital assumes the status of an object of study, like any other, to be wrapped up and delivered by the investigating intellect (which itself remains uninterrogated), or even a "digitization of philosophy," in which the act of doing philosophy is subject to reinvention as something like "distributed intelligence," merely a marketing slogan, or even as my forebears might have called it "rhizomatic theory" or "schizo-culture."

The project here was of a rather different nature. The intent was not so much to appropriate one term to the other, not so much to apply the metaphysical as-structure and attempt to think digital-as-philosophy or philosophy-as-digital. Instead the intent was to apply the *in-structure,* a structure more suitable for generic immanence: digital-in-philosophy and philosophy-in-digital. The applicability of such an approach to future writing on those other things—computers, software, networks, or the Web—will make itself evident in different ways and at different times.

What was discovered during the course of this journey, in which both the digital and the analog have played a role, is that any exploration of the digital—as cleaving, distinction, rivenness, or alienation—will necessarily place new demands on metaphysics, because metaphysics will be held to account, summoned to explain its own rivenness. Here we have answered that call *not* by explaining metaphysics in terms of more metaphysics, an approach that succeeds in forestalling the urgency of the question but ultimately explains very little. Instead metaphysics was described as an event and modal condition of the one. The one is, in this sense, the finite a priori of the real, defined in the various ways previously discussed including the principle of identity ($a = a$) and the principle of insufficient attribution or casting.

By discussing all of this under the name of Laruelle and his signal contribution to contemporary thinking, I do not pretend to recast Laruelle as a digital philosopher, or an analog one for that matter. A digital or analog Laruelle would make very little sense indeed, him being the theorist who has most avoided distinction, most avoided any kind of becoming-discrete.

On the contrary, what Laruelle proves is that digitality is not destiny. He illustrates that the same kind of indecision shown to philosophy can also be shown to digitality. Digitality is much too sufficient to allow for any kind of destiny.

So if it is destiny we seek, or the generic, or love, or nature, or the common, we ought better to leave digitality behind (and analogy too). For the key to our destiny is not so much zeros and ones, but ones and twos, the one becoming two and the two returning as one. Only by refusing the sufficiency of the digital will we discover the promise of an immanent materialism.

Acknowledgments

Principal writing for this book began in summer 2011 and concluded in early October 2012. Yet early inspiration for the volume dates to a few months earlier. On October 29, 2010, I conducted a seminar on the work of François Laruelle in Brooklyn at the Public School New York. The resulting short text, "François Laruelle, or The Secret," was included in a series of five pamphlets titled *French Theory Today: An Introduction to Possible Futures* (Brooklyn: Public School New York, 2011). Let me acknowledge and thank everyone who attended the seminar and those involved in the publication: editor Sarah Resnick, designers Kamomi Solidum and Anne Callahan, and contributors Taeyoon Choi, David Horvitz, Nicola Masciandaro, Jackson Moore, Dominic Pettman, Stephen Squibb, Eugene Thacker, and Prudence Whittlesey. My individual contributions to the Public School pamphlets were subsequently reorganized and published in French as *Les nouveaux réalistes: Philosophie et postfordisme* (Paris: Editions Léo Scheer, 2012). I am grateful to the Public School New York and Léo Scheer for supporting this material and allowing it to reappear here, folded inside the Introduction.

A first attempt to bridge Laruelle and digitality was presented at the Miguel Abreu Gallery in New York on April 6, 2011, with Laruelle in attendance. These rudimentary thoughts were expanded into a lecture titled "Marxism without Digitality" given at Duke University on January 21, 2012, under the invitation of the Literature Program, as well as a presentation on January 24 in a colloquium at the University of Pennsylvania hosted by Avi Alpert and Danny Snelson. These initial explorations were reorganized into a formal lecture titled "10 Theses on the Digital"— my attempt at a pun—given first in Erich Hörl's Medienwissenschaft colloquium at the Ruhr-Universität Bochum in Germany on May 9, 2012, and then again under the invitation of Matthew Fuller at Goldsmiths, University of London, on May 14. I thank these hosts for their support and for the feedback I received during my respective visits.

The bulk of chapter 5 was written for Briankle Chang and Zachary McDowell at the University of Massachusetts Amherst, where I was invited to give a talk, originally titled "Deleuze and Computers," on December 2, 2011. The lecture was subsequently published as "Computers and the Superfold" in *Deleuze Studies* 6, no. 4 (November 2012): 513–28. It reappears here in altered and expanded form.

Additional material was written in response to two invitations from Anthony Paul Smith, whom I recognize for his generosity and intellectual camaraderie. Chapter 6 first appeared as "Laruelle, Anti-capitalist," in *Laruelle and Non-philosophy,* edited by John Mullarkey and Anthony Paul Smith (Edinburgh: Edinburgh University Press, 2012): 191–208. Material from a second essay titled "The Autism of Reason," written for a special issue on Laruelle in the journal *Angelaki* 19, no. 3 (2014), has been incorporated into several different chapters.

Chapter 7 was originally developed for two different seminars organized in part by Ed Keller, Nicola Masciandaro, Eugene Thacker, and Daniel Colucciello Barber, all of whom I acknowledge and thank for their friendship and boundless powers. As such the chapter incorporates material from "What Is a Hermeneutic Light?" in *Leper Creativity: Cyclonopedia Symposium,* edited by Ed Keller, Nicola Masciandaro, and Eugene Thacker (Brooklyn: Punctum Books, 2012), 159–72, and "Rocket: Present at Every Point of the Remote," in Daniel Colucciello Barber et al., *Dark Nights of the Universe* (Miami: Name, 2013), 89–100.

A part of chapter 8 first appeared as "Laruelle and Art" in *continent.* 2, no. 4 (2013): 230–36. I especially thank Miguel Abreu, who furnished me with obscure texts without which the chapter would not have been possible.

The opening section of chapter 9 first appeared as a review in *Parrhesia* 16 (2013): 102–5.

Portions of the fully drafted manuscript were again presented at the Public School New York during a class on Laruelle that Taeyoon Choi helped organize over four weekends in April 2013. These discussions were extremely useful, and I thank everyone who attended, in particular Jesse Newberg.

I benefited greatly from three fine research assistants during the preparation of the book: Shane Brennan, Jason LaRivière, and Hannah Zeavin. All three will recognize traces of themselves throughout the volume, just as I do.

This book would not have seen the light of day without Douglas Armato of the University of Minnesota Press and Cary Wolfe, the Posthumanities book series editor. I thank them both for supporting the project. A number of friends and colleagues read and commented on the penultimate draft of the manuscript. Among them I am particularly grateful to Daniel Colucciello Barber, Seb Franklin, Steven Shaviro, Jason Smith, Eugene Thacker, and McKenzie Wark. More than anyone I am grateful to Juliet Jacobson.

Notes

PREFACE

1. See Carla Lonzi, "Let's Spit on Hegel," originally published in *Revolt Femi-nize*, and translated in *Italian Feminist Thought: A Reader*, eds. Paola Bono and Sandra Kemp, 40–59 (Oxford and Cambridge: Basil Blackwell, 1991).

2. In a rare moment of autobiographical reflection, Laruelle cites two formative events from his youth, renouncing Hegel and watching an Antonioni film: "I wrote a master's thesis, 'The Absence of Being,' after having seen a film, Antonioni's *La Notte*. At first I was going to write something on the young Hegel. But after I came back from vacation, having seen *La Notte*, and I told my supervisor, Paul Ricoeur, that I renounced Hegel! (Not that the young Hegel isn't interesting . . .) So yes, that film was also a turning point, curious things like that happen" (François Laruelle, *From Decision to Heresy: Experiments in Non-Standard Thought*, ed. Robin Mackay [New York: Sequence, 2012], 3).

INTRODUCTION

1. François Laruelle, "Obscénité de la philosophie," in *Théorie-Rébellion: Un ultimatum*, ed. Gilles Grelet (Paris: L'Harmattan, 2005), 123. This and all subse-quent unattributed translations from the French are my own. I have not been pedantic about returning to the French on every single occasion and will cite an English translation if it happens to be the way in which I first encountered the text.

2. François Laruelle, *The Concept of Non-photography / Le concept de non-photographie*, trans. Robin Mackay (Falmouth, U.K., and New York: Urbanomic and Sequence, 2011), 123.

3. François Laruelle, "The Truth according to Hermes: Theorems on the Secret and Communication," trans. Alexander R. Galloway, *Parrhesia* 9 (2010): 18–22. Par-enthetical citations refer to this edition, giving both page number and thesis number. For a much longer examination of hermeneutics, difference, deconstruc-tion, and the non-interpretable, see Laruelle's essay "Anti-Hermes," in *Text und*

Interpretation: Deutsch-französische Debatte, ed. Philippe Forget, 78–114 (Munich: Fink, 1984).

4. See Quentin Meillassoux, *After Finitude: An Essay on the Necessity of Contingency,* trans. Ray Brassier (London: Continuum, 2008).

5. A note on the capitalization of terms like "the One" and "Being": It is not necessary to be overly fastidious about observing correct capitalization in every instance, and the reader should not extract anything particularly revelatory from such fluctuations, but suffice it to say that I follow the convention, often seen in the translations of Heidegger and others, of using the capitalized "Being" to refer to the ontological status of things, which is to say the presence as such of things, while reserving the lowercase "being" (or more commonly "a being," "beings," or less ambiguously "entities") to refer to actually existing things. As Heidegger himself specified, the use of the uppercase is nothing special and is not meant to bestow an aura of grandeur to these kinds of words. Indeed the capitalization of nouns happens differently in German than in English or French. As for Laruelle and the distinction between "one" and "the One"—the former a mundane number or a simple pronoun, the latter a more generic condition of identity—I tend to deviate from the example set in Laruelle. He capitalizes the One, yet my preference, when not citing Laruelle directly, is to set it lowercase whenever possible. In my view a capitalized One unnecessarily inflates the importance of the concept, ironically endowing it the same kind of transcendental sufficiency that Laruelle seeks to withhold.

6. In fact Laruelle performs surgery on phenomenology in an effort to resurrect it in non-standard form. So phenomenology's central conceit that Being is given over to the thought-world of man, establishing the fundamental structures of perception, projection, orientation, absorption, attention, and solicitude, is replaced by what Laruelle calls "vision-in-One." Vision-in-One refers essentially to a non-standard phenomenology. The basic logic of perception, projection, orientation, and so on is abstracted from its humanness and collapsed back into a structure of generic immanence. Thus Laruelle's vision is no longer a vision of the world, or a solicitude toward the other, but a vision within the one, a solicitude within immanence. Doing this also allows Laruelle to modify the classical ecstatic notion of existence as ex-ist (being out of). Quite cleverly Laruelle replaces ecstatic existence with the term in-One. The "ex" of exist becomes "in" and the "is-ness" becomes One: so not "exist" but "in-One."

7. In his robust critique of Laruelle, fueled by a skepticism toward the way in which Laruelle lumps all of philosophy into a single, uniform "decision," Ray Brassier traces the origins of the concept of philosophical decision to Heidegger. "Heidegger exemplifies the decisional structure Laruelle has in mind"; indeed, in Brassier's view, it would be apt "to characterize Laruelle's non-philosophy as the *terminus ad quem* of Heidegger's delimitation of metaphysics" (Ray Brassier, *Nihil Unbound: Enlightenment and Extinction* [New York: Palgrave Macmillan, 2007], 126, 127). In a similar vein, Quentin Meillassoux has critiqued Laruelle on the grounds that Laruelle fails to escape the circle of correlationist reflection: "If, like

Laruelle, you posit something outside the circle of objectivity—in his case the Real outside 'Philosophy'—this Real will still be, according to me, in the circle of correlationism. Because it will be a posited Real: a Real posited by reflection outside of representation" (Quentin Meillassoux, in Ray Brassier et al., "Speculative Realism," *Collapse* 3 [November 2007]: 307–449, 418).

8. See François Laruelle, *Principes de la non-philosophie* (Paris: PUF, 1996), and François Laruelle, *Philosophie non-standard: Générique, quantique, philo-fiction* (Paris: Kimé, 2010).

9. John Mullarkey, *Post-continental Philosophy: An Outline* (London: Continuum, 2006), 133.

10. Malabou has elaborated the concept of plasticity across a number of books. See, in particular, Catherine Malabou, *Plasticity at the Dusk of Writing: Dialectic, Destruction, Deconstruction*, trans. Carolyn Shread (New York: Columbia University Press, 2010).

11. François Laruelle, "A Summary of Non-philosophy," *Pli* 8 (1999): 138–48, 143.

12. Although Laruelle does not often speak of digitality per se, he does indeed spend a great deal of time in *Philosophie non-standard* discussing discretization and particularity in quantum theory, including the distinction between particles and waves. Particles and waves are central to quantum mechanics, of course, but Laruelle also uses the terms to talk about the oscillations between discretization and generic continuity. In his view, particles or corpuscles are more affiliated with philosophy and its tendency toward decision and digitality, while waves or undulations are more affiliated with the generic and its quantic and immanent qualities.

13. The particular quotation in question is somewhat longer when viewed in context: "The splitting of a single whole and the cognition of its contradictory parts (see the quotation from Philo on Heraclitus at the beginning of Section III, 'On Cognition,' in Lasalle's book on Heraclitus) is the *essence* (one of the 'essentials,' one of the principal, if not the principal, characteristics or features) of dialectics" (V. I. Lenin, "On the Question of Dialectics," in *Collected Works*, vol. 38 [Moscow: Progress Publishers, 1972], 359).

14. Alain Badiou, *The Century*, trans. Alberto Toscano (Cambridge: Polity, 2007), 60.

15. Mao Tsetung, "A Dialectical Approach to Inner-Party Unity," trans. anonymous, *Selected Works of Mao Tsetung*, vol. 5 (Peking: Foreign Languages Press, 1977). For an overview of some of the relevant vocabulary, see Li Kwok-sing, ed., *A Glossary of Political Terms of the People's Republic of China*, trans. Mary Lok (Hong Kong: Chinese University Press, 1995), 139–40, 521–22.

16. Ai Hengwu and Lin Qingshan, "'Dividing One into Two' and 'Combining Two into One': Some Realization Gained in the Study of Chairman Mao's Thought in Materialistic Dialectics," trans. anonymous, *Guangming Daily*, May 29, 1964, http://marxistphilosophy.org/ailin64.pdf, 1.

17. See Guy Debord, *The Society of the Spectacle,* trans. Donald Nicholson-Smith (New York: Zone Books, 1994); Pierre Macherey, "Un se divise en deux," in

Histoires de dinosaure: Faire de la philosophie, 1965–1997, 64–73 (Paris: PUF, 1999); Pierre Macherey, "Georges Bataille: Materialism Inverted," in *The Object of Literature,* trans. David Macey, 112–31 (Cambridge: Cambridge University Press, 1995), but particularly 125–27; Bruno Bosteels, "On the Subject of the Dialectic," in *Think Again: Alain Badiou and the Future of Philosophy,* ed. Peter Hallward, 150–64 (London: Continuum, 2004); Bruno Bosteels, "One Divides into Two," in *Badiou and Politics,* 110–56 (Durham, N.C.: Duke University Press, 2011); Alenka Zupančič, *The Shortest Shadow: Nietzsche's Philosophy of the Two* (Cambridge, Mass.: MIT Press, 2003); and Michael Hardt and Antonio Negri, *Commonwealth,* 290–95 (Cambridge, Mass.: Harvard University Press, 2009).

The work of Lardreau and Jambet represents a slightly different development, irreducible to either analysis or synthesis. (See Guy Lardreau and Christian Jambet, *L'Ange: Pour une cynégétique du semblant* [Paris: Éditions Grasset, 1976].) In their fantastical hunt for an "angelic" Marxism, Lardreau and Jambet continued to fight against the Hegelian synthesis, keeping a fidelity to what they viewed as the more Marxist moment of analysis (1 → 2). Yet, in arriving at the two, Lardreau and Jambet sought to elevate the two as such, preserving it as a kind of perpetual contradiction of opposites, immune to subsequent counter forces of synthesis, but nevertheless still susceptible to a higher, "angelic" realization. Lardreau and Jambet's allegiance to the two produces something slightly different from struggle, rather an "eternal dual between the Master and a Rebel whose independence from that Master can be asserted only through the radically disincarnate figure of the Angel . . . in other words, a radically antidialectical take on the Leninist model of history as epic struggle" (Peter Starr, *Logics of Failed Revolt: French Theory after May '68* [Stanford, Calif.: Stanford University Press, 1995], 93). In such a revolutionary model, rooted in the angelic, not the dialectical, Lardreau and Jambet describe a mode of revolt that cannot simply flip back into mastery, cannot simply be recuperated by authority. In fact Lardreau and Jambet also pitted themselves against sexual liberation and the unfettering of desire, a somewhat counterintuitive move that would differentiate them from those operating in the wake of May 1968, based on the assumption that desire and sexual liberation are too easily recuperated.

After the failure of figures like Yang Xianzhen and beyond the escapades of Lardreau and Jambet, the first coherent alternative to the Marxist hegemony of two over one are the postwar followers of Spinoza, most notably Althusser, Macherey, and Deleuze. In Macherey, for example, as in Althusser, the basic choice is not so much Marx or Hegel but another choice entirely. The true alternative is Hegelian-Marxism *or Spinoza.* In such an alternative Spinoza is held up as a materialist, like Marx, but a materialist within whom the divisions and distinctions of the dialectic give way in favor of a pervasive immanence of nature.

18. Alain Badiou, *The Rational Kernel of the Hegelian Dialectic: Translations, Introductions and Commentary on a Text by Zhang Shiying,* trans. Tzuchien Tho (Melbourne: re.press, 2011), 60.

19. Hardt and Negri, *Commonwealth,* 294.

20. Gilles Deleuze and Félix Guattari, *A Thousand Plateaus,* trans. Brian Massumi (Minneapolis: University of Minnesota Press, 1987), 5.

21. In his more recent writing, Laruelle has moved slightly closer to the computer while still remaining apart from it. Laruelle prefers to speak of a "matrix," which may observe certain physical or mathematical principles but has little to do with the modern computer. "I would rather talk about a *generic matrix* or even a collider, producer and detector of new thought particles, than about a computer devoted to formal calculation" (23), he notes in *Philosophie non-standard,* the large methodological centerpiece of a trio of late works—*Introduction aux sciences génériques* (Paris: Pétra, 2008), *Philosophie non-standard,* and *Anti-Badiou: Sur l'introduction du maoïsme dans la philosophie* (Paris: Kimé, 2011)—devoted to, among other things, algebraic principles, quantum mechanics, and the generic. "The generic matrix has certain aspects like the computer: a hardware side . . . and a software side from either the algebraic . . . or the philosophical. . . . But it functions differently"; we need not a *transcendental* machine, he writes, alluding to Turing's invention, but an "immanental" machine (*Philosophie non-standard,* 23, 24).

22. Laruelle, *Introduction aux sciences génériques,* 28.

23. François Laruelle, "L'ordinateur transcendantal: Une utopie non-philosophique," in *Homo ex machina* (Paris: L'Harmattan, 2005), 13.

1. THE ONE DIVIDES IN TWO

1. Alain Badiou, *Being and Event,* trans. Oliver Feltham (New York: Continuum, 2005), 24.

2. Ibid., 23.

3. Ibid.

4. Indeed the claim "The one is not" eventually leads Badiou to an ontology of the void. The important aspect of Badiou's intervention is that he solidly configures the one as "merely" a structure or operation of being, what he calls the "count-as-one." Badiou's one is thus not a land beyond, not a pseudonym for God, and not some kind transcendental state of pre-being. "What has to be declared is that the one, which is not, solely exists as *operation.* In other words: there is no one per se, only the count-as-one. The one, being an operation, is never a presentation" (ibid., 24).

5. Alain Badiou, *Deleuze: The Clamor of Being,* trans. Louise Burchill (Minneapolis: University of Minnesota Press, 2000), 52.

6. The violence is most spectacular during Badiou's discussion of Deleuze's notion of univocity, which he likens to a suspended "simulacra" of being. "Strangely, this consequence has a Platonic, or even Neoplatonic air to it," Badiou concludes tartly. "Deleuzianism is fundamentally a Platonism with a different accentuation" (Badiou, *Deleuze,* 26). The irony, of course, is that Deleuze had long construed himself as the most extreme form of anti-Platonist, by way of a total rejection of the dialectic, idealism, and classical metaphysics in general, making him essentially incompatible with Plato.

7. Badiou, *Deleuze,* 78.

8. Gilles Deleuze, *Difference and Repetition,* trans. Paul Patton (New York: Columbia University Press, 1994), 35, 36.

9. Ibid., 304.

10. "... one Being and only for all forms and all times, a single instance for all that exists, a single phantom for all the living, a single voice for every hum of voices and every drop of water in the sea" (Gilles Deleuze, *The Logic of Sense,* trans. Mark Lester [New York: Columbia University Press, 1990], 180). This chapter of *The Logic of Sense* also illustrates why it would not be entirely correct to label Deleuze's defense of univocity a "monism." He says clearly that there is not one and the same being. He endorses the opposite position, in fact, that there is a multiplicity of different beings. Univocity does not state that there is one substance, or that there is, ultimately, a single thing in which Being consists. So while Deleuze proposes a multiplicity of pure becoming, what he delightfully calls "the primary order which grumbles beneath" (125), he also states that this multiplicity carries across its many permutations the same one sense. Univocity thus designates an identity of commonality between being's events *and* being's sense. On this score *The Logic of Sense* is a much more radical work of ontology than even *Difference and Repetition,* because it demonstrates that the theory of sense is ultimately a theory of being, that being is a vocalization or expression, that "Being is Voice" (179). It demonstrates why, in order to talk about being, Deleuze felt obligated to talk about *language.*

11. Deleuze, *The Logic of Sense,* 180.

12. To be sure, Laruelle's one is not "extra" in the sense of being higher or more external than Being: "In reality it is not the One that is separated from Being, it is Being that is separated from the One. . . . *We do not exit from philosophy into the One; we describe the vision-in-One of philosophy*" (François Laruelle, *Philosophies of Difference: A Critical Introduction to Non-philosophy,* trans. Rocco Gangle [London: Continuum, 2010], 155). Laruelle's one should also not be confused with the All, because the one is finite and insufficient, while the All typically refers to a totality, an infinity, a multiplicity, or some other kind of sufficient whole.

13. Laruelle, "A Summary of Non-philosophy, 141.

14. There is, of course, an active tradition within intellectual history of categorizing Hegel as the consummate thinker of immanence. Badiou sums it up nicely: "All of Hegel can be found in the following: the 'still-more' is immanent to the 'already'; everything that is, is already 'still-more'" (Badiou, *Being and Event,* 162). Although cognizant of this alternate tradition, I think it necessary to differentiate between, shall we say, weak and strong theories of immanence. Philosophies of weak immanence (here Hegel) give allowance to excess or supplement, corralling the "still more" back into the essence of what "already" is. By contrast, strong theories of immanence (Laruelle) give no quarter to the "still more." The "still more" is by definition ecstatic; it must step beyond and exceed the entity whatsoever it is. Within this more radical conception of immanence—"radical" in Laruelle's lexicon meaning roughly "more fully determined"—nothing ever has to go outside itself in order to realize itself. That being the core motto of Hegelianism, I think it

unfitting to label Hegel a thinker of immanence, at least in the stronger or more radical variety espoused by Laruelle.

15. See, for example, Laruelle, *Principes de la non-philosophie*, 6.

16. Immanence is territory that Laruelle seeks to win for himself. In a number of places he discusses the tradition of philosophical immanence only to show how none of the existing philosophies of immanence is adequate. Michel Henry is most laudable in Laruelle's eyes, but even Henry is not rigorous enough. See, for example, the section titled "Mésaventures de l'immanence (de Spinoza à M. Henry)" in François Laruelle, *Introduction au non-marxisme* (Paris: PUF, 2000), 40–43; or Laruelle's "Réponse à Deleuze" in François Laruelle, *La non-philosophie des contemporains* (Paris: Kimé, 1995), 49–78, in which Laruelle responds rather forcefully to a small but friendly footnote that mentions him in *What Is Philosophy?* one of Deleuze's last books (with Guattari).

17. Jacques Lacan, *On Feminine Sexuality: The Limits of Love and Knowledge—The Seminar of Jacques Lacan, Book XX,* trans. Bruce Fink (New York: Norton, 1998), 47.

18. Ibid.

19. Ibid.

20. Ibid., emphasis added.

21. Whitehead calls this "the bifurcation of nature." See Alfred North Whitehead, *The Concept of Nature* (New York: Prometheus, 2004).

22. Laruelle, "The Truth according to Hermes," 22.

23. Badiou, *Deleuze,* 78.

24. Luce Irigaray, *The Forgetting of Air in Martin Heidegger,* trans. Mary Beth Mader (Austin: University of Texas Press, 1999), 17, 2.

25. Alfred North Whitehead, *Process and Reality: An Essay in Cosmology* (New York: Free Press, 1978), 19.

26. See, for example, Laruelle, *Principes de la non-philosophie*, 1.

27. Laruelle, *Introduction aux sciences génériques*, 25, emphasis removed.

28. In such contexts it is easy to see why Deleuze was drawn to biological principles of asexual reproduction such as cutting, grafting, cloning, and rhizomatic propagation. Just as Laruelle's clone is what we might call "riven-without-rivenness," the rhizome of Deleuze and Guattari propagates only via a kind of "blind" or nonsynthetic repetition. See the opening sections of Deleuze and Guattari, *A Thousand Plateaus.*

29. Laruelle, *Philosophie non-standard,* 95.

30. Michel Henry, *The Essence of Manifestation,* trans. Girard Etzkorn (The Hague: Nijhoff, 1973), 719.

31. Immanuel Kant, *Prolegomena to Any Future Metaphysics That Can Qualify as a Science,* trans. Paul Carus (Chicago: Open Court, 1902), 85.

32. Martin Heidegger, "The Principle of Identity," in *Identity and Difference,* trans. Joan Stambaugh (Chicago: University of Chicago Press, 1969), 31.

33. Martin Heidegger, "Time and Being," in *On Time and Being,* trans. Joan Stambaugh (Chicago: University of Chicago Press, 1972), 19.

34. Eugene Thacker, *In the Dust of This Planet: Horror of Philosophy, Vol. 1* (Winchester, UK: Zero Books, 2011), 5, 6. See also Eugene Thacker, "The Insomnia of Thought," *Black Annals* (forthcoming).

35. In no way should the real be understood as some sort of primitive, cosmological soup. In this book words like *equiprimorder, co-original,* or *prior* should carry in the reader's ear absolutely no connotation of a past time in which things were simpler and humans existed in a state of nature, nor anything like a brute Darwinism in which primitive forces fight and evolve from simpler states to more advanced states. And when we speak of oneness it is not out of romanticism or nostalgia for some lost state of integrity or completeness, but simply through a reversal of the rivenness of being. Following apophatic reason: if being is digital, the one must be analog; if being is transcendental, the one must be immanent. Indeed, chapter 10 shows how both the digital and the analog are equally interesting and useful. These protestations, of course, may not dispel such interpretations, just as Heidegger's unambiguous protestations about the non-normative nature of his *Verfallen* (falling, lapsing, slouching, ensnarement) are thoroughly unconvincing to me. But at least the protestations are on the record.

36. Deleuze, *Difference and Repetition,* 37.

2. The Standard Model

1. For an examination of this dynamic see, in particular, Kristin Ross, *Fast Cars, Clean Bodies: Decolonization and the Reordering of French Culture* (Cambridge, Mass.: MIT Press, 1996).

2. François Laruelle, "Du noir univers: Dans les fondations humaines de la couleur," *La Décision philosophique* 5 (April 1988): 107–12, 111.

3. Laruelle, *Principes de la non-philosophie,* 28.

4. A number of contemporaries are exploring the relationship between philosophy and autism. See, in particular, Erin Manning, "The Shape of Enthusiasm," *Parallax* 17, no. 2 (2011): 84–109, and Steven Shaviro, *The Universe of Things: On Speculative Realism* (Minneapolis: University of Minnesota Press, 2014). Some thinkers and scientists within disability studies are endorsing a model of "neurodiversity" in which autism is not considered deficient or necessarily disabling but rather simply one neurological configuration among others. By contrast the nonstandard method would suggest a model more along the lines of "neurocommonality" or "generic thought."

5. Such a method is referred to as *apophatic* or *privative reason,* or alternately as the *via negativa.* Laruelle himself does not shun the *via negativa* as a viable methodology: radical immanence "is defined *negatively* through an exclusion of ecstatic or phenomenological distance" (Laruelle, *Philosophie non-standard,* 159).

6. Laruelle, *Introduction au non-marxisme,* 69.

7. Laruelle himself has not received enough credit for what is perhaps the most ambitious aspect of his entire project: a unified theory to fuse science and philosophy. See, in particular, the second chapter of *Principes de la non-philosophie.*

A more recent work, *Philosophie non-standard,* devoted to what Laruelle calls a "generic science," also takes up this task in earnest. Generic science comes from a series of convictions: "(1) that philosophy's critique of representation during the Twentieth Century is still an unfinished project, and that philosophy itself is incapable of realizing this critique as long as it elevates *one science to a fundamental methodological position* (Newton for Kant, number theory for Husserl, set theory for Badiou), (2) that the point of science in general is not to generate the most virtuosic critique of philosophy, but that science in general carries with it an indifference toward philosophy, a prior-priority *[avant-priorité]* capable of (under) determining critique, (3) in particular that, among the sciences, historical materialism, psychoanalysis, and quantum mechanics are the closest to establishing a Generic Science of philosophy itself . . . , (4) that the critique of philosophy, or criticism more broadly construed as our contemporaries practice it, must change its nature and must no longer be 'first critique,' but rather lined up behind a fore-first science *[science avant-première]*" (Laruelle, *Philosophie non-standard,* 185). Although some might be skeptical of the way in which Laruelle has begun to talk about quantum mechanics in recent books, it's best to think of his sudden penchant for twentieth-century physics in terms of a larger relationship between scientific formalism and philosophical rationalism. As he suggests, some sort of generic science is at the core of all inventive thought: "Husserl needed the science of psychology as a waypoint toward the autonomy of the transcendental, Kant needed newtonian physics as passage toward the *a priori* and the transcendental, Heidegger needed ontological difference to get to *Ereignis,* Plato needed mathematics to get to philosophy. Today we need quantum physics and particularly its use of imaginary numbers in order to pass on to the generic" (Laruelle, *Philosophie non-standard,* 257–58). Laruelle has thus not anointed quantum mechanics as some sort of special meta-discourse able to speak in the voice of being. Rather, quantum theory is merely a particularly convenient way to obtain a generic science, in part because quantum theory already speaks the language of the generic (via concepts like non-commutativity or superposition). Still, quantum theory remains just as "philosophical" as philosophy itself, and thus requires its own non-standard parallel (the task of *Philosophie non-standard*).

8. Laruelle, *Philosophie non-standard,* 174.

9. See, for instance, chapter 16 of Badiou, *Being and Event,* 173–77. Brassier has also suggested a useful mixture of Badiou and Laruelle: "The full-force of Badiou's ontological thesis—viz., that being is nothing—is only realized when it is supplemented by the transcendental hypothesis which we have extracted from Laruelle. . . . We will distinguish the void as unilateral duality from the being-nothing in which it is rooted as indivisible zero. Where dialectics proceeds by the One dividing into two, unilateralization consists in the two of the void effectuating the zero of being-nothing. Non-dialectical negation is this 'voiding' and the logic of its effectuation is that of the unilateral duality, the irreversible cut" (Brassier, *Nihil Unbound,* 148).

10. See Henry, *The Essence of Manifestation,* 44, 45, 41.

11. The fourfold schema described here is not meant to duplicate or emulate Laruelle's own "four discourses of the One," consisting of the Master, the Stranger,

Life, and the Rebel. The first two he describes in terms of philosophy and non-philosophy, while the second two are attached to the names Michel Henry and Gilles Grelet respectively. "(1) The philosopher or the Master is complacent in the World and is himself a World . . . ; (2) The Stranger . . . is that clone of being-in-struggle-with-the-World . . . ; (3) Life is the refusal and contempt for the World . . . and in this way Life distinguishes itself from the World that it does not want to know; (4) The Rebel is in-hatred of the World" (François Laruelle, *Struggle and Utopia at the End Times of Philosophy,* trans. Drew S. Burk and Anthony Paul Smith [Minneapolis: Univocal, 2012], 181). Although there is some superficial resemblance between the Master and differential being or the Rebel and dialectical being, it would be a mistake to compare the two models because they derive from different premises and thus result in incompatible maps.

12. Laruelle, *Principes de la non-philosophie,* 5. See also 7, 45, and 52.

13. G. W. F. Hegel, *Encyclopedia of the Philosophical Sciences: Part One, The Science of Logic,* trans. William Wallace (Oxford: Oxford University Press, 1975), 115.

14. Deleuze, *The Logic of Sense,* 53.

15. Ibid., 125.

16. Alain Badiou, *Manifesto for Philosophy,* trans. Norman Madarasz (Albany: State University of New York Press, 1999), 108–9.

17. François Laruelle, *Introduction aux sciences génériques* (Paris: Pétra, 2008), 39, 40. Such a litany is what others refer to as "anti-philosophy." In his translator's introduction to Badiou's *Ethics,* Peter Hallward provides a useful description of anti-philosophy, starting with his own list of figures: "Saint Paul's 'discourse of Life' (as opposed to the pretensions of Greek philosophy); Pascal's *charité* (against rational and institutional intellect); Rousseau's sincerity (against the science of Voltaire and the Encyclopédistes); Kierkegaard's redemptive choice (against Hegel's synthesis); Nietzsche's 'active' force (against the 'theoretical' *ressentiment* of the philosopher-priest); the early Wittgenstein's inarticulable, otherworldly Meaning (against speculative idealism); Heidegger's letting-be (against the technocratic manipulation of beings)—these are all so many efforts to set an ineffable *Value* against mere theory, a genuine *Act* against the feeble abstractions of philosophy (see Alain Badiou, *Saint Paul* [Paris: PUF, 1997], 62). *Showing* here prevails over *saying:* anti-philosophy reveals, where philosophy explains. Every 'anti-philosophical act consists of letting become apparent "what there is", to the degree that "what there is" is precisely that which no proposition is able to say' (Alain Badiou, 'Silence, solipsisme, sainteté' [*BARCA ! Poésie, Politique, Psychanalyse* 3 (1994): 13–53], 17)" (Peter Hallward in Alain Badiou, *Ethics: An Essay on the Understanding of Evil,* trans. Peter Hallward [London: Verso, 2001], xxxix–xl).

18. Laruelle, *Introduction aux sciences génériques,* 59–60, see also pages 125–27 for a longer discussion of the one and the two. It is technically incorrect and certainly overly simplistic to assert that Laruelle is "against the two" or "for the one." Admittedly Laruelle thinks that philosophy generally enforces a "law of the two" based in bifurcation, reflection, auto-position, etc. Yet non-philosophy cannot be

understood as a simple rejection of the two and a return to the one. Laruelle describes non-philosophy as *a theory of the immanent one and the unilateral two.* This preserves a notion of the one that is not transcendental, and a notion of the two that is not representational.

In fact, a useful conversation could be staged here between Laruelle and Jacques Rancière around Rancière's concept of *partage* (distribution, sharing, or parceling out; see Jacques Rancière, *Le partage du sensible: esthétique et politique* [Paris: La Fabrique, 2000], published in English as *The Politics of Aesthetics: The Distribution of the Sensible*, trans. Gabriel Rockhill [New York: Continuum, 2004]). Contra Rancière, Laruelle does not speak of distributions or arrangements, at least not in the way they are typically discussed. Rather, he impoverishes the transcendental core of *partage* and renders it generic, unilateral, and immanent: "The radically unequal or complimentary distribution is what we call unilateral, . . . [It's] an immanence without exception, without any kind of distribution or parcelling out *[partage]*" (Laruelle, *Philosophie non-standard*, 172). Thus, in the wake of Laruelle a number of things become possible. One is able, for the first time in recent memory, to cease thinking about distributed networks and begin thinking about unilateral networks. One is able to cease contemplating the many distributions of the sensible and begin thinking the *compression* of the sensible.

19. Ibid., 150.

20. Laruelle, *Principes de la non-philosophie*, 227, 228. One particularly interesting demonstration of this method of non-philosophical cloning is Laruelle's short, experimental piece "Variations on a Theme in Heidegger." Starting from one of the most important and often-quoted passages in Heidegger's *Being and Time*, the section in which Heidegger describes the ontic distinctiveness of *Dasein* in terms of it *being* ontological, Laruelle repeats and modulates Heidegger's language through sixteen successive paragraphs, like a musician circling back through various motifs, until Heidegger's claims become more or less globally transformed into non-philosophy. As Laruelle summarizes at the end, "Two series of variations divide up the Philosophical Decision and open it up to 'non-philosophy.' On the one hand, variations on the circle or the circle as variation: Being-as-being, Saying-as-said, *Lógos*-as-differe(a)nce, Desire-as-lack, Everydayness-as-subject and even Difference-as-One. . . . And on the other hand, in effect, variations that affect the ontical itself, either as being, as Other, as lack, as substitute—in short, as One. . . . When at last man—through the Vision-in-the-One that he 'is,' prior to all comprehension of Being—sees the circle of circles pass by again, it's so he can glimpse it as it passes outside and under the One, above and even 'over' him, like a cloud over the moon, or like the sun of reason over the inalterable opacity of man. It is then that philosophy floats, indifferent, through the air of 'non-philosophy'" (François Laruelle, "Variations sur en thème de Heidegger," *La Décision philosophique* 1 [May 1987]: 86–94, 93–94).

21. Laruelle, *Principes de la non-philosophie*, 273. Indeed, during his summary of the axioms and theorems of non-philosophy, Laruelle combines all of the following

figures into a unilateralized, transcendental identity: Plato, Aristotle, Leibniz, Kant, Fichte, Marx, Heidegger, Wittgenstein, and Gödel (ibid., 276–77).

22. Laruelle, *Philosophie non-standard*, 206.

23. François Laruelle, *The Concept of Non-photography / Le concept de non-photographie*, trans. Robin Mackay (Falmouth, U.K., and New York: Urbanomic and Sequence, 2011), 99.

24. Laruelle himself suggests the $n = 1$ formula and others like it including $A + A = A$. "In immanence, one no longer distinguishes between the One and the Multiple, there is no longer anything but n = 1, and the Multiple-without-All. No manifold watched over by a horizon, in flight or in progress: everywhere a true chaos of floating or inconsistent determinations. . . . Between Identity and Multiplicity, no synthesis by a third term . . ." (Laruelle, *The Concept of Non-photography*, 98–99).

These formulae illustrate the principle of *idempotence*. From the Latin meaning "having the same power" or "the capacity of being the same," an operation is idempotent when it produces a result of the same. For example, addition is idempotent with reference to zero because $1 + 0 = 1$, $2 + 0 = 2$, etc. "Idempotence is essentially a superposition ($1 + 1 = 1$ or $A + A = A$), a summation that is *almost* barren, an addition that produces the same kind of result or preserves its own truth. We may thus label it a non-ecstatic superposition" (Laruelle, *Philosophie non-standard*, 471; for idempotence see also 294–302).

Regarding such formulae it is important to remember that in Laruelle "and" typically means "equals." Just as Deleuze tends to recast negative operations as affirmative or creative, Laruelle recasts additive operations as revelations of identity or equality. Hence in Laruelle the expression "this *and* that" really means "this *is* that." The idempotent formula encapsulates it well: $1 + 1 = 1$ is simply a more verbose way of stating $1 = 1$. Likewise for vector or wave addition the addition of two waves simply produces a new wave. This is one of the key ways in which Laruelle differs from Deleuze. Recall Deleuze's discussion of the conjunctive series designated as "and, and, . . ." The conjunctive series is different from Laruelle's idempotent formula in two important ways. First, Deleuze eliminates the algebraic nature of the formula by eliminating the two sides held in balance by an equals sign. Second, Deleuze extends the expression off into the distance, allowing the proliferation of addition to continue unfettered. (Such is sufficient proof, according to Laruelle, of Deleuze's ultimate inability to think immanence fully.) In other words, Deleuze's ontology is a *calculus,* that is, differential units summed together while approaching infinity. Yet Laruelle's ontology is an *algebra,* that is, finite determinations of identity. Deleuze seeks the infinite expression of difference, while Laruelle the finite determination of equality. See, inter alia, Laruelle, *Philosophie non-standard*, 302–3.

25. Laruelle, *The Concept of Non-photography,* 10.

26. From comments made by Laruelle during a panel discussion at Miguel Abreu Gallery, New York, N.Y., April 6, 2011. In his late work, particularly *Philosophie non-standard,* Laruelle spends considerable time examining quantum mechanics

and the scientific theories of particles, waves, superposition, non-commutativity, and complementarity.

3. THE DIGITAL

1. Although digitality has received less attention, analogy is indeed a perennial theme in Western thought. In one of the more accomplished recent studies of philosophy and culture, Kaja Silverman begins from the perspective of analogy rather than difference, alterity, negation, or other themes more common to critical theory (see Kaja Silverman, *Flesh of My Flesh* [Stanford, Calif.: Stanford University Press, 2009]). Unlike Laruelle, Silverman considers analogy more important than identity, and she does us a great service in parsing the many fine distinctions among analogy, metaphor, correspondence, and resemblance (see, in particular, her chapter 7 [168–221]). Yet like Laruelle, Silverman recognizes the importance of *finitude* compared to the more abstract or idealist postures of transcendental metaphysics: "Finitude is the most capacious and enabling of the attributes we share with others, because unlike the particular way in which each of us looks, thinks, walks, and speaks, that connects us to a few other beings, [finitude] connects us to *every* other being. Since finitude marks the point where we end and others begin, spatially and temporally, it is also what makes room for them—and acknowledging these limits allows us to experience the expansiveness for which we yearn, because it gives us a powerful sense of our emplacement within a larger Whole" (4).

2. A notorious challenge for translators, Leonardo Tarán renders the passage modestly but appealingly as "for the same thing can be thought and can exist" (*Parmenides: A Text with Translation, Commentary, and Critical Essays* [Princeton: Princeton University Press, 1965], frag. 3, line 1). Alternate versions by other translators include "For to think and to be is one and the same thing," or "Thinking and Being are the same thing," or even simply "Non-Being is inconceivable," which despite its awkwardness would certainly follow from the claims made by Parmenides in fragment 2.

3. Bernard Stiegler, *For a New Critique of Political Economy*, trans. Daniel Ross (Cambridge: Polity Press, 2010), 31–32, 33.

4. François Laruelle, *Le principe de minorité* (Paris: Aubier, 1981), 5.

5. Laruelle discusses Fichte on a number of occasions, particularly his treatment of the "I" (the Self) and the relation "I = I" (Self = Self) only to dismiss Fichte's "I" as an "intellectual intuition" unable to achieve true immanence within the real. See, for example, Laruelle, *Principes de la non-philosophie*, 105–6 and 168–85.

6. Recall that tautology, although merely useless for many, is more malevolent for others, symptomatic of the depraved circularity of modern life. Marx, for example, begins his explication of the general formula for capital with the tautological expression M-M, or money-money, a contracted form of the C-M-C-M-C-M chain (commodity-money-etc.). This allows him to inject the concept of surplus into the chain, resulting in a cycle of M to M' (money to money prime)

where money is "not spent . . . [but] advanced" (Karl Marx, *Capital, vol. 1: A Critique of Political Economy,* trans. Ben Fowkes [London: Penguin, 1976], 249). Later, theorists like Jean Baudrillard and Guy Debord would lament the closed circuits of society and culture precisely for their seemingly impervious, tautological, and therefore repressive effects. "The spectacle is essentially tautological, for the simple reason that its means and its ends are identical" (Guy Debord, *The Society of the Spectacle,* trans. Donald Nicholson-Smith [New York: Zone Books, 1994], 15 [para. 13]). Laruelle, for his part, is content to shrug off such nefarious connotations. Immanence is too seductive a prize for him. Laruelle maintains that the tautological identity formula (viz. One-in-One) is the only true expression of immanence.

7. Gilles Deleuze, *Cinema 1: The Movement-Image,* trans. Hugh Tomlinson and Barbara Habberjam (Minneapolis: University of Minnesota Press, 1986), 1.

8. Here, as elsewhere, Deleuze takes inspiration from Henri Bergson. Contrasting ancient and modern scientific approaches, Bergson writes that "ancient science thinks it knows its object sufficiently when it has noted of it some privileged moments, whereas modern science considers the object at any moment whatever." Time is the key factor, because "modern science must be defined preeminently by its aspiration to take time as an independent variable." See Henri Bergson, *Creative Evolution,* trans. Arthur Mitchell (Mineola, N.Y.: Dover, 1998), 330, 336, emphasis removed.

9. The chief avatar of such an image regime, at least in *Cinema 2,* is Hans-Jürgen Syberberg. Deleuze describes "a new computer and cybernetic race, automata of computation and thought, automata with controls and feedback" (264–65), and singles out the "disingenuous" nature of electronic images: "a new image can arise from any point whatever of the preceding image" (Gilles Deleuze, *Cinema 2: The Time-Image,* trans. Hugh Tomlinson and Robert Galeta [Minneapolis: University of Minnesota Press, 1989], 264–65).

10. To this end, Élie During, in his book *Faux raccords: La coexistence des images* (Arles: Actes Sud, 2010), proposes the intriguing concept of the "volume-image."

11. See Deleuze, *Cinema 1,* 11.

12. Ibid., 111.

13. Deleuze, *Cinema 2,* 100, emphasis removed.

14. Ibid., 101.

15. Laruelle, "Du noir univers," 112.

16. McKenzie Wark's term for the reverse panopticon is *transopticon.* See McKenzie Wark, *Telesthesia: Communication, Culture and Class* (Cambridge: Polity Press, 2013), 207 and passim. An early instance of the reverse panopticon—in the form of a circular photographic studio—was built by François Willème in Paris in the early 1860s.

17. Laruelle is essentially an *illiberal* thinker in that he does not cede center stage to the unfettered freedoms of an empowered individual. Consider his discussion of the generic as fulfillment. "The generic means 'fulfillment,' just as we might speak of a 'fulfillment of the Law'" (Laruelle, *Philosophie non-standard,* 141

and repeated on 423). By alluding to Romans 13:8–10, "Whoever loves others has fulfilled the law," Laruelle means to indicate that the generic entails a determination of elemental conditions, not a liberation from the constraints of those conditions. "Whoever loves others has fulfilled the law" means essentially: whoever commits to loving the other has fulfilled the generic determination that "all are lovable" or "love is the radical medium of all." One must *fulfill* the generic law, therefore, not flee from it. One must *force* the generic, not liberate the transcendental, as liberal thinkers suggest.

This gets to the core of the distinction between a promiscuous or *liberal* ontology and a prophylactic or *radical* ontology. The liberal seeks a state of natural freedom with a minimum of laws, while the radical accepts at least a modicum of discipline, law, or commitment in order better to adhere to the generic common. A promiscuous ontology assumes a kind of ontological anarchy rooted in contingency and the seeming absence of law, while a prophylactic ontology posits axiomatically some sort of "foundation," law, or way. Promiscuous ontologies may seem attractive at first glance, because they are adept at corroding and collapsing even the most odious of normative hierarchies (patriarchy, orientalism, heteronormativity). Yet promiscuous ontologies have a danger of falling into a tyranny of structurelessness, in which "all that is solid melts into air" and things are caught up in the *larger* movements of an invisible engine of power. To be sure, prophylactic ontologies, if improperly wrought, also have their own dangers; they can easily slip into priggish moral philosophy, ontological essentialism, or even a kind of quasi-fascism. The key is to craft the non-foundation in such a way that it avoids these dangers. Deleuze's solution is to make the foundation immanent, multiple, and infinite. Badiou does something similar: transcendental, multiple, and infinite. Laruelle's solution is slightly different: the non-foundation of the one is immanent and generic, but also finite.

4. Events

1. Martin Heidegger, "The End of Philosophy and the Task of Thinking," in *On Time and Being*, 67.

2. Heidegger, "The Principle of Identity," in *Identity and Difference*, 26.

3. See, in particular, Georges Bataille, "Formless," in *Vision of Excess: Selected Writings, 1927–1939*, trans. Allan Stoekl (Minneapolis: University of Minnesota Press, 1985), 31, and Yve-Alain Bois and Rosalind E. Krauss, *Formless: A User's Guide* (New York: Zone Books, 2000).

4. See, for example, Laruelle, *Principes de la non-philosophie*, 213.

5. For his part, Badiou does not shy away from the image of the hero, as he admits at the end of *Logics of Worlds*: "I am sometimes told that I see in philosophy only a means to reestablish, against the contemporary apologia of the futile and the everyday, the rights of heroism. Why not? Having said that, ancient heroism claimed to justify life through sacrifice. My wish is to make heroism exist through the affirmative joy which is universally generated by following consequences through. We could say that the epic heroism of the one who gives his life is supplanted by

the mathematical heroism of the one who creates life, point by point" (Alain Badiou, *Logics of Worlds: Being and Event, 2,* trans. Alberto Toscano [London: Continuum, 2009], 514).

6. Indeed Laruelle is rather dismissive of the Deleuzian event: "Deleuze gives a standard, philosophically average description of the event because he brings together all its transcendental conditions in perfect equilibrium." See François Laruelle, "Identity and Event," trans. Ray Brassier, *Pli* 9 (2000): 174–89, 176.

7. Ibid.

8. Even Laruelle must expend much energy to demonstrate the extreme immanence of the one. For if the one is immanent to itself, why even suggest that it must "remain within" itself? Why instill even a modicum of doubt that there might exist a beyond to the one? To say that the one is immanent is, on the merits, not exactly true, because immanence speaks in the language of transcendence ("remaining") even as it negates transcendence in favor of inherent pervasiveness ("within"). And the one is absolutely incompatible with the transcendental—not that the transcendental is the negation of the one, but simply that the one is so pervasive and supersaturated in its identity that it absolutely preempts any transcendental whatsoever, except those cloned directly from its identity.

9. Deleuze, *Difference and Repetition,* 304, emphasis added.

10. Laruelle states his entire theory of the event succinctly as follows: "We distinguish between three modes of the event: 1. the intra-philosophical event or event-object of philosophies; 2. the world-Event with its philosophical form, or 'philosophy' insofar as it constitutes the prototypical or originary event; 3. a rigorous theory (that of the world-Event) as *non-philosophical Advent [Avènement];* one which is still primary but dependent on a cause of the last-instance" (Laruelle, "Identity and Event," 184). The first is thus the normal day-to-day level of events as relations and decisions. The second is philosophy itself, as a decision (the philosophical decision), and hence as an event superimposed into and coterminous with the world. The third mode, however, is the non-philosophical mode that withdraws from the evental decision in order to theorize the event itself as unilateral identity. "The Advent is no longer in excess of the World as given, because such an excess now belongs to the World. . . . The Advent comes neither from afar nor from on high. It emerges as a radical solitude that it is impossible to manipulate, to dominate, to reduce, like the solitude of great works of art. . . . It no longer announces anything, it is neither absence nor presence nor even an 'other presence', but rather unique solitude given-in-One in-the-last-instance. . . . The Advent is not more absolute than the philosophy-Event, which is already absolute, but it is radical. It is not more 'originary' in some vague manner, it is archi-originary or radically first" (ibid., 186, 187).

11. Deleuze, *The Logic of Sense,* 148.

12. Heidegger, "The Principle of Identity," 37, emphasis added.

13. Jean Baudrillard, *Passwords,* trans. Chris Turner (London: Verso, 2003), 61. Much more could be done on the relationship between Baudrillard and Laruelle,

particularly around the question of Baudrillard's concepts of fatal strategy, hyper-reversibility, and structural indifference. In a certain sense, Baudrillard invented a kind of proto-non-standard method *strictly within the available discourse of post-structuralism.*

5. Computers

1. François Laruelle, "Lettre à Deleuze," *La Décision philosophique* 5 (April 1988): 101–6.

2. François Dosse, *Gilles Deleuze and Félix Guattari: Intersecting Lives,* trans. Deborah Glassman (New York: Columbia University Press, 2010).

3. Gilles Deleuze, "Le 'Je me souviens' de Gilles Deleuze," *Le Nouvel Observateur* (November 16–22, 1995): 51. As Deleuzians are keen to point out, the aged Deleuze spoke of an upcoming book project devoted to "the grandeur of Marx," a book that unfortunately was never realized during his lifetime.

4. Jean-Louis Baudry et al., "La révolution ici maintenant: Sept points," *Tel Quel* 34 (October 1968): 3–4.

5. See, for example, the account given in Bernard Dionysius Geoghegan, "From Information Theory to French Theory: Jakobson, Lévi-Strauss, and the Cybernetic Apparatus," *Critical Inquiry* 38 (Autumn 2011): 96–126.

6. Parenthetical citations refer to Gilles Deleuze, "Postscript on Control Societies," in *Negotiations, 1972–1990,* trans. Martin Joughin (New York: Columbia University Press, 1995). Those seeking the French should consult Gilles Deleuze, *Pourparlers, 1972–1990* (Paris: Les Éditions de Minuit, 1990). Note that the original French essay first appeared a couple months prior in *L'Autre Journal* (May 1990) and bore a slightly shorter title, "Les sociétés de contrôle." The essay was thus never intended as a "postscript" to anything in particular, and only gained the appellation as a result of being bundled at the tail end of *Pourparlers.*

7. Deleuze, Guattari, and Foucault participated in the famous "Schizo Culture" conference held at Columbia University in 1975. Burroughs gave a talk at the conference titled "The Impasses of Control."

8. Laruelle heaps scorn on this kind of techno-science, or what he terms "world-research," an umbrella for all manner of think tanks, skunk works, innovation labs, R&D departments, research parks, government labs, nonprofit policy institutes, and university science initiatives. "Regarding the population of researchers, World-Research is a way of controlling them as 'subjects' adjunct to research initiatives and subjected to a specifically liberal and capitalist dominion over science" (Laruelle, *Introduction aux sciences génériques,* 31).

9. Today the expression "Web surfing" is common; however, because he was writing just prior to the advent of the Web, Deleuze's frame of reference would have included television and the phenomenon of channel surfing, as well as the actual sport of wave surfing. In an earlier piece titled "Mediators," also included in *Negotiations,* Deleuze says a bit more about surfing. "The kind of movements you find in sports and habits are changing. We got by for a long time with an energetic

conception of motion, where there's a point of contact, or we are the source of movement. Running, putting the shot, and so on: effort, resistance, with a starting point, a lever. But nowadays we see movement defined less and less in relation to a point of leverage. All the new sports—surfing, windsurfing, hang-gliding—take the form of entering into an existing wave. There's no longer an origin as starting point, but a sort of putting-into-orbit. The key thing is how to get taken up in the motion of a big wave, a column of rising air, to 'get into something' instead of being the origin of an effort" (Deleuze, *Negotiations,* 121). The surfing image also appears in *What Is Philosophy?* During their itemization of the features of conceptual personae, Deleuze and Guattari describe the dynamic features as follows: "If moving forward, climbing, and descending are dynamisms of conceptual personae, then leaping like Kierkegaard, dancing like Nietzsche, and diving like Melville are others for philosophical athletes irreducible to one another. And if today our sports are completely changing, if the old energy-producing activities are giving way to exercises that, on the contrary, insert themselves on existing energetic networks, this is not just a change in the type but yet other dynamic features that enter a thought that 'slides' with new substances of being, with wave or snow, and turn the thinker into a sort of surfer as conceptual persona" (Gilles Deleuze and Félix Guattari, *What Is Philosophy?* trans. Hugh Tomlinson and Graham Burchell [New York: Columbia University Press, 1994], 71).

10. In *Anti-Badiou: Sur l'introduction du maoïsme dans la philosophie* and other recent work, Laruelle has turned to quantum mechanics, particularly the principles of superposition and non-commutativity. English translator Robin Mackay has rendered Laruelle's *quantiel* as "quantware," mimicking the relationship between *logiciel* and software. See François Laruelle, *Anti-Badiou: On the Introduction of Maoism into Philosophy,* trans. Robin Mackay (London: Continuum, 2012).

11. Gilles Deleuze, *Francis Bacon: Logique de la sensation* (Paris: Éditions de la Différence, 1981). The French edition was expanded and reissued in 1984, then reprinted in Alain Badiou and Barbara Cassin's book series at Éditions du Seuil in 2002. The original French edition is in two volumes: volume 1 contains Deleuze's text, while volume 2 contains several reproductions from Bacon's paintings. The current French edition consolidates the volumes and contains only seven color plates. The English edition, which unfortunately features no imagery at all, was published in 2004 as Gilles Deleuze, *Francis Bacon: The Logic of Sensation,* trans. Daniel Smith (Minneapolis: University of Minnesota Press, 2004).

12. Published in the same year as Deleuze's *Francis Bacon,* Laruelle's *Le principe de minorité* also has something to say about digitality. Laruelle mentions three different kinds of multiplicities, (1) "discrete or arithmetic" multiplicities, (2) continuous multiplicities, which he associates with Difference, and (3) what he calls "dispersive multiplicities," which he also labels "Unary Multiplicities or Minorities," claiming that they are "the absolute concept or the essence of multiplicities" (p. 6). The first two are clearly code words for digital and analog: the realm of discrete arithmetic is the realm of the digital, while the realm of the continuous is the realm of the analog. What is so provocative, then, is the third term—that there

should be a third term. The provocation will eventually lead Laruelle away from digitality, precisely because it will lead him away from philosophy.

13. Deleuze, *Francis Bacon*, 95.

14. Deleuze, *Difference and Repetition*, 211.

15. Deleuze, *Francis Bacon*, 93.

16. Ibid., 95.

17. Ibid.

18. A few other relevant references exist such as Deleuze and Guattari's mention of "three ages" in their introduction to *What Is Philosophy?*: "The three ages of the concept are the encyclopedia, pedagogy, and commercial professional training" (12). See also Félix Guattari, "Modèle de contrainte ou modélisation créative," *Terminal* 53 (April–May 1991): 43.

19. Deleuze, *Negotiations*, 174, 175.

20. Gilles Deleuze, "Having an Idea in Cinema," in *Deleuze and Guattari: New Mappings in Politics, Philosophy and Culture,* ed. Eleanor Kaufman and Kevin Jon Heller (Minneapolis: University of Minnesota Press, 1998), 18, translation modified. This text also appears in a different form under the title "What Is the Creative Act?" in Gilles Deleuze, *Two Regimes of Madness: Texts and Interviews 1975–1995,* trans. Ames Hodges and Mike Taormina (New York: Semiotext(e), 2006), 312–24.

21. Gilles Deleuze "Qu'est-ce que l'acte de création?" http://www.webdeleuze .com/php/texte.php?cle=134&groupe=Conf%E9rences&langue=1). The reference to Minitel does not appear in the version of the essay collected in Gilles Deleuze, *Deux régimes de fous: Textes et entretiens 1975–1995* (Paris: Les Éditions de Minuit, 2003), and hence neither in the English translation contained in *Two Regimes of Madness.*

22. As Frédéric Astier notes in his doctoral thesis, Deleuze mentioned the superfold in his seminars on Foucault held on March 18 and 25, 1986. See Frédéric Astier, "La philosophie orale de Gilles Deleuze et son rôle dans l'élaboration de son œuvre écrite" (PhD thesis, Université Paris 8, Vincennes-Saint-Denis, France, December 3, 2007), 290–91. I thank Adeline Gasnier for bringing this to my attention. Toward the ending of the March 25 session Deleuze reiterates some of the ideas that would reappear in book form, specifying that the superfold is the fold *sur le dehors* (over the outside; a fold that incorporates the outside), an allusion to Foucault's concept of the "thought of the outside." See Gilles Deleuze, *Cours du 25 mars 1986. Sur Foucault. Le pouvoir: année universitaire 1985–1986.* 9., track 4; 41 min., 13 sec.; audio recording; from Bibliothèque nationale de France, http://gallica .bnf.fr/ark:/12148/bpt6k128388k. Deleuze's March 18, 1986, seminar is even more explicit: the historical shift from God to man to superman corresponds directly to the processes of unfolding (God), folding (man), and superfolding (superman). See Gilles Deleuze, *Cours du 18 mars 1986. Sur Foucault. Le pouvoir: année universitaire 1985–1986.* 8., track 1; 11 min., 15 sec.; audio recording; from Bibliothèque nationale de France, http://gallica.bnf.fr/ark:/12148/bpt6k1283876.

23. Gilles Deleuze, *Foucault,* trans. Seán Hand (Minneapolis: University of Minnesota Press, 1988), 92, 93.

24. Ibid., 130.

25. Ibid., 131–32. Just as Nietzsche's *Übermensch* is rendered alternately in English as "overman" or "superman," one might translate Deleuze's *surpli* as "overfold" as well as "superfold."

26. Gilles Deleuze, *The Fold: Leibniz and the Baroque,* trans. Tom Conley (Minneapolis: University of Minnesota Press, 1993), 6.

27. Laruelle has integrated fractals and what he calls "generalized fractality" into his work to great effect. See in particular his *Théorie des identités: Fractalité généralisée et philosophie artificielle* (Paris: PUF, 1992), and *The Concept of Non-photography.*

28. Such is the argument contained in Laruelle, "L'ordinateur transcendantal," 5–19.

29. Ibid., 13.

6. Capitalism

1. Louis Althusser, *Lenin and Philosophy: And Other Essays,* trans. Ben Brewster (New York: Monthly Review Press, 2001), 57.

2. Ibid., 52.

3. Fredric Jameson, *Representing* Capital: *A Reading of Volume One* (New York: Verso, 2011), 47, 23.

4. Ibid., 22.

5. At a revealing moment, Laruelle stresses that his kernel is "real" or "symptomatic" but never "rational," framing everything against an Althusserian backdrop. "Althusser's 'error,'" he writes, "is to have searched in Marx for the rational (and thus philosophical and idealist) kernel of the Hegelian dialectic; whereas, in all philosophers, one must first identify the real symptomatic kernel" (Laruelle, *Introduction au non-marxisme,* 46).

In the following passage Laruelle also evokes Marx's famous kernel metaphor, and as he often does Laruelle uses the analogy of non-Euclidean geometry to outline the position of non-philosophy vis-à-vis philosophy, or in this case non-Marxism vis-à-vis Marxism: "Such a project, in the spirit of a 'non-Euclidean' marxism, consists in producing, on the bases of this certain ingredient = X [i.e. the non-philosophical ingredient in marxism], the universal non-marxist kernel not *of* marxism but *for it and starting from it* simultaneously as symptom and model, in general as 'material'" (ibid., 6). In this way Laruelle's book on Marx finally fleshes out the larger claim, commonly heard in non-philosophy, that philosophy must stand as "material" for non-philosophy. With this book it is clearer what exactly Laruelle means by "material"; he means the material infrastructure, and further he means materialism as a bridge joining philosophy with scientific non-philosophy.

6. In a surprising turn of phrase, Althusser expresses a Laruellean impulse *avant la lettre* when in a 1976 lecture he writes that "to support our argument by comparison with the revolutionary State, which ought to be a State that is a 'non-State'—that is, a State tending to its own dissolution, to be replaced by forms of free

association—one might equally say that the philosophy which obsessed Marx, Lenin and Gramsci ought to be a 'non-philosophy'—that is, one which ceases to be produced in the form of a philosophy, whose function of theoretical hegemony will disappear in order to make way for new forms of philosophical existence" (Louis Althusser, "The Transformation of Philosophy," trans. Thomas Lewis, in *Philosophy and the Spontaneous Philosophy of the Scientists, and Other Essays* [London: Verso 1990], 264). But even earlier, in February 1968, he had already called for a "non-philosophy" during his explanation of the syntax of the title "Lenin *and* Philosophy": "Not Lenin's philosophy, but Lenin *on* philosophy. In fact, I believe that what we own to Lenin, something which is perhaps not completely unprecedented, but certainly invaluable, is the beginnings of the ability to talk a kind of discourse which anticipates what will one day perhaps be a non-philosophical theory of philosophy" (Althusser, *Lenin and Philosophy*, 14). Or a few lines earlier when Althusser anticipates Laruelle's emblematic preference for the preposition *in* instead of the preposition *of*, indeed not just a preference but an absolute mandate: Althusser tells the audience assembled at the Société Française de Philosophie that his talk "will be a talk *in* philosophy. But this talk in philosophy will not quite be a talk *of* philosophy. It will be, or rather will try to be, a talk *on* philosophy" (ibid., 13). Had he been present, Laruelle would most certainly have agreed with such an elevation of *in* over *of*.

7. Although the political import of Laruelle's work is distributed in a complex fashion across his entire body of work, two books, *Le principe de minorité* and *Une biographie de l'homme ordinaire: Des Autorités et des Minorité* (Paris: Aubier, 1985), are notable for their description of dispersive or "minoritarian" multiplicities and the minority individuation or minoritarian thought of the "ordinary man" as he exists in a determinative relation to states, authorities, and worlds.

In the non-Marxism book, Laruelle speaks of these categories of subjecthood in terms of a "subject-in-struggle." This subject would be a "non-proletarian" or "universal stranger" summoned not from the call for "workers of the world to unite!" but rather from a call to remain "unified" in immanent identity. See Laruelle, *Introduction au non-marxisme*, 118, as well as all of chapter 6 (109–39).

An additional, shorter text is relevant here too, Laruelle's "précis" of non-Marxism, "Pour un marxisme clandestin" (manuscript, undated), which reiterates and amplifies the issues first broached in the 2000 book.

8. Innumerable are the ways in which philosophers have tried to normalize materialism in order to make it more palatable, writes Laruelle. He lists several of the guilty parties: normalization "by existentialism (Sartre), by structure (Althusser), by the transcendental phenomenology of auto-affecting life (Henry), by the transindividual as a synthesis of the collective and the individual (Balibar), by deconstruction of its 'specters' (Derrida), by contractuality and metastructure (Bidet)" (Laruelle, *Introduction au non-marxisme*, 33).

9. Ibid., 5, emphasis removed.

10. Laruelle is admittedly somewhat vulnerable to the same critique that Rancière makes of Althusser in *Althusser's Lesson*. In that book Rancière indicts Althusser

on the grounds of intellectual elitism, that Althusser, by making Marx more scientific, was only making Marxism "safe" for university professors and other elite technicians. See Jacques Rancière, *La leçon d'Althusser* (Paris: Gallimard, 1974), 35.

11. For an extensive discussion of science and philosophy see chapter 2 in Laruelle, *Principes de la non-philosophie*. In the non-Marxism book, Laruelle attacks Althusser directly, devoting a number of pages to how the Althusserian concepts of "problematic" and "epistemological break" should be superseded by "unified theory." See Laruelle, *Introduction au non-marxisme*, 78–83.

12. Laruelle, *Introduction au non-marxisme*, 22.

13. To help explain this sense of "universal capitalism," Laruelle writes that "the real universal object of non-marxism will be capitalism *plus* the entire set of its philosophical conditions structured in their 'essence,' which is to say 'universal' capitalism in the radical sense of the term, the synthesis of capitalism and the essence of philosophy under the auspices, the one and the other, of 'World'" (ibid., 8). In other words, one cannot simply examine capitalism itself, one must look at the "World" produced from the grand collaboration between capitalism and philosophy. Laruelle admits, then, that the subject of his non-Marxism book is, in the most general sense, "philosophically universal capitalism" (ibid., 9).

14. Ibid., 145.

15. Ibid., 10.

16. Ibid., 42.

17. Karl Marx, *The Eighteenth Brumaire of Louis Bonaparte* (New York: International Publishers, 1963), 47.

18. Karl Marx, *Early Writings*, trans. Rodney Livingstone and Gregor Benton (London: Penguin, 1974), 425.

19. Ibid.

20. Laruelle discusses *force de travail* and *force (de) pensée* together in *Introduction au non-marxisme*, 111–15.

21. Ibid., 39.

22. Ibid., 27.

23. Ibid., 40.

24. The DLI logic in Laruelle is indeed unique. Heidegger's being-unto-death is perhaps another instance of this unusual logic, to the extent that being-unto-death requires the construction of a relation with an event, one's death, from which it is impossible to achieve a reciprocated relation in return. See, in particular, the second half of Heidegger, *Being and Time*. Heidegger writes that death is non-relational and yet nevertheless still "mine": "Death is the possibility of the absolute impossibility of Dasein" (294).

25. See, in particular, Badiou's discussion of the communist hypothesis in Alain Badiou, *The Meaning of Sarkozy*, trans. David Fernbach (London: Verso, 2008) and Alain Badiou, *The Communist Hypothesis*, trans. David Macey and Steve Corcoran (London: Verso, 2010). According to Badiou the communist hypothesis existed already, under modernity at least, during two historical periods, 1792–1871 from the French Revolution to the Paris Commune, and 1917–76 from the Russian

Revolution to the end of the Cultural Revolution in China. Based on this periodization, Badiou forecasts the appearance of a third historical phase for the communist hypothesis.

Marx's "mole," originally from a passage in *The Eighteenth Brumaire of Louis
Napoleon*—"The revolution is thoroughgoing. . . . It does its work methodically. . . .
When it has done this second half of its preliminary work, Europe will leap from
its seat and exultantly exclaim: Well grubbed, old mole!" (Marx, *The Eighteenth
Brumaire of Louis Napoleon*, 121; Marx was paraphrasing from *Hamlet*: "Well said,
old mole! canst work i' the earth so fast?" [Act 1, Scene V])—has been revived most
recently in Michael Hardt and Antonio Negri, *Empire* (Cambridge, Mass.: Harvard
University Press, 2000), 57–58. In contrast to the old mole of the nineteenth and
early twentieth centuries, Hardt and Negri propose a new metaphor of the snake,
suggesting that today's political events, with their "infinite undulations" (57), can
strike like a snake at any time and from any place against the very core of Empire.

26. Laruelle, *Introduction au non-marxisme*, 17.

27. Ibid., 7.

28. Althusser, *Lenin and Philosophy*, 36. The Hegelian undertones here—a science of logic as pure thought—are ironic given Althusser's antipathy for Hegel.

29. Karl Korsch, *Three Essays on Marxism* (New York: Monthly Review Press,
1972), 65, emphasis removed.

30. Laruelle, *Introduction au non-marxisme*, 38.

31. Ibid., 37.

32. Gilles Deleuze, *Kant's Critical Philosophy*, trans. Hugh Tomlinson and Barbara Habberjam (London: Athlone Press, 1984), 11.

33. Kant, *Prolegomena*, 1, 24, 25, 26, 31, and passim.

7. THE BLACK UNIVERSE

1. See, in particular, the second chapter of Laruelle, *Principes de la non-
philosophie*, titled "First Science as Unified Theory of Science and Philosophy, or
Democracy within Thought" (43–93).

2. Laruelle, "Du noir univers," 107–12, 111. Since its inaugural issue, Laruelle's
journal *La Décision philosophique* was organized in two sections, a more or less
straightforward opening section, followed by a shorter, more informal ending section dubbed "Experimentation; Fiction; Hyper-speculation." If the main articles in
the journal resembled traditional attempts to grapple with philosophy from a non-
standard point of view, the ending section touted actual examples of what it would
mean to write non-philosophically. "Du noir univers" ("On the Black Universe")
appeared in the hyper-speculative, experimental section of the journal, bundled in
the pages immediately following Laruelle's notorious five-page "Letter to Deleuze."

3. Ibid., 112.

4. Ibid., 111.

5. Deleuze, *Cinema 2*, 200.

6. François Laruelle, "Biographie de l'oeil," *La Décision philosophique* 9 (1989):
93–104, 96.

7. Ibid.

8. Using internal quotations from Kandinsky, Michel Henry writes that "black is a nothingness bereft of possibilities. It is a future 'without hope' and a death 'as if the sun had become extinct'. It comes 'full circle', a 'spent funeral-pyre', something motionless, like a corpse, which is dead to all sensations'" (Michel Henry, *Seeing the Invisible: On Kandinsky,* trans. Scott Davidson [London: Continuum, 2009], 78–79).

9. Ibid., 97.

10. Ibid., 99.

11. Heidegger, *Being and Time,* 171.

12. In an essay devoted to media theory, written concurrently with this book, I describe such modes of mediation at greater length: the two, the one, and the multiple are three discrete "middles" condensed into the three Greek divinities Hermes, Iris, and the Eumenides. See "Love of the Middle" in Alexander R. Galloway, Eugene Thacker, and McKenzie Wark, *Excommunication: Three Inquiries in Media and Mediation,* 25–76 (Chicago: University of Chicago Press, 2013).

13. Reza Negarestani, *Cyclonopedia: Complicity with Anonymous Materials* (Melbourne: re.press, 2008), 26.

14. Athanasius Kircher was known to have a catoptric chest "completely filled with a treasure of all sorts of delicacies, fruits, and precious ornaments," as described by his student Kaspar Schott: "You will exhibit the most delightful trick if you [introduce into the chest] a live cat, as Fr. Kircher has done. While the cat sees himself to be surrounded by an innumerable multitude of catoptric cats, some of them standing close to him and others spread very far away from him, it can hardly be said how many jokes will be exhibited in that theatre, while he sometimes tries to follow the other cats, sometimes to entice them with his tail, sometimes attempts a kiss, and indeed tries to break through the obstacles in every way with his claws so that he can be united with the other cats, until finally, with various noises, and miserable whines he declares his various affections of indignation, rage, jealousy, love and desire." See Georgio de Sepibus, *Romani Collegii Musaeum Celeberrimum . . .* and Kaspar Schott, *Magia Universalis,* quoted in Michael John Gorman and Nick Wilding, "Techica Curiosa: The Mechanical Marvels of Kaspar Schott (1608–1666)," in Kaspar Schott, *La "Technica Curiosa"* (Florence: Edizioni dell'Elefante, 2000), 260, 274.

15. Franciscus Aguilonius, *Opticorum Libri Sex, philosophis juxta ac mathematicis utiles* (Antwerp: Plantin Press, 1613), bk. 1, pp. 31, 33.

16. Quoted in Martin Jay, *Downcast Eyes: The Denigration of Vision in Twentieth-Century French Thought* (Berkeley: University of California Press, 1994), 73.

17. Eugene Thacker, "Three Questions on Demonology," in *Hideous Gnosis: Black Metal Theory Symposium 1,* ed. Nicola Masciandaro, 179–219, (New York: Glossator, 2010), 186.

18. Negarestani, *Cyclonopedia,* 28.

19. Laruelle, "Du noir univers," 111.

20. Far from rejecting the color spectrum outright, Laruelle embraces it, recasting color as the "material" for non-philosophical thinking. Every philosophy contains a special hue, Laruelle suggests, a special color of thought that differentiates it from others around it. "Another non-philosophical effect has to do with the color of thought," he notes. "We obtain such color via the superposition of philosophical styles. . . . The signature claims of a given philosophy have a certain wavelength with a determined propagation frequency or period, and this distinguishes them from the same claims made by other authors while still allowing one to be superpositioned on top of another. This is how we acquire a certain color of thought from out of the pile of individual concepts—but not merely a new thought system or rigid doctrine, never just a Marxist color, a zen color, or a phenomenology color. Thought is a prism first, a spectrum of radiation. Only 'later' is it a system" (Laruelle, *Philosophie non-standard,* 478).

21. Laruelle, *The Concept of Non-photography,* 77.

22. Ibid., 34.

23. Laruelle, "Biographie de l'oeil," 98.

24. Ibid.

25. Laruelle, *The Concept of Non-photography,* 95, 12.

26. Ibid., 47.

27. Laruelle, "Du noir univers," 112.

28. Laruelle, "Biographie de l'oeil," 96.

29. Ibid., 99.

30. Ibid.

31. Ibid.

32. Ibid., 102.

8. Art and Utopia

1. François Laruelle, "A Light Odyssey: La découverte de la lumière comme problème théorique et esthétique" (undated typescript), 1. The text was written for an exhibition of James Turrell's work at le Confort Moderne in Poitiers, France, in the early 1990s. Although more specific details are elusive, it was likely published in 1991 on the occasion of James Turrell's exhibition "Heavy Water" at at le Confort Moderne.

A number of secondary sources are available on Turrell and his work, including Craig Adcock, *James Turrell: The Art of Light and Space* (Berkeley: University of California Press, 1990), and Georges Didi-Huberman, *L'Homme qui marchait dans la couleur* (Paris: Minuit, 2001). While acknowledging his use of light, Didi-Huberman characterizes Turrell primarily as an artist of space and movement.

2. "First Light: Twenty Etchings by James Turrell" (press release), Museum of Modern Art, New York (July 1990).

3. Quoted in Amanda Boetzkes, *The Ethics of Earth Art* (Minneapolis: University of Minnesota Press, 2010), 119, emphasis added.

4. Laruelle, "A Light Odyssey," 1.

5. Ibid.

6. Ibid., 6.

7. Ibid., 8. On the topic of phenomenological revealing, Laruelle also notes that "when a subject is in a 'Turrellean' mode, its affect does not allow for a light that would be hidden and/or unveiled" (ibid., 9). The key issue for Laruelle is that philosophy prohibits any kind of direct thought in light. Rather philosophy tends toward reflections *on* light. "Light is the medium most favored by philosophy, and so philosophy—by way of ontology and phenomenology—must be understood as love of light more than light itself, just as philosophy is love of wisdom more than wisdom itself" (ibid., 5).

8. Ibid., 10.

9. Ibid., 14.

10. Ibid., 20. To be clear, Laruelle uses the term *identity* to mean something very particular, the immanent common. As has been stressed throughout, his use of the term should not be confused with the way *identity* is used in discourses on identity politics or postmodern subject formation, particularly because these discourses typically use identity as a way to examine difference, not the common.

11. Ibid., 5.

12. Laruelle, *The Concept of Non-photography,* and François Laruelle, *Photo-Fiction, a Non-standard Aesthetics / Photo-fiction, une esthétique non-standard,* trans. Drew Burk (Minneapolis: Univocal, 2012).

13. Laruelle, *Photo-Fiction,* 4, translation modified.

14. Ibid.

15. Laruelle, *The Concept of Non-photography,* 11.

16. Laruelle, *Photo-Fiction,* 37. See also the first chapter in section 2 of Laruelle, *Philosophie non-standard,* devoted to the flash and the principle of sufficient light (95–105).

17. Laruelle, *Photo-Fiction,* 6, translation modified. For idiosyncratic if not pedantic reasons my preference is to reverse the word order of some of Laruelle's hyphenated terms and render *photo-fiction* as "fiction-photography" or "fiction-photo." In greater deference to the original French, translator Drew Burk has opted to follow Laruelle's word order. For more on Laruelle's use of the term *fiction,* see chapter 16 of Laruelle, *Philosophie non-standard,* 479–504.

18. Laruelle, *Photo-Fiction,* 55, translation modified. Given that photography indexes and orients itself reflexively in relation to a world, Laruelle is intent on labeling all of photography, and indeed philosophy, as characteristically modern, modernist even. "Photography is the Modernist art par excellence," he remarks. But fiction-photography is different; "fiction-photography *[photo-fiction]* is precisely the passage from an exemplarily modern aesthetics to a contemporary and inventive aesthetics that conjugates the arts and unfolds them" (ibid., 38–39, translation modified). Thus by way of generic extension or generalization, fiction-photography avoids modernism's penchant for both meta-reflection and narcissistic autonomy—that old chestnut "art for art's sake." In this way, Laruelle might be characterized not so much as modern or antimodern but *alter-modern,* because he asserts a nonreflexive autonomous real that is not contrary to the modern but exists alongside it.

Like Laruelle, Henry is also essentially an anti- or alter-modern thinker. He exhibits a certain superficial distrust of modern technology, of course, as is the case of those he writes about (Husserl, Heidegger, Schopenhauer, Kandinsky). But Henry's alter-modernity is more fundamental than that. Consider those emblematic modern assertions: the medium is the message; the form determines the content; the conditions of possibility of thinking determine what can be said and thought. These kinds of claims are *the* emblematic form of modernity, whether the early modern thought of Galileo or Descartes, or a more contemporary Kant, Foucault, or McLuhan. Yet as an alter-modern, Henry argues precisely the reverse: content determines form; Inner Necessity determines composition; spirit determines matter; will or affect determines representation.

19. Laruelle, *The Concept of Non-photography,* 8.

20. Ibid., 94.

21. Ibid., 12.

22. François Laruelle, *Struggle and Utopia at the End Times of Philosophy,* 12.

23. See, for example, Laruelle, *Struggle and Utopia at the End Times of Philosophy,* where he is explicit about the connection between non-philosophy and the utopia narratives common in science fiction: "In passing from the world to the Universe without horizon, and from a terrestrial technics to utopian technology, the future of humanity comes to be of the utmost importance for science fiction, which tears it away from its traditional foundational tasks in the World and consecrates it to utopia" (4). However, Laruelle considers standard utopias to be oriented toward the past, whatever chronology they might propose, while nonstandard utopia is properly future oriented because of its axiomatic and oracular logic.

24. August von Briesen was born August 16, 1935, in Budapest, Hungry, to a German father and a Hungarian mother. His life was marked by a series of upheavals, and he eventually emigrated out of Hungary to England in the wake of the Soviet invasion of Hungary in 1956. He lived in a few different countries before settling in France in 1972. The biographic record is uncertain, and von Briesen himself was secretive about his own name and origins; however, it is possible his birth name was József Kovács or József Kovács-Gömöri. His death at the age of sixty-eight is shrouded in pathos; he died alone in poverty in Paris, where he succumbed to the heat wave of 2003. "At the end of his life," the newspapers recounted at the time, "the Hungarian emigre was living off of the meal vouchers provided by the local social services office of the 16th arrondissement. He died at the age of 68 in his small attic apartment on the Avenue Foch" ("Le destin tragique d'August von Briesen" [obituary], *Le Parisien* [September 11, 2003], http://www.leparisien.fr /societe/le-destin-tragique-d-august-von-briesen-11–09–2003–2004380805.php.) The summer heat wave claimed a number of lives that year, particularly among the elderly. It was feared that he would be buried in potter's field, because his body went unclaimed for some time before eventually being identified. After his death a certain Mr. Yves Pozzo di Borgo put forth a petition that the city acquire a work by von Briesen for the Musée National d'Art Moderne at the Centre Pompidou.

However, according to the transcript of a 2004 city council debate, various attempts to track down von Briesen's heirs were unsuccessful, and they were unable to make the acquisition.

25. See Michel Henry, "Graphie de la subjectivité," in François Laruelle, ed., *Réflexions philosophiques sur l'oeuvre d'August von Briesen* (Paris: Fondation Brandenburg-Neumark, 1984): 25–60, which was reprinted with minor changes as Michel Henry, "Dessiner la musique: Théorie pour l'art de Briesen," *Le Nouveau Commerce* 61 (Spring 1985): 49–106, and again reprinted in Michel Henry, *Phéno-ménologie de la vie, Tome III: De l'art et du politique* (Paris: PUF, 2004): 241–82; Henry, *Seeing the Invisible*; and Marcelin Pleynet, "Musical Drawing and Graphic Drawing in the Work of August von Briesen," trans. Stephen Bann, in Laurent Michel, ed., *Briesen: L'offrande musicale* (Geneva: Musée de l'Athénée, 1981).

26. Laruelle, *Réflexions philosophiques sur l'oeuvre d'August von Briesen*, 175.

27. Ibid., 176.

28. Although his pencil drawings seem to have garnered the most attention, at least from Henry and Laruelle, von Briesen did not work exclusively in that medium. He worked commercially as an illustrator, designing the covers of books, and he was a moderately successful painter as well, painting a number of landscapes and interiors. In addition to the small pencil drawings of music, his images of music were also reproduced in large form: "1985 was designated the European Year of Music by the Council of Europe, and for this occasion August von Briesen created two 40 by 40 foot [12 × 12 m] color paintings of Mozart's opera 'Don Giovanni,' one each for the first and second acts. Six other color paintings were done in the same format for Brahms' Symphony number 4. Two canvasses at the same size, this time in black and white, depicted Bach's Goldberg Variations" (ibid).

29. Henry, "Graphie de la subjectivité," 32.

30. Ibid.

31. Ibid., 38, 42, emphasis added.

32. François Laruelle, "Réflexions philosophiques sur l'oeuvre d'August von Brie-sen," in Laruelle, *Réflexions philosophiques sur l'oeuvre d'August von Briesen*, 14.

33. Ibid., 16. Music must have had an almost synesthetic power over von Brie-sen. "Barthes said, 'there must be something wrong with me, I see language.' Von Briesen could easily say, 'there must be something wrong with me, I draw music. . . . As a listener I don't hear the music so much as see it, but as an artist, I don't see music, I listen at the very depths of drawing'" (ibid., 20).

34. Henry, "Graphie de la subjectivité," 54, emphasis removed.

35. Pleynet, "Musical Drawing and Graphic Drawing in the Work of August von Briesen," 96, 90. "The drawing offers us a sensory image not the image of a melodic line but that of a sonorous space which has already been established" (96).

36. Laruelle, "Réflexions philosophiques sur l'oeuvre d'August von Briesen," 16. In his essay on the transcendental computer, Laruelle makes a distinction between the automaton and what he calls the "unimaton." Making a play on words with the prefixes *auto-* and *uni-*, Laruelle seeks to highlight the auto-relational nature of

philosophy and the uni-relational nature of non-standard philosophy. See Laruelle, "L'ordinateur transcendantal, 5–19.

37. Laruelle makes a number of references to "black boxes," "black music boxes," and even a musical *camera obscura*, Latin for "dark chamber." "Von Briesen likes to work 'in the dark,'" by sitting in the orchestra pit rather than with the audience, "because he knows that in the pit he is positioned just at the point where he can, despite everything, *manifest as a whole and without remainder the musical real*" (Laruelle, "Réflexions philosophiques sur l'oeuvre d'August von Briesen," 14).

38. François Laruelle, "La plus haute des contemplations," in *Réflexions philosophiques sur l'oeuvre d'August von Briesen*, 154.

39. Laruelle, "Réflexions philosophiques sur l'oeuvre d'August von Briesen," 16.

40. Ibid., 12.

41. Ibid., 12, 14. At times Laruelle adopts an almost Deleuzian vocabulary and describes the way in which "philosophers like Bergson, Merleau-Ponty, and Nietzsche have described this world of flows, of vibrations and rhythms, of condensations and dissipations, of variations in intensity that come before the perceptual and pictorial order" (Laruelle, "La plus haute des contemplations," 150). Von Briesen's style is not simply that of a "romantic interiority" or a "musical nostalgia," but rather a more remote and "splendid world of multiplicities" (ibid., 164).

42. Laruelle refuses to contextualize von Briesen within the tradition of the avant-garde, modernist or otherwise. "Rather than calling [von Briesen's work] a kind of *musico-graphical 'happening' or action-drawing*, which would still only be a superficial interpretation of the work . . . we might rather label it a kind of *free-floating graphicality* (just as psychoanalysts speak of a 'free-floating attention')" (ibid., 158).

43. For an author who is keen to suppress or obfuscate his own philosophical lineage, particularly so after the earliest phases of his career, Laruelle's writings on von Briesen overflow with a profoundly Nietzschean sensibility: "Von Briesen is animated by an almost excessive *will-to-draw [vouloir-dessiner]*. He expresses himself through a permanent struggle with the music . . . . A willful drawing, but even more than willful, the drawing of the will, the *will-to-draw* directly within present conditions, the gesture *burns within the moment*" (Laruelle, "Réflexions philosophiques sur l'oeuvre d'August von Briesen," 16, 18). The Nietzschean influence is perhaps not surprising given Laruelle's early book on Nietzsche (*Nietzsche contra Heidegger: Thèses pour une politique nietzschéenne* [Paris: Payot, 1977]) and the role that Nietzsche plays in *Les philosophies de la différence* (Paris: PUF, 1986). Laruelle's writings on von Briesen come near the start of the period of what Laruelle has labeled "Philosophy II" (1981–95), the phase of his writings that marks the beginning of non-philosophy proper. The Nietzsche book was published in 1977 and marks the end of "Philosophy I," the first period of his work, which he admitted several years later was still "placed under the authority of the Principle of Sufficient Philosophy" (Laruelle, *Principes de la non-philosophie*, 39).

As for the topic of Nietzsche and music, "we know that Nietzsche composed music, which at any rate was likely not that good, but what would a 'Nietzschean'

music be if it existed? . . . Music becomes Nietzschean with von Briesen, or at the
very least it ceases to be reactive, ceases to be a mere 'appendage' relying on the
canvas and its graphical methods in order to 'come to the surface'" (Laruelle,
"Réflexions philosophiques sur l'oeuvre d'August von Briesen," 12).

Henry makes the connection explicit as well, linking von Briesen with both
Schopenhauer and Nietzsche: "Schopenhauer is, along with Nietzsche, one of the
rare philosophers with whom von Briesen felt a profound affinity" (Henry,
"Graphie de la subjectivité," 28). Or by von Briesen's own admission: "As a child I
was fragile and weak, beaten down and humiliated. But now I have become strong.
I possess a terrible force. For instance I would kill anyone if they so much as
touched my children. . . . I was already Nietzschean before I even read Nietzsche
for the first time" (ibid., 38).

44. Ibid., 36.

45. Ibid., 34.

46. Hal Foster concisely summarizes the present conjuncture in his article
"Post-Critical" published in *October* 139 (Winter 2012): 3–8.

47. For more on theories of aesthetic immanence in the French tradition, see
Mikel Dufrenne, *The Phenomenology of Aesthetic Experience* [1953], trans. Edward
Casey et al. (Evanston, Ill.: Northwestern University Press, 1973); Étienne Souriau,
"A General Methodology for the Scientific Study of Aesthetic Appreciation," trans.
Van Meter Ames, *Journal of Aesthetics and Art Criticism* 14, no. 1 (September 1955):
1–18; and Gérard Genette, *The Work of Art: Immanence and Transcendence,* trans.
G. M. Goshgarian (Ithaca, N.Y.: Cornell University Press, 1997). It is known that
Deleuze's explorations into the immanent aesthetics of cinema were at least partially influenced by Dufrenne (see Deleuze, *Cinema 1,* 231 n. 16). And Genette himself cites Souriau on the "plurality of modes of existence" (12). Although Genette
devotes considerable attention to the topic of aesthetic immanence in his book, the
concept comes across quite differently from that of Laruelle. For Genette, immanence is essentially a way of describing the specific fixed materiality of a work of
art, and is thus a synonym for "material objects" (31) or "unique objects of immanence" (32). "Autographic objects of immanence, which consist in physical things
or events, fall, naturally, within the province of the senses, lending themselves to
direct perception through sight, hearing, touch, taste, smell, or a combination of
two or more of the senses" (29). Genette borrows the term *autographic* (and its
companion, *allographic*) from Nelson Goodman, *Languages of Art: An Approach
to a Theory of Symbols* (Indianapolis: Hackett, 1976).

48. Philosophical realism concerns whether or not reality exists independently
of the observer, and realism carries its own meaning in law, international relations,
and several other fields. In the arts, realism bears a profusion of different and
sometimes divergent meanings. Realism in literature and fine art refers to the
depictions of the conditions of everyday life that emerged in nineteenth-century
France particularly after 1848 with Courbet and others, or in literature with Balzac
or Flaubert. *Social* realism, as in Walker Evans's photographs of the American

Great Depression, extends and modulates these concerns by focusing on the conditions of the disenfranchised. In a different sense, the *socialist* realism of socialist and communist countries orients itself around the revolutionary or post-revolutionary subject, as in Gladkov's novel *Cement* (1925) depicting post-revolutionary Russia or the Stalinist architecture of the Palace of Culture and Science in Warsaw. Further, the post–World War II films of Visconti, Rossellini, de Sica, and others represent a slightly different approach to realism. Known as Italian *neorealism,* such films were notable for shooting on location, using inexpensive cameras and sound equipment, casting nonprofessional actors, and focusing on poverty and other proletarian themes. For some deeper reflection on these many issues, see in particular T. J. Clark, *The Painting of Modern Life: Paris in the Art of Manet and His Followers* (Princeton, N.J.: Princeton University Press, 1999), and the chapter "The Existence of Italy" in Fredric Jameson, *Signatures of the Visible* (New York: Routledge, 1992), 155–229. John Mullarkey has also explicitly described the relation between Laruelle and Italian neorealism in his essay "The Tragedy of the Object: Democracy of Vision and the Terrorism of Things in Bazin's Cinematic Realism," *Angelaki* 17, no. 4 (2012): 39–59.

49. Although there is not enough room in the present volume to grant Henry the necessary attention that he deserves, suffice it to say that Henry represents a very different kind of immanence, and indeed a very different kind of phenomenology. Like other phenomenologists, a central concept for him is revelation. Yet Henry does not seek a revelation of the world. Instead, like Laruelle, Henry seeks an "immanent revelation" interior to the human self, because, as he puts it, the truth of man is "more original than the truth of Being" (Henry, *The Essence of Manifestation,* 41). Thus Henry displays not so much an immanence of matter, but an immanence of life, spirit, or Ego. "To want 'to bring to light' the foundation is the ultimate ontological absurdity," Henry claims, rebuffing Heidegger and other likeminded phenomenologists. "The universal light is not the homeland of all phenomena. The 'invisible' is the mode of a positive and truly fundamental revelation" (ibid., 42, 44). Henry's term for this is *affect;* Schopenhauer, a great influence on Henry, calls it *will.*

Art is never art of what is seen, only what is unseen. As Henry says of both Kandinsky and von Briesen, to paint is to paint the *invisible* because what is rendered is always an affect, a will, an internality, an immanence, a life: "The content of painting, of all paintings, is the Internal, the invisible life that does not cease to be invisible and remains forever in the Dark. . . . To paint is to show, but this showing has the aim of letting us see what is not seen and cannot be seen. The means of painting . . . sink into the Night of this abyssal subjectivity that no ray of light can enter and that no dawn will ever dissipate" (Henry, *Seeing the Invisible,* 10).

Henry's commitment to abstraction is formidable in the Kandinsky book. He maintains that even the material support of painting, not just its compositional content, is abstract. Even the points and lines on the canvas are pure abstractions. "The means by which [painting] expresses this invisible content—forms and colours—are themselves invisible" (ibid., 9). Ultimately he agrees with Laruelle on the question of utopia and the withdrawal from the world: "'Abstract' no longer refers to what is derived from the world at the end of a process of simplification or complication or at the end of the history of modern painting: instead, it refers to what was prior to the world and does not need the world in order to exist. It refers to the life that is embraced in the night of its radical subjectivity, where there is no light or world" (ibid., 16).

50. Deleuze has been the most influential of all the late twentieth-century theorists of immanent or realist aesthetics, inspiring a new generation of writers focused on the direct, material, and real conditions of art. See, in particular: Brian Massumi's two books, *Parables for the Virtual: Movement, Affect, Sensation* (Durham, N.C.: Duke University Press, 2002) and *Semblance and Event: Activist Philosophy and the Occurent Arts* (Cambridge, Mass.: MIT Press, 2011); Elizabeth Grosz, *Chaos, Territory, Art: Deleuze and the Framing of the Earth* (New York: Columbia University Press, 2008); and Steven Shaviro, *Without Criteria: Kant, Whitehead, Deleuze, and Aesthetics* (Cambridge, Mass.: MIT Press, 2009). A lesser-known text, parallel to Deleuze and cited by him, is Bernard Cache's 1983 book on geography, architecture, and topological theory titled *Earth Moves: The Furnishing of Territories,* trans. Anne Boyman (Cambridge, Mass.: MIT Press, 1995).

51. See Martin Heidegger, *Poetry, Language, Thought,* trans. Albert Hofstadter (New York: HarperCollins, 1971).

52. Deleuze's aesthetics centralizes the role of production and desire while minimizing or eliminating representational and metaphysical structures. A number of contemporary thinkers have explored the centrality of production and creativity in philosophy, whether aesthetic or more strictly ontological. See, in particular, Iain Hamilton Grant, *Philosophies of Nature after Schelling* (London: Continuum, 2006) and Steven Shaviro, *Without Criteria,* in which, in an unorthodox reading, Shaviro suggests that Kant's aesthetics was itself already immanent or nonrepresentational. A more classical text, Meyer Abrams, *The Mirror and the Lamp: Romantic Theory and the Critical Tradition* (Oxford: Oxford University Press, 1953), examines a broad range of aesthetic theories within romanticism, including reflective and expressive models. More recently the architect Lars Spuybroek, in his *The Sympathy of Things: Ruskin and the Ecology of Design* (Rotterdam: NAi, 2012), has made an impassioned plea for a return to John Ruskin as a way to grapple with the reality of objects in an age of technological mediation.

53. Laruelle, "La plus haute des contemplations," 154, 158.

54. Deleuze, *Difference and Repetition,* xx. In fact the opening of *Difference and Repetition* has a bit of a non-philosophical tinge: difference "in itself" (28).

55. Laruelle, "La plus haute des contemplations," 170, emphasis removed.

56. Ibid.

57. Ibid., 160.

58. Laruelle, "Réflexions philosophiques sur l'oeuvre d'August von Briesen," 18. "The art work, von Briesen himself, and we the viewers together make a circle, a circle of self contemplation combining both extreme passivity and extreme activity,

the circle of the 'eternal return.' It is the fulfillment, at and the same time the destruction, of the old notion of the 'correspondence of the arts'" (Laruelle, "La plus haute des contemplations," 160).

59. Ibid., 166.

60. Ibid., 162.

61. Laruelle, "Réflexions philosophiques sur l'oeuvre d'August von Briesen," 10.

62. Ibid.

63. Laruelle, "La plus haute des contemplations," 164.

64. Ibid., 170. Indeed Laruelle's non-standard aesthetics is driven largely by a withdrawal from and unilateralization of the basic terms put forth in Kant's *Critique of Judgement,* including questions of taste, reflection, aesthetic judgment, and the constitution of the aesthetic regime. See, in particular, François Laruelle, "Le problème d'une pensée-art ou d'une non-esthétique" (typescript, undated), and François Laruelle, "Qui est artiste?" (typescript, undated).

65. The work of von Briesen "isn't nihilist in its destruction of the musical and graphical fetish, so much as ascetic and affirmative" (Laruelle, "Réflexions philosophiques sur l'oeuvre d'August von Briesen," 20).

66. Laruelle, "La plus haute des contemplations," 170.

67. Ibid. See also the discussion of the common in Henry, "Graphie de la subjectivité," 25–60.

68. Laruelle, "Réflexions philosophiques sur l'oeuvre d'August von Briesen," 18.

69. Here I side with Ray Brassier, who views Laruelle's chief innovation as that of developing a nondialectical, post-Hegelian logic of relation. See chapter 5 of Brassier, *Nihil Unbound,* 118–49. As Brassier puts it, Laruelle's innovation is "fundamentally formal: it consists in the invention of a new kind of transcendental logic whose conceptual depth (if not extensive breadth) at once equals and challenges that of Hegel's dialectical logic" (148). Although, while Brassier characterizes Laruelle's logic primarily in terms of negation, I find it more apt to characterize the non-standard logic in terms of identity ($a = a$ or the One-in-One).

70. Fredric Jameson, "In Soviet Arcadia," *New Left Review* 75 (May–June 2012): 119–27, 125.

71. Ibid.

9. ETHICS

1. See François Laruelle, *Théorie générale des victimes* (Paris: Mille et une nuits, 2012), subsequent parenthetical citations refer to this edition.

2. The heart of the book, occupying approximately one-quarter its length, is the opening chapter on "The Victim-in-Person." This is followed by a series of shorter chapters that expound on additional themes: the role of the intellectual, the "weak force" of the victim, crime and punishment, animals and animality, victims' resurrection and insurrection, and ultimately Laruelle's thoughts on some of the most significant historical instances of victimization such as the Holocaust, Christ's crucifixion, and crimes against humanity. These more topical chapters are bookended by two thin sections at the start and finish of the book. First is

an opening section, "Some Theoretical Preparations and Precautions" (Laruelle, *Théorie générale des victimes*, 10–20), which "fixes the coordinates of the book in a slightly more rigorous way, its vocabulary and its method" (9) using the techniques of non-standard philosophy. As we have seen, Laruelle's project is notoriously idiosyncratic, often entirely unassimilable to any philosophical precedent. For the most part, the non-standard jargon and methods that tend to saturate his books are significantly toned down in the body of this text. However, here in the opening pages, Laruelle dips into a more technical idiom. Likewise, a closing section, "Recollection of the Entire Argument" (196–210), does not so much summarize the book as restate and elaborate some of its claims using, again, the slightly more rigorous terminology and phrasing of Laruelle's non-standard philosophy.

3. Victims are thus never "saved." We should cease to speak of things like survivors or casualties. Victims are, in Laruelle's words, *resurrected*. That is, they participate in a unidirectional and inaugural human event. "Victims alone . . . deserve resurrection, and likely they alone have the power to do it" (Laruelle, *Théorie générale des victimes*, 33, emphasis removed). But here Laruelle risks being misunderstood because of his choice of words. He is drawn to the term *resurrection* not for its religious connotations so much as the powerful logic it describes. Just as his claim "We are all victims" has nothing to do with the doctrine of original sin, and just as his call for compassion has nothing to do with the tradition of humanist charity (with its adjacent ills of self-righteousness or priggish patronization), resurrection has nothing to do with the miracle of Christian rebirth. Or if it does, at least Laruelle is attempting to perform a powerful heresy against those sources, refashioning their logics into a parallel, non-standard form. "Neither natural phenomenon nor religious miracle, generic resurrection is materiel rather than material, vectorial rather than spiritual. It means a new insurrection each time, in each relaunching or superposition, of immanent lived reality, passing over and bringing down the most excessive moments of monotheistic transcendence" (155).

4. Alain Badiou, *Logics of Worlds*, 4.

5. For Laruelle, there are not Badiousian truths so much as "the algebraic objectivity of human lived experience" (Laruelle, *Théorie générale des victimes*, 53). Real human experience is thus not so much a fact but a variable, not so much an object but a formal relation, just as the algebraic equation $x = 2y$ tells how x and y are related without saying anything about what x and y actually are. (Indeed, here on these pages, Laruelle's concept of superposition closely resembles Deleuze's concept of the virtual.) Such an outcome is appealing to Laruelle because it eschews the need for dialectical synthesis. Instead entities withdraw into a condition of "duality" or "fusion." Thus in opposition to Badiou's "dialectical materialism," Laruelle proposes what he calls a "materialized algebra" of elements held as variables in superposition with each other.

6. The various permutations of the subject are complex in Laruelle. His main goal is to clone and unilateralize the transcendental subject. First off, Laruelle does not begin from the one. Instead he begins from philosophy, from, say, the

philosophical notion of the Ego. From the outset, the Ego may remain in a fully immanent state, what Laruelle calls the Ego-in-Ego. Or the Ego can also split into historically and philosophically specific conditions, the modern Ego, for example, as seen in the Cartesian contract between thought and being *(cogito ergo sum)*. In this sense, the "transcendental dialectic" or "amphibology" between Ego and subject takes on a specific, regional profile, which is to say a *certain type of subject* grounded in the pact between thought and being. "The principle of 'Modernity,' of 'Spirit,' is the amphibious quality of the Ego and the subject, their reduction one to the other," writes Laruelle. "This subject is the synthesis—but more or less immediate or mediatised then differentiated—of Being and thought" (Laruelle, *Principes de la non-philosophie,* 99). There are four terms at play: Ego and subject, but also thought and Being. When the Ego takes the form of the Cartesian subject, that subject consists of a riven core in which thought and Being are interrelated and "amphibiously" intermixed. Laruelle is offended by the local amphibology of thought and Being within the Cartesian subject, but he is also offended by the larger amphibology of subject and Ego. What Laruelle seeks is a theory of the subject rooted in an immanent Ego (the Ego-in-Ego). In other words, the antinomy itself does not ground anything at all; its very auto-positionality—I am a subject in relation to the transcendental Ego, and the transcendental Ego manifests itself in individual subjects like me—is evidence of its vain and bloated self-sufficiency. The antinomy itself must be explained. And in this sense, the Ego–subject antinomy is the philosophical fodder that allows non-philosophy to begin its work. As Laruelle says, "We must explain theoretically why the philosophies of the Ego and the subject are enmeshed" (ibid., 97).

Thus Laruelle does not begin from the one. He begins from philosophy, in this case with the Ego-subject relation in Descartes. Then, second, by virtue of the force (of) thought he asserts axiomatically the identity of both Ego and subject (something like $E = s$). This constitutes the first movement into non-philosophy proper. It asserts the transcendental identity that is "before" or "more generic" than both Ego and subject. "A theory of the subject is only possible on the basis of an invalidation of the confusion of the Ego with the subject or with the structure of the Philosophical Decision: the Ego is no longer subject but rather Real, and the subject is 'emptied' too of its mixtures with the Ego (but not of the Ego itself)" (ibid., 99). Asserting the identity of Ego and subject ($E = s$) is what invalidates the confusion. Only by virtue of Cartesianism being so auto-reflexive—the self as it orients back on the self—can Cartesianism indicate to Laruelle the way forward toward a generic identity of the Ego. In other words the very narcissism of the Cartesian subject becomes the raw ingredients for immanence within the non-philosophical Ego. And finally, according to the principle of unilateral duality, he aprioristically converts the identity into a duality (i.e., converts $E = s$ into $E–s$). This finally describes non-philosophy proper. In fact during the process the one never really enters in. It only appears "in the last instance," because at the end there arrives a condition of the generic real.

7. Laruelle's use of Christ and resurrection comes to a climax in the book's provocative ending section, where he talks directly about specific instances of victimization, first with the Holocaust, then again with Christ's crucifixion, and ultimately with crimes against humanity. Yet Laruelle does not address human rights, genocide, crimes against humanity, the Holocaust, or other matters of world-historical importance in any sustained way. This is not a book about political events and the waves of violence and trauma they produce. For better or worse he remains stubborn on the question of theory: Laruelle's non-standard philosophy can and must move forward using theory and theory alone. Analyses of events such as the Shoah or the crucifixion of Jesus are only useful for him to the extent that they can be rejiggered as theoretical constructs. So although this book perhaps veers closer to the newspaper headlines than past Laruelle projects, it is still properly labeled a "general theory" of victims, not a tally sheet of the dead or a manifesto for breaking the bonds of subjugation.

8. See Badiou, *Logics of Worlds,* 397–447.

9. Ibid., 420.

10. The friend/foe distinction is closely associated with the work of Carl Schmitt. See, in particular, Carl Schmitt, *The Concept of the Political,* trans. George Schwab (New Brunswick, N.J.: Rutgers University Press, 1976).

11. Louis Althusser, *Lenin and Philosophy,* 13. Ironically the word *science* derives etymologically from a root meaning to cut or divide.

12. Guy Debord, *The Society of the Spectacle,* trans. Donald Nicholson-Smith (New York: Zone Books, 1994), 41.

13. Heidegger, *Being and Time,* 51.

14. Tiqqun, *Introduction to Civil War,* trans. Alexander R. Galloway and Jason E. Smith (Los Angeles: Semiotext[e], 2010), 206.

15. Ibid., 214.

16. Heidegger, *Being and Time,* 150.

17. Ibid., 149.

18. Ibid., 167.

19. Brassier's critique of Laruelle hinges on precisely this point, that Laruelle privileges his own special "suspending instance" in the form of radical immanence. See Brassier, *Nihil Unbound,* 122.

20. Laruelle says something similar in the opening pages of *Philosophies of Difference:* "The canonical enunciation: *Everything is (Water, Earth, Fire, etc.)....* the Milesian enunciation, itself, makes apparent the oldest concrete philosophical matrix, a matrix of the empirico-transcendental parallelism and/or circle ... the empirico-transcendental Circle that is the essence not only of metaphysics, but of the attempts to 'surpass,' 'overcome,' 'turn' or 'deconstruct' metaphysics as well and that altogether surpasses, as circle, any attempts to distend it, split it, break it, etc.... It is to think the real as all (*the* all: not only the universal, but an absolute or unifying universal) and thus, inversely, the *all* of the real as still an element of the real, indeed as Other" (Laruelle, *Philosophies of Difference,* 6). To be clear, Laruelle is not against a unified theory; his opposition is to any kind of "absolute"

or "unifying" tendency that would make the All a transcendental sufficiency substitutable for all reality, thereby isolating and incorporating alterity within itself. By contrast the Laruellean one is insufficient or generic in its universality.

10. THE GENERIC

1. "Science and philosophy meet in the universality of the synthetic *a priori,*" writes Laruelle, giving credit to Kant's centrality in modern philosophical discourse. "As an example of a non-philosophical undertaking, we focus directly on the problem of the *a priori.* We take the 'synthetic *a priori* judgment,' which Kant revealed to be the basic essence and algorithm of philosophy in the form of a hybrid between metaphysics and science, and treat it as our material." See Laruelle, *Principes de la non-philosophie,* 321, 314.

2. See, for example, the sections on the singular and the generic in Badiou, *Being and Event,* or the chapter titled "Whatever" in Giorgio Agamben, *The Coming Community,* trans. Michael Hardt (Minneapolis: University of Minnesota Press, 1993), 1–2. Although he is not a "subtractivist" per se, Laruelle can, in a very general sense, be included in this tradition to the extent that he endorses a generic state of immanence, whether it be the real as One-in-One or humanity as Stranger or Man-in-person *[Homme-en-personne].* See, for example, Laruelle, *Introduction aux sciences génériques.* On the term "Man-in-person," see also François Laruelle, *Future Christ: A Lesson in Heresy,* trans. Anthony Paul Smith (London: Continuum, 2010), 2, 5, 20, and passim, and François Laruelle, *L'ultime honneur des intellectuels* (Paris: Les éditions Textuel, 2003), 26, 50, and passim.

3. Hardt and Negri, *Empire,* 212.

4. Hardt and Negri, *Commonwealth,* 152.

5. Peter Hallward, *Badiou: A Subject to Truth* (Minneapolis: University of Minnesota Press, 2003), 163.

6. Badiou, *Manifesto for Philosophy,* 143. For more on Badiou's theory of subtraction see Alain Badiou, "On Subtraction," in *Conditions,* trans. Steven Corcoran (London: Continuum, 2008), 113–28. See also Badiou, *Being and Event,* particularly Part VII on the generic.

7. Michel Foucault, "Of Other Spaces," trans. Jay Miskowiec, *diacritics* 16, no. 1 (Spring 1986): 22–27.

8. See Marc Augé, *Non-places: Introduction to an Anthropology of Supermodernity,* trans. John Howe (London and New York: Verso, 1995). Augé laments a new kind of world that anthropologists must acknowledge and make sense of: "[a] world where people are born in the clinic and die in hospital, where transit points and temporary abodes are proliferating under luxurious or inhuman conditions (hotel chains and squats, holiday clubs and refugee camps, shantytowns threatened with demolition or doomed to festering longevity); where a dense network of means of transport which are also inhabited spaces is developing; where the habitué of supermarkets, slot machines and credit cards communicates wordlessly, through gestures, with an abstract, unmediated commerce; a world thus surrendered to solitary individuality, to the fleeting, the temporary and ephemeral" (78).

9. See chapter 7 in Deleuze, *Cinema 1*. Deleuze's any-space-whatever and Augé's non-place are sometimes confused by English readers, because of a mistake in Deleuze's English translation attributing the term "any-space-whatever" to a certain Pascal Augé. The attribution should read Pascal Auger, the French experimental filmmaker and former student of Deleuze.

10. Deleuze, *Cinema 1*, 112.

11. Like Heidegger's use of the phrase "It gives" *(es gibt)*, Levinas uses the neutral expression "There is" *(il y a)* as a way to reference the "phenomenon of impersonal being" (Emmanuel Levinas, *Ethics and Infinity: Conversations with Philippe Nemo*, trans. Richard Cohen [Pittsburgh: Duquesne University Press, 1985], 48). Levinas also explores the conditions of impersonal selfhood and otherness by way of the latinate terms "ipseity," meaning itselfness, selfhood, or that-one-hood, and "Illeity," a strange coinage literally meaning He-hood that Levinas uses to refer to the remote absent trace of God. "The ipseity of the I consists in remaining outside the distinction between the individual and the general. . . . The I is thus the mode in which the break-up of totality, which leads to the presence of the absolutely other, is concretely accomplished. It is solitude par excellence" (Emmanuel Levinas, *Totality and Infinity: An Essay on Exteriority*, trans. Alphonso Lingis [Pittsburgh: Duquesne University Press, 1969], 118). For more on Illeity see Emmanuel Levinas, *Otherwise than Being: Or Beyond Essence*, trans. Alphonso Lingis (Pittsburgh: Duquesne University Press, 1998), 162.

12. Jean-François Lyotard, *The Inhuman: Reflections on Time*, trans. Geoffrey Bennington and Rachel Bowlby (Stanford, Calif.: Stanford University Press, 1991).

13. Ibid., 187, 7.

14. Deleuze, *The Logic of Sense*, 52, emphasis removed.

15. Ibid., 102.

16. Deleuze and Laruelle both profit from subtleties in the French term *personne* that can mean both "person" and "no one" (*elle n'est personne* [Deleuze, *The Logic of Sense*, 116]). Thus the "person" in Deleuze is actually an impersonal being, or perhaps more simply an "imperson." Contrast this also to the Deleuzian concept of the "dividual."

17. See, for example, Laruelle, *Future Christ*.

18. Heidegger, *Identity and Difference*, 66.

19. See, for example, Alphonso Lingis, *The Community of Those Who Have Nothing in Common* (Bloomington: Indiana University Press, 1994), and Jacques Rancière, *Disagreement: Politics and Philosophy*, trans. Julie Rose (Minneapolis: University of Minnesota Press, 1999).

20. See, for instance, the account given in Marcelo Bucheli, *Bananas and Business: The United Fruit Company in Colombia, 1899–2000* (New York: New York University Press, 2005).

21. "What does it mean to force philosophical properties into their generic states?" Laruelle asks near the beginning of *Philosophie non-standard*, 127. The forcing of a passage from the transcendental to the immanent entails five steps: (1) specify whatever is transcendental in any given philosophical work, (2) define

the particular attributes in which the transcendental operates, in particular the internal hierarchy they produce, (3) render such attributes insufficient by under-determining them, (4) fuse the hierarchical attributes under the condition of immanence, and (5) extrapolate back to the real appearance or symptom (Laruelle, *Philosophie non-standard*, 128–29).

22. Alain Badiou, "On the Truth Process," http://www.egs.edu/faculty/alain-badiou/articles/on-the-truth-process/. For a more technical definition of forcing see Badiou, *Being and Event*, particularly Parts VII and VIII (327–435).

23. David Graeber makes such an argument rather convincingly in his *Debt: The First 5000 Years* (Brooklyn: Melville House, 2011). See in particular the discussion of "everyday communism" (94–102).

24. Jo Freeman, "The Tyranny of Structurelessness," http://www.jofreeman.com/joreen/tyranny.htm.

25. Eugene Thacker and I have written more about this in our book *The Exploit: A Theory of Networks* (Minneapolis: University of Minnesota Press, 2007).

Index

abstraction, xxviii, 120, 128, 164–65, 171, 257n49

advent, 14–16, 20–21, 82–83, 94, 111, 218, 242n10

aesthetics, xiv–xv, xviii, 93, 147, 156–58, 160, 164–68, 170–73, 183, 219; aesthetic theory, 164–65, 171; non-representational, 164, 166, 168; realist, xviii, 171. *See also* non-standard aesthetics

affirmation, 30, 33–34, 38–39, 42, 57, 88–89, 95, 204

"Afrum-Pronto" (Turrell), 153

Agamben, Giorgio, 55, 57, 105, 191, 197

Ai, Hengwu, xxxi

algebra, xxiv, 7, 181, 231n2, 238n24, 260n5. *See also* mathematics; number

alienation, xxix, 5, 12–14, 16, 29, 52–53, 70, 80, 85, 116, 159, 205

All, the, xii, 19, 53, 192, 232n12, 262n20

Althusser, Louis, xv, xxix, 115–21, 123–24, 126–28, 186, 246n6, 247n10

amphibology, 10, 89, 260n6

analog, xiv, xxviii–xxix, xxxi–xxxiii, 33, 38, 51–52, 55–63, 69–71, 75, 77–79, 82–84, 89, 94, 98, 101, 103–4, 183, 185–87, 190–91, 199, 205, 214–15, 219–21; event, 59–60, 75, 77–79, 83; integration, 84, 214; paradigm, 103–4; relation, 69, 78

analysis, xxviii–xxxiii, 95, 195–96, 229n17; laws of, 59

anarchism, 212–13; ontological, 240n17

Anti-Badiou (Laruelle), 180, 231n21, 244n10

anticapitalism, 119, 127

Anti-Oedipus (Deleuze and Guattari), 99, 105

anti-philosophy, 236n17

Antonioni, Michelangelo, 65, 199, 227n2

any-space-whatever, 64–66, 199, 264n9

apophatic reason, 234n5, 234n35

a posteriori, 16–18, 130

appropriation, 33, 218; structure of, 11; event of, 14–15, 88, 94, 110. *See also Ereignis*

a priori, xv, 13, 16–19, 21–22, 28, 45–46, 58–59, 88, 130, 146, 171, 196–97, 221

Aristotle, 59, 136, 192

Arnold, Matthew, 135

art, 40, 104, 133, 135–36, 153–57, 160–72

as-structure, 28–29, 76, 82, 220

267

234n35, 236n11, 236n18, 242n8; and being, xxvi, 5–6, 8, 12, 16, 20, 28, 45; and the clone, xxvi–xxvii, 18, 20, 27, 63, 125, 127, 172, 193; as identity, 6, 8, 18, 28, 46–47, 58–59, 61–63, 76, 78, 84, 127, 147, 196, 204; and the two, xxix–xxx, xxxiii, 12, 35, 46, 52–53, 56, 60–61, 70, 78, 89, 94, 206, 219, 236n18. *See also* being; identity; Not-One; One-and-the-Same; One-as-Multiple; One-in-One; One Two; univocity
One-and-the-Same, 34, 39–41, 44, 58. *See also* being: generic
One-as-Multiple, 34, 37, 39, 56–58. *See also* being: continuous
One-in-One, xxxiii, 59, 196–97, 201. *See also* one, the
One Two, 33–36, 54, 204. *See also* being: differential
ontology, xiii, xxvi, xxxiv, 3, 7, 14, 32, 38, 51, 56, 69, 82–83, 93, 102, 108, 118–19, 122, 126, 144, 165–67, 172, 195–96, 198, 202, 205–6, 219–20; crypto-ontology, 44, 144–45; of the digital, 51, 220; ontological darkness, 44, 144; ontological difference, 45, 196; onto-logical principle, 11–13, 20; poetic, 166–67, 205–6. *See also* promiscuous ontology; prophylactic ontology
opacity, 44, 140–44, 147, 189, 197–98; opaque body, 139, 142–43
OPEC (Organization of the Petroleum Exporting Countries), 172
Opticorum Libri Sex (d'Aguilon), 142
optics, 140, 142, 146–47
Order of Things, The (Foucault), xi
orientalism, 154, 240n17
orientation, 14, 34, 43, 117, 121, 147, 154, 155, 158, 228n6, 252n18

panopticon, 68–69
parallel, xviii, xxxv, 44–46, 60–62, 68, 158–59, 188, 219; parallelism, 27, 41,

60–61, 70, 159, 219, 262n20; parallelity, 61–62, 70, 219; world, 179
Paris, 125, 160–61
Parmenides, 3–7, 10–11, 19, 46, 52, 77, 137, 239n2
particle, 35–36, 48; quantum theory of, 229n12; subatomic, 77
person, xv, 40–42, 56, 62, 73, 127, 148–49, 179–82, 199–201, 205, 213, 264n16; in person, xiii, 179–81; per-sonhood, 40, 177, 182; third person, 17. *See also* impersonal; Man-in-person
pessimism, cosmic, 144–45
petroleum, 139, 145
Phaedrus (Plato), 52
phenomenology, xi, xxii–xxiii, 10, 28, 32, 53, 66–67, 76, 85, 116–17, 121, 137–38, 142, 147, 155, 159, 162, 166–67, 170, 189, 191, 228n6
philosophical decision, xviii–xix, xxiv–xxv, 9, 11–12, 20, 34, 89, 130, 149, 173, 192–93, 228n7
Philosophies of Difference [Les philoso-phies de la différence] (Laruelle), 85, 168, 232n12, 255n43, 262n20
philosophy, xiii–xv, xvii–xix, xxi–xxv, xxvii, xxx, xxxii–xxxv, 3, 5, 7–14, 16, 18, 21, 25–32, 34, 38–41, 44–48, 51–54, 56, 58, 77, 80, 82–86, 89, 94–95, 98–101, 104, 110, 115, 117–24, 127–30, 134–35, 146–48, 154–60, 166–68, 171, 178–80, 182–83, 186, 189–90, 195–97, 218–21; best response to, xvii, 120; and capitalism, 120–21; and digi-tality, xix, 179; and non-philosophy, xxxv, 95; philosophical method, xxviii, 33; philosophical sufficiency, 124, 170; philosophical world, xiv, 89. *See also* standard model
Photo-Fiction: A No-Standard Aesthetics (Laruelle), 156–58, 252n17, 252n18

photography, 133, 146–47, 155–58, 160,
172, 252n18; photographic apparatus,
157, 172; photographic image, 64, 159

Plato, xvii, 6, 12, 29, 35, 52–54, 76, 98,
129, 134, 157, 165, 191, 231n6, 234n7,
237n21

Platonism, 4, 8, 38–39, 146

plenum, 47, 144

Pleynet, Marcelin, 160, 162

Plotinus, 5

"Poetically Man Dwells" (Heidegger),
167

politics, 40, 42, 46, 80, 85, 87–88, 104–
5, 118–19, 122, 133, 183, 185–90, 202–7,
209–11, 214, 219; political action,
206, 209; political distinction, xix,
190; political economy, 18, 128.
See also ethics

postmodernism, 171, 189

"Postscript on Control Societies"
(Deleuze), 96, 98–100, 104–9, 243n6

post-structuralism, xxii, xxvi, 8, 25, 46,
54, 87, 103, 119, 137, 142

pragmatism, 187, 192

"Preface (to *A Contribution to the
Critique of Political Economy*)"
(Marx), 122

prepositions, 13, 26–28, 246n6

prevent, 16–21, 60, 70, 78, 82–83,
86–89, 94, 133, 217–19

principle of identity. *See* identity:
principle of

"Principle of Identity, The"
(Heidegger), 15

*Principle of Minority, The [Le principe
de minorité]* (Laruelle), 55, 244n12,
247n7

principle of sufficient digitality, xxxiv,
207. *See also* digital

principle of sufficient economy, 120–21,
182

principle of sufficient philosophy,
xxiv–xxv, 11, 89, 120–21, 182. *See also*
philosophy

principle of sufficient reason, 11, 82,
110, 184

*Principles of Non-Philosophy [Principes
de la non-philosophie]* (Laruelle),
xxiv, 34, 234n7, 237n21, 239n5,
248n11, 249n1, 255n43, 260n6, 263n1

process, 38–39, 79, 84–85, 112, 185,
207–10

process philosophy, 84–85, 119

Proclus, 5

production: mode of, 127, 174, 179;
relations of, xxviii, xxxi, 122

Prokofiev, Sergei, 161

proletariat, xxxiii, 42, 115, 128; dictatorship of, xii; proletarianism, 203

promiscuous ontology, 46, 196, 240n17

prophylactic event, 60. *See also*
prevent

prophylactic ontology, xii, 21, 195–96,
217, 240n17. *See also* prevent

protocol, 80, 210, 214; protocological
control, 86

psychoanalysis, 85, 101, 146–47

quantum mechanics, xxiv–xxv, 181–82,
188, 217, 229n12, 231n21, 234n7,
238n26, 244n10

queer communism. *See* communism:
queer

Rambo, John, 25

Rancière, Jacques, 55, 236n18, 247n10

Rawls, John, 204–5

real, the, xix–xxi, xxiv, xxvi–xxviii, 5, 8,
10, 16–21, 34, 44, 68, 75, 84, 88, 95,
121, 134, 147, 163, 165, 170, 172, 188,
198, 209, 219, 221, 228n7, 234n35,
262n20; digitization of, 12

realism, xxvii–xxviii, 80, 84, 88, 165–
66, 168, 171–72, 256n48, 258n50.
See also aesthetics: realist

Reinhardt, Ad, 135–36

representation, xxiv–xxv, xxvii, 6, 13,
16, 34–35, 40, 43, 58, 67, 89, 102, 111,

ALEXANDER R. GALLOWAY is professor of media, culture, and communication at New York University. His books include *The Interface Effect, Gaming: Essays on Algorithmic Culture* (Minnesota, 2006), and *Protocol: How Control Exists after Decentralization.*